TEXTS & DOCUMENTS

A Series of the Getty Research Institute Publication Programs

The TEXTS & DOCUMENTS series offers to the student of art, architecture, and aesthetics neglected, forgotten, or unavailable writings in English translation.

Edited according to modern standards of scholarship and framed by critical introductions and commentaries, these volumes gradually mine the past centuries for studies that retain their significance in our understanding of art and of the issues surrounding its production, reception, and interpretation.

Eminent scholars guide the Getty Research Institute for the History of Art and the Humanities in the selection and publication of TEXTS & DOCUMENTS. Each volume acquaints readers with the broader cultural conditions at the genesis of the text and equips them with the needed apparatus for its study. Over time the series will greatly expand our horizon and deepen our understanding of critical thinking on art.

Julia Bloomfield, Thomas F. Reese, Salvatore Settis, *Editors*
Kurt W. Forster, *Consultative Editor*, TEXTS & DOCUMENTS
The Getty Research Institute Publication Programs

THE MODERN FUNCTIONAL BUILDING

TEXTS & DOCUMENTS

Published by the Getty Research Institute for the History of Art and the Humanities

INTRODUCTION BY ROSEMARIE HAAG BLETTER

TRANSLATION BY MICHAEL ROBINSON

THE MODERN
FUNCTIONAL
BUILDING
ADOLF BEHNE

THE GETTY RESEARCH INSTITUTE PUBLICATION PROGRAMS
Julia Bloomfield, Thomas F. Reese, Salvatore Settis, *Editors*
Kurt W. Forster, *Consultative Editor,* TEXTS & DOCUMENTS

TEXTS & DOCUMENTS
Architecture
Harry F. Mallgrave, Editor

The Modern Functional Building

Stanislaus von Moos, Editorial Consultant
Lynne Kostman, Managing Editor
Michelle Ghaffari, Manuscript Editor
Diane Mark-Walker, Copy Editor

Published by
The Getty Research Institute for the History of Art and the Humanities,
Santa Monica, CA 90401-1455
© 1996 by The Getty Research Institute for the History of Art and the Humanities
All rights reserved. Published 1996
Printed in the United States of America

02 01 00 99 98 97 96   7 6 5 4 3 2 1

Translated from
Adolf Behne, *Der moderne Zweckbau*, Die Baukunst, ed. Dagobert Frey
(Munich: Drei Masken Verlag, 1926). Copyright 1926 by Drei Masken Verlag A.G., Munich.

Published by arrangement with Friedr. Vieweg & Sohn
Verlagsgesellschaft mbH.

Library of Congress Cataloging-in-Publication Data is to
be found on the last printed page of this book.

Contents

Acknowledgments

I would like to thank Stanislaus von Moos for his careful and insightful reading of my text. My particular appreciation goes to Mary McLeod for her unstinting assistance and her thorough and sympathetic suggestions and comments made during various stages of this project. Thanks are also due to Robin Middleton for his support, to Frederic J. Schwartz and K. Gutschow for useful bibliographical information, and to Gabrielle Esperdy for her tremendous help in tracking down some of the more obscure bibliographic entries. Further, Harry Mallgrave's consistent and superb overview is most appreciated, as well as Julia Bloomfield's patience during the production of this text and the precise and attentive editing of Michelle Ghaffari, Lynne Kostman, and Diane Mark-Walker. Lastly, I want to thank my husband, Martin Filler, for helping me to keep my sanity and to keep my Germanisms in check.

—RHB

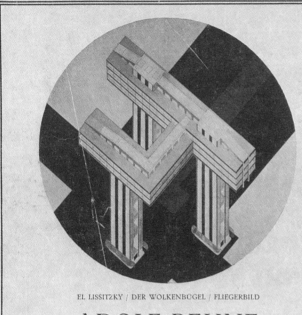

Jacket of the first edition of Adolf Behne's *Der moderne Zweckbau* (Munich: Drei Masken Verlag, 1926). Collection J. Bloomfield, Santa Monica. Photo: John Kiffe.

Introduction

Rosemarie Haag Bletter

Adolf Behne's *Der moderne Zweckbau* (*The Modern Functional Building*) presciently unmasked many of the ideologies of functionalism, rationalism, and European Modernism of the 1920s. Written in 1923 (though not published until 1926),[1] it preceded the later German publications of Walter Gropius, Ludwig Hilberseimer, Walter Curt Behrendt, and Bruno Taut and sheds much light on them.[2] Today the Anglo-American audience remains largely familiar with European Modernism through the narrow focus of Henry-Russell Hitchcock and Philip Johnson's *The International Style*, 1932, although Hitchcock's earlier *Modern Architecture: Romanticism and Reintegration*, 1929, had presented a somewhat more varied picture of recent developments.[3] By contrast, arguments about Modernism were articulated in surprisingly rich and complex ways in the aforementioned European works of the 1920s.

Behne's *Der moderne Zweckbau* is crucial for understanding modernist polemics contextually, especially those later subsumed under the notion of functionalism. In a general sense, the increasing concern with purpose and *Sachlichkeit* in early Modernism signifies the change from older, aristocratic value systems to an emphasis on everyday and common experience as the new paradigm. Behne's text is also helpful in reconsidering some of the standard assumptions and questions about this period, especially the presumption of a visually coherent style. Instead of emphasizing the external appearance of buildings, German texts dealing with Modernism in the 1920s identified the new architecture through its underlying conceptual premises. Contemporary expression was therefore seen as a reflection of philosophical attitudes toward modernity, and this view allowed for greater visual diversity — perhaps only because an exact correspondence between idea and form was difficult to establish.

The three-year delay in the publication of *Der moderne Zweckbau* reveals much about the competitive nature of early Modernism. Gropius had sought Behne's assistance in preparing the Bauhaus exhibition *Internationale Architektur* in 1923; but when Behne in turn asked Gropius to change the content or delay the publication date of the book of the same title (the first entry in the Bauhausbücher, or Bauhaus book series, which was projected for publication in 1924) because of its similarity to Behne's own work, Gropius refused. Gropius's decision to start a book series hampered Behne's efforts on other fronts as well. When Behne shortly thereafter approached J. J. P. Oud (whose work Behne had promoted in 1922 in his monograph on Dutch architecture) and asked him for material for his own book, Oud responded that he would prefer to have his work published in the Bauhaus book series. He clearly expected more publicity and credibility given the Bauhaus's institutional backing.

Nevertheless, books such as Gropius's *Internationale Architektur,* 1925, portrayed contemporary architecture — as did Behne — in an astonishingly varied way. Frank Lloyd Wright's Larkin Building and Erich Mendelsohn's equally massive-looking double house in Berlin were included among *Internationale Architektur*'s illustrations. Hilberseimer's *Internationale neue Baukunst* (New international architecture), which appeared in 1927 under the auspices of the German Werkbund, was similarly diverse in scope. Its examples ranged from an apartment house by Jan Wils to housing by Taut, in addition to unexecuted schemes by Russian Constructivists. In *Die neue Baukunst in Europa und Amerika* (simultaneously published in English as *Modern Architecture*), 1929, Bruno Taut was also extraordinarily inclusive in his selection of examples.

Whereas several of these books alluded to the perceived internationalism of contemporary architecture, only Behrendt's *Der Sieg des neuen Baustils* (The victory of the new building style), 1927, treated the new architecture as a style, as would Hitchcock and Johnson's later study.[4] Notwithstanding his title, even Behrendt presented a varied picture of contemporary architecture, one that included works by Hans Poelzig, Mendelsohn, and Willem Dudok. He saw Wright's Robie House and Henry van de Velde's theater at the Werkbund exhibition of 1914 as the key precedents to modern architecture; and he presented an organic plan by Hugo Häring next to Ludwig Mies van der Rohe's De Stijl–inspired plan for a brick country house so that side-by-side they appeared as equally central examples of the new style. But because German proselytizers of Modernism tended to downplay the aesthetic aspects of architecture, their criteria depended less on visual elements than did Hitchcock and Johnson's work. Reinforcing this attitudinal difference was the fact that contemporary architecture was commonly referred to in Germany as "Neues Bauen" (new building), just as in Holland it was known as "Nieuw Bouwen."[5]

It is not entirely clear why the term *Neues Bauen* became prevalent in the 1920s. The word *modern* was more commonly used prior to 1923, as for example in Karl Scheffler's *Moderne Baukunst,* 1907, or, for that matter, Behne's *Der moderne Zweckbau.*[6] Possibly under the influence of the general Expressionist conception of the new man, and more specifically the *Neues Bauen* exhibition of 1920 at J. B. Neumann's gallery in Berlin,[7] and the popularization after 1923 of Gustav Hartlaub's "Neue Sachlichkeit" (conceived by him as a further evolution of Expressionism, not a reaction to it), the term *neu* attained wide currency among the German avant-garde. Taut's *Die neue Wohnung* (The new dwelling), 1924, suggests the link to Expressionism.[8] *Neu* seems to have implied change and the progressivism associated with the new movement more clearly than the term *modern.* The latter seems almost to have been perceived as a neutral chronological marker synonymous with *contemporary.* Behne himself signifies the shift from *modern* to *neu* in his *Neues Wohnen — Neues Bauen* (New dwelling — New building), 1927, and the emphasis on the new is apparent in the titles of Hilberseimer's *Internationale neue Baukunst,* Behrendt's *Der Sieg des neuen Baustils,* or Taut's *Bauen — Der neue Wohnbau* (Building — The new domestic architecture), 1927.[9]

It is also possible that *neu* carried political overtones that had prewar origins in Germany. The weekly newspaper of the Social Democrats was called *Die neue Zeit.* Behne wrote an essay for this paper in 1914 on the representation of workers in art. His first book (subsequent to publication of his doctoral thesis) was titled *Zur neuen Kunst* (Toward the new art) and was published in 1915 by *Der Sturm. Modern* in a political context may have meant simply "of the present time," whereas *neue Zeit* — and by implication *neu* — suggested a rupture with past times.

Such contextual or regional shifts in terminology do not apply in the same way to the Anglo-American sphere, where *modern* continued to be the preferred term. It is significant that Taut's *Die neue Baukunst in Europa und Amerika,* 1929, appeared in its English edition of the same year under the title *Modern Architecture.* And Behrendt, the author of *Der Sieg des neuen Baustils,* 1927, later, while living in America, wrote *Modern Building,* 1937.[10] There are, however, subtle variations even within the more general discussion of "modern" developments, as Alan Colquhoun has recently pointed out.[11] Whereas in England in the 1950s the avant-garde of the 1920s was generally referred to as the *Modern Movement* — suggesting a degree of activism and ongoing development — today we tend to prefer *Modernism,* a word that seems to denote a historical period.

To understand the ideology and intricacies of the modernist debate that fueled the Neues Bauen, one needs to study more closely the polemics of books by the aforementioned German authors. For this purpose Behne's *Der moderne Zweckbau* is the most revealing text. It fully explores and carefully sets the stage for later arguments and for the development of concepts such as *Sachlichkeit* (objectivity, functionalism) and *Zweck* (purpose, function). In this respect Behne's role is comparable to that of Hartlaub in the staging of the exhibition of 1925 on the Neue Sachlichkeit in painting.[12] Beyond that, Behne, a critic of both art and architecture, was also an astute observer of the contemporary scene. Although his writings do not have the acerbic consistency of Adolf Loos, many of his essays and books contain sharp, perceptive comments and critiques of the Werkbund, Expressionism, and the Bauhaus, as well as the work of close friends. He was not a practicing architect, yet he was not exactly a completely detached observer. Behne was a major participant in Expressionist architectural groups after World War I. Like Sigfried Giedion, he had the advantage of an academic education in art history and a close acquaintance with nearly all of the principal architects of his time.

Adolf Bruno Behne was born in Magdeburg on 13 July 1885, the son of an architect. When he was a year old his parents moved with him and his two older brothers, Erich and Karl, to Berlin. He grew up in one of the working-class districts of eastern Berlin near the Centralviehhof (main slaughter-house) and attended a *Gymnasium* from which he graduated in 1905. His academic training commenced with the study of architecture at the Technische Hochschule (Polytechnic school) in Berlin-Charlottenburg, but in 1907 he decided to study art history at the Friedrich-Wilhelm Universität. After a stay in Italy, he produced his dissertation, "Der Inkrustationsstil in Toscana" (The incrustation style in Tuscany), in 1912. Among his teachers were Heinrich Wölfflin (with whom Giedion had also studied) and Georg Simmel, the great philosopher and sociologist. Thereafter he taught in a *Hochschule* as well as a *Volkshochschule* (an adult education program), and he became part of the Volksbildungsbewegung (People's education movement). This movement was concerned with furthering education outside of academic institutions, and it remained an interest for Behne throughout his career. In 1913 he married Elfriede Schneider, the daughter of a railroad engineer, whom he had met through the mathematics club at the university. They had two daughters—Karla, born in 1913, and Julia, born in 1921.[13]

Before the war Behne also belonged to the Choriner Kreis (Chorin circle), a group of young writers, artists, and architects that met on weekends for walks in the woods around the small town of Chorin near Berlin. Max Beckmann and Taut were also members of the group, and Behne formed a long-lasting friendship with Taut.[14] Among Behne's earliest articles were those in *Die Hilfe* — the weekly journal published by Friedrich Naumann, a politician, former Protestant pastor, and one of the key organizers of the Werkbund. Naumann had founded *Die Hilfe* in 1894 as the organ of the progressive wing of the Christian-Social movement. He had been interested in using the arts to improve the quality of products because he believed that doing so "would raise the value of labor, improve the worker's status, increase his joy in work, and thus reverse the trend to proletarianization hitherto associated with the advance of capitalism."[15] Together with the sociologist Max Weber, with whom he was closely associated, Naumann rejected the Marxist view that economics is the central factor in social change. Both men stressed the plurality and interdependence of causes.

Behne's name appears for the first time as a member of the Werkbund in 1913, the year after he received his doctorate. Before World War I he published articles on the work of Peter Behrens and Taut. His articles appeared in *Der Sturm, Die Weltbühne, Sozialistische Monatshefte,* and *Das neue Frankfurt,* among many other periodicals. He wrote frequently on the role of the museum in the general education of the public and more specifically on the ambiguous nature of the framed picture in the museum setting. Since the museum imposes a change in context on all works of art, he saw the common concern with "original" art as a false issue. In his essay "Das reproduktive Zeitalter" (The reproductive era) of 1917, he seems to prefigure Walter Benjamin's well-known thesis about the effect of mass produced images on art.[16] Behne was also interested in advertising and its wide-ranging effects on culture: he once referred to Mendelsohn's urban buildings as *Reklamearchitektur* (advertising architecture). He did not, however, see eye-to-eye with the prevailing Werkbund policy imposing aesthetic standards on all aspects of daily life. Advertising, he wrote in 1924, was as central to a modern economy as money, and any attempt to control it through aesthetic regulations was bound to be counterproductive in that it would treat advertising as a purely formal problem. On the one hand, Behne did not believe that using art to mask a subject was necessarily good.[17] On the other hand, he wrote about films as art as early as 1921, and he included the important role of film in his discussion of pedagogy.[18]

As noted above, Behne's first book, *Zur neuen Kunst,* was published in 1915 by *Der Sturm,* the major disseminator of contemporary, and particularly Expressionist, art. An excerpt from the book titled "Expressionistische Architektur" appeared in the magazine *Der Sturm* in the same year. This essay was among the earliest attempts to define Expressionism, and it certainly was the first to do so within the context of architecture. Behne's description of Expressionism was not narrowly Germanic or medievalizing, and his essay included Cubism and Futurism as equally important aspects of this contemporary expression.[19]

In 1915 Behne also wrote an article in *Die Tat* entitled "Der Hass der Neutralen" (The hatred of the neutrals), in which he complained about the lack of support for Germany during the early war years. He returned the idea of an "avant-garde" to its original military meaning when he wrote that those who did not commit themselves were fearful of the new. Behne was hardly alone in this attitude. The sociologist Weber described the war as "great and wonderful," and Thomas Mann saw it as "purification, liberation . . . an immense hope."[20]

Behne's position during the war years has led to a diverse set of assessments concerning his political beliefs. Iain Boyd Whyte in his otherwise exceptionally informative *Bruno Taut and the Architecture of Activism*, 1982, uses this essay and Behne's association with the Choriner Kreis (among other things) to show that he (and Taut) were essentially conservative.[21] Following the Marxist, or more correctly Stalinist, argument of Georg Lukács in his attack on Expressionism of 1934 (by this time he had become an apologist for Stalinism), Whyte finds conservatism endemic. Lukács viewed Expressionism as counterrevolutionary because it was a product of imperialist capitalism and therefore responsible for fascism. According to the Lukácsian formula, the association of Behne and Taut with the Choriner Kreis establishes them as conservative, because the group's back-to-nature component can be regarded as part of the *Wandervögel* Movement, which began in the 1890s. By the 1930s this movement was clearly an extension of the National Socialists' nationalism and racialism; however, before World War I, it was perhaps patriotic but not nationalist.[22] As with the Werkbund, however, political uniformity cannot be ascribed to the members of any large organization. By the same token, one cannot say that the Expressionists or modernists were all liberal. A similar restrictive Lukácsian formula led Magdalena Bushart in *Der Geist der Gotik und die Expressionistische Kunst* (The spirit of the Gothic and Expressionist art), 1990, to categorize Behne as an opportunist because of his later shift in political opinion.[23] But not all changes of attitude reflect ulterior motives. Walter Benjamin, for instance, who was generally recognized as a Marxist in the 1920s, had participated in the German youth movement before 1914.[24]

6

Lukács's reductive argument was countered in the late 1930s by one of his former friends, the Marxist philosopher Ernst Bloch (they had met in Simmel's seminar). Bloch wrote that Lukács's opinions were based primarily on literary Expressionism, as opposed to painting and architecture. He argued further that Expressionism did in fact question basic social values and asserted the constructive value of utopianism. Bloch also found the Expressionists' inclusion of folk art from many countries more meaningful than the Neoclassicism that Lukács had endorsed.[25] Most contemporary Neo-Marxist historians such as Manfredo Tafuri and Francesco Dal Co cite only Lukács and not Bloch, thereby overlooking the vigorous debate and disagreements about a politically engaged art that took place in the 1920s and 1930s.[26] Possibly because of Lukács's influence on recent literary criticism, his opinions about Expressionist literature have been carried over into the other arts of the period with which, however, he was not as familiar.

Whyte is correct when he maintains that a shift in beliefs took place as World War I progressed. Some, like Taut, became pacifists. Behne joined the alternative service as a medical orderly during the war. As early as 1914 three of Behne's lectures were published by the educational committee of the Social Democratic Party (SPD), and he wrote for the party's weekly, *Die neue Zeit*.[27] In 1917, on the other hand, he wrote a book that was published under the auspices of the Dürerbund, a fairly conservative educational association for the appreciation of art founded in 1902. In 1917 he also wrote an essay in praise of the Russian Revolution.[28] It is clear that at the beginning of his career his interest in a populist approach to art colored most of his associations. However, sometime during these early years he joined the SPD, and in 1913 he had begun writing for *Sozialistische Monatshefte*, which publicized the international socialist movement. After the war he joined the USPD, the Independent Social Democratic Party and the schismatic left wing of the majority Socialists; this group had been founded in 1917 to call for an end to the war and to help politicize the labor force.[29]

Lukács, in fact, had coupled his critique of Expressionism with an attack on the USPD. In his opinion the USPD's attitude toward revolution, like that of the Expressionists, was half-hearted. Lukács's scorn directed at Expressionists and the USPD reflects the uneasy alliance between these groups and the Spartacists — from 1919 on the Communists (KPD) — and their later extreme doctrinal split. By the late 1920s the KPD and the USPD had become archenemies. But in the last year of the war the Spartacists were loosely associated with the USPD,[30] and in reality the USPD participated in the mislabeled

"Spartacus Uprising" of January 1919. Both the SPD and the KPD were working-class parties. The KPD, however, contained more unskilled and unemployed workers. The parties' respective social programs reflected the differences in their makeups. The Social Democrats sought to develop orthodox Marxism into a *Volkssozialismus* (popular socialism) and *Kultursozialismus* (cultural socialism) within the capitalist system; the Communists, however, demanded radical change and regarded any reform as illusory. Much of the energy of the labor movement was dissipated by the intense enmity between these parties. After 1928 the change of policy of the Soviet Communist Party and the Comintern imposed complete separatism on the KPD, which became openly confrontational with the SPD.[31] If one talks about the fate of the Weimar Republic and the responsibility for the onset of fascism, a great deal of blame can be meted out not just to conservatives but also to the Communists for their refusal to form an alliance with the Socialists.

Lukács's simultaneous attack of Expressionism and the USPD in 1934 must therefore be viewed not just in contrast with Bloch's response but even more as an instance of the hard-left approach of the German KPD and its ongoing internecine struggle with the competing workers' party, the Social Democrats. By the end of the war Behne had become unquestionably associated with the USPD. In 1919 he complained in an article titled "Unsere moralische Krisis" (Our moral crisis), published in the *Sozialistische Monatshefte,* that nothing had changed and that there had really been no break with old attitudes of nationalist arrogance.[32] At the same time, Behne, although often critical of German society, retained the Social Democrats' belief in the possiblity of reform. While some of his books were addressed to a cultural elite, many more of his publications in the 1920s were directed to a larger audience. Among these were his introductions to art and contemporary art respectively, both published in 1925 by the Arbeiter-Jugend Verlag, *Die Überfahrt am Schreckenstein: Eine Einführung in die Kunst* (The passage to the Schreckenstein: An introduction to art) and *Von Kunst zur Gestaltung: Eine Einführung in die moderne Kunst* (From art to design: An introduction to modern art). His deep commitment as a teacher to the *Volkshochschule* Movement is another indication of his general agreement with the Social Democrats' attempt to develop a popular and cultural socialism.[33]

Does Modernism Equal Functionalism?

For many architectural historians, even those who are well acquainted with German developments in the 1920s, Modernism and functionalism have become nearly synonymous.[34] Within the comparatively brief period of Modernism, however, functionalism assumed many guises. Although it is not within the scope of this essay to do justice to the complexity of functionalist beliefs in modern architecture, some arguments about functionalism are useful to consider in order to understand both the underlying conventions of functionalism in the 1920s and the considerable misunderstandings that have become embedded in postmodern discussions.

Two extreme positions regarding functionalism help to introduce succinctly the conflicting issues of the history of the term and current reactions to it. Characteristic of the positive view of functionalism in the 1950s is Edward Robert de Zurko's excessively broad and uncritical history *Origins of Functionalist Theory*, 1957. Typical of the early postmodernist reaction against functionalism is David Watkin's rather narrowly conceived *Morality and Architecture*, 1977. The shared assumption in both works is that functionalism is synonymous with Modernism.

Using a rather circular argument, de Zurko writes that "the literature of functionalism consists largely of the writings of recognized functionalists (such as Horatio Greenough, Louis Sullivan, and Taut)."[35] Whereas de Zurko's book is perhaps too inclusive regarding ideas of purpose and utility, Watkin's tone is that of a postmodern scold. He belittles Le Corbusier's *Vers une architecture*, 1923, because, in Watkin's words, "What is simple, supposedly functional, and materialistic in aim, light in colour, and immediately apprehensible in form enjoys advantages in terms of health and morality over other different or more complex solutions. Thus it must be imposed on society as soon as possible if we are to avoid revolution." He goes on to insist that the apocalyptic overtones of Le Corbusier's functionalist argument were later exaggerated by Taut in his *Modern Architecture*, 1929, and cites the following passage from Taut to prove his point:

> If everything is founded on sound efficiency, this efficiency itself, or rather its utility, will form its own aesthetic law. A building must be beautiful when seen from outside if it reflects all these qualities.... The architect who achieves this task becomes a creator of an ethical and social character; the people who use the building for any purpose, will, through the structure of the house, be brought

9

to a better behaviour in their mutual dealings and relationship with each other. Thus architecture becomes the creator of new social observances.[36]

If Watkin himself takes on a moralizing voice in his critique of moralizing theories (in this instance a Puginian trust in social control through architecture), de Zurko is more open-minded than most modernist historians in his belief that "modern discussions of functionalism show a dual approach: the rational and the poetic." He cautions also that "the frequency of statements by modern architects regarding functionalism indicates that functionalism is neither a clear and unchallenged law of architecture nor a spent force, but a vital concept requiring clarification."[37]

Important for understanding modern functionalism and Behne's attempt to categorize the various tendencies is de Zurko's discussion of two major nineteenth-century functionalist trends: the mechanical and the organic analogies. The former uses machines as a paradigm for aesthetic theory and is a response to the Industrial Revolution. Although the latter trend draws its references from nature and the former employs models of mechanical production, both could be invoked together. A clear and early example is the theory of the American sculptor Horatio Greenough, who in 1843 proposed a functionalist approach to architecture in order to create what he thought of as a tabula rasa, or hedge against the influence of the older European styles. He believed that functionalism could foster an indigenous American approach to design and recommended, "Let us consult nature, and in the assurance that she will disclose a mine richer than was ever dreamed of by the Greeks." He went on to say that "the law of adaptation is the fundamental law of nature in all structure." Together with this organic justification, Greenough drew a parallel between natural selection and the production of man-made artifacts in general and machines in particular, "If we compare the form of a newly invented machine with the perfected type of the same instrument, we observe, as we trace it through the phases of improvement, how weight is shaken off where strength is less needed, how functions are made to approach without impeding each other, how straight becomes curved, and the curve is straightened, till the straggling and cumbersome machine becomes the compact effective and beautiful engine."[38]

In addition to the organic and mechanical paradigm, Greenough, through his close relationship with Ralph Waldo Emerson, gave his ideas an ethical dimension as well. Behne would also address all three functional concepts present in Modernism — the organic, the mechanical, and the social — but

10

whereas he described the first two in his role as a historian of the 1920s, he only advocated a type including a social dimension. His advocacy of a social functionalism, in fact, resembles Louis Sullivan's polemics.

Sullivan's dictum "form follows function," stated first in 1888, employed two components of Greenough's functionalism. Its Lamarckian organicism is the most evident, and disregarding Greenough's mechanical analogy, Sullivan gave the ethical aspect of functionalism greater importance. Although initially indebted to Transcendentalism as much as to Greenough, Sullivan came under the influence of Chicago School pragmatic realism and John Dewey's utilitarian instrumentalism in the 1890s. These philosophies assumed a complex interrelationship between human thought and action and the environment. This interrelationship contrasts with the simple behaviorist model of Pugin, in which the environment affects human action but not vice versa. Hugh Dalziel Duncan explains the Chicago School and Sullivan's dictum thus, "Forms arise in attempts to solve problems in social action, form and function are real, not because of their relationship to an essence outside of or beyond action, but *within* action in society."[39]

The distinctly utilitarian ethics of "form follows function" do not seem to have—on the surface at least—a direct relationship with Central European ideas in the early twentieth century. However, Behne's stress on the social implications of functionalism, despite his rejection of "utilitarianism" as he understood it, cannot be divorced altogether from the social meaning of utilitarianism or from Sullivan's understanding of function as a social tool.

Because "form follows function" is such an easy-to-recall, alliterative, and concise phrase, it has unfortunately been remembered far too often. In popular usage throughout the second half of the twentieth century, it has usually been forgotten that the phrase was coined by Sullivan, and today it is frequently associated with European Modernism in general or, just as often, with the Bauhaus specifically. In fact, "form follows function" and "Bauhaus functionalism" have become imprecise, interchangeable clichés that are used either descriptively by modernists or critically by postmodernists as a presumed shorthand for Modernism.

In Hitchcock and Johnson's *The International Style*—so important for introducing an American audience to European Modernism—this confusion had not yet occurred. Hitchcock and Johnson, in fact, tried to discredit modern functionalism for its lack of aesthetic concerns:

Some modern critics and groups of architects both in Europe and in America deny that the aesthetic element in architecture is important, or even that it exists. All aesthetic principles of style are to them meaningless and unreal. This new conception, that building is science and not art, developed as an exaggeration of the idea of functionalism.

In its most generally accepted form the idea of function is sufficiently elastic. It derives its sanctions from both Greek and Gothic architecture, for in the temple as well as in the cathedral the aesthetic expression is based on structure and function.[40]

They held Hannes Meyer, in particular, responsible for a contemporary doctrinaire functionalism, because he was an "anti-aesthetic functionalist" who claimed that the basis of all design must be economic.

Lewis Mumford in an essay of 1951, "Function and Expression in Architecture," saw the failure of modern architecture, by contrast, to be its lack of symbolic communication. He identified an excessive reliance on a machine aesthetic and a misunderstanding of "form follows function" as the central problem in the later development of Modernism:

> Now all this is not to say that the doctrine that form follows function was a misleading one. What was false and meretricious were the narrow applications that were made of this formula. Actually, functionalism is subject to two main modifications. The first is that we must not take function solely in a mechanical sense, as applying only to the physical functions of the building. Certainly new technical facilities and mechanical functions required new forms; but so, likewise, did new social purposes and new psychological insights.[41]

For Mumford the modern period is an "age of deep psychological exploration and heightened social responsibility." It is not just the age of Albert Einstein, Henry Bessemer, and Frederick Taylor but also the age of Charles Darwin, Henri Bergson, Sigmund Freud, and Pyotr Alekseyevich Kropotkin.

Mumford's analysis is similar to that of Joseph Hudnut in his essay "The Post-Modern House," 1945.[42] Hudnut was then the dean of Harvard's influential Graduate School of Design and was responsible for bringing Gropius to Harvard. He criticized the use of a dogmatic functionalism and structural invention for its own sake. As early as 1931 (that is, before Hitchcock and Johnson), he had complained that the doctrine of functionalism could be obfuscating and mystifying if a rigid utilitarianism became the sole principle of design. He regarded as naive the belief that beauty is automatically created by building logically, the shibboleth of "form follows function." If this were correct, no school of architecture would have to concern itself with the teaching of beauty; it would be enough to teach economics, business, and the cost of materials.

The present-day misunderstanding of modernist functionalism does not in fact spring from either Taut's or Hannes Meyer's conception; it is based on an overly narrow definition of function as a single issue that is presumed to be a practical design response within a specific building, one that does not seem to embrace environmental, social, or economic factors. In this later, simplistic version of functionalism, biological and utilitarian ideas have become not only hopelessly abbreviated, frozen, and canonical but also nearly meaningless.

One problem with interpreting functionalism as if it were a law or mathematical theorem (the belief that there is indeed a specific form for each possible function) is that it is based on a fundamental misapprehension of design procedures. In truth, a single function — if it can ever be completely segregated conceptually from all other functions — can be interpreted by the architect in many appropriate formal expressions. Nevertheless, "form follows function" in its popular conception may be difficult to dislodge because it provides a semblance of rules in an area where there are none.

Not all architectural histories that address functionalism are as extreme as de Zurko's in their apparent unpolemical neutrality or as hotly polemical as Watkin's. For instance, Heinrich Klotz in *The History of Postmodern Architecture*, 1988, makes a fair assessment of the difference between the functionalism of classical Modernism and a later "vulgar" or "doctrinaire" functionalism. He even takes time to discuss the less well-known organic functionalism of Häring, a form of modernist functionalism that Behne also deals with at length. The postmodern reaction against Modernism — as well as the consequent tendency to present Modernism in an overly simplistic form — has been most apparent in the Anglo-American sphere, whereas elsewhere attitudes have reflected a calmer evolutionary approach. In this context it is significant that Klotz's book, when it was first published in Germany in 1984, was called *Moderne und Postmoderne: Architektur der Gegenwart*.[43] The German title suggests that Modernism and postmodernism are simultaneously present in contemporary architecture; in the title of the American version Modernism has been banished.

Whereas de Zurko described the progress of functionalism uncritically, Colquhoun in his *Essays in Architectural Criticism: Modern Architecture and Historical Change*, 1981, assessed the possible meaning of functionalism in a few words but with far greater cogency:

> Positivism, in separating pure instrumentality from meaning, impelled architecture simultaneously toward eclecticism and functionalism. Ever since the late eighteenth century, architecture has oscillated between two poles of thought: that according to which all styles are possible and that according to which all styles are forbidden — between synchronic and diachronic relativism. But diachronic relativism — the belief in the continuous evolution of architectural form — can be seen, from another point of view, as the continuation of the eighteenth-century search for the origins of architecture. There is still the sense of a return to the primitive statement unsullied by the historical accumulation of metaphor. We see then that the origins of modern functionalism lie in a very complex intermixture of the notion of architecture as relative and evolutionary and the notion of architecture as based on natural law.[44]

Equally suggestive, Stanford Anderson in his essay "The Fiction of Function," 1987, has argued that "'functionalism' is a weak concept, inadequate for the characterization or analysis of any architecture." He continues: "It may be useful to recognize 'functionalism' to the extent that one can find some naive functionalist arguments to contrast with Hitchcock and Johnson's antifunctionalist rhetoric. However, any serious examination of the buildings at issue will reveal that none of them, whatever the surrounding rhetoric, can be explained functionally. It was a fiction that function provided a crucial line of demarcation within modern architecture."[45] He goes on to describe functionalism in modern architecture as a specific form of fiction — not a lie but a storyline that was used to describe a vision of the world that is richer and broader than the postmodern, truncated notion of functionalism projected onto Modernism. Of course, postmodernists demonized Modernism in the same manner that modernists demonized nineteenth-century eclecticism — another form of fictionalizing the past, in this case with Gothic horror stories. Anderson's suggestion for studying the functionalist storyline of the modernists will allow us to comprehend their understanding and self-presentation vis-à-vis theory and architecture in its widest implications. Modernist texts need to be examined, therefore, in order to discover both their constructive and constructed fiction.

To date, a general awareness of specific modernist books is inadequate, perhaps because so few of these texts of the 1920s have been translated. Taut's *Modern Architecture* was the only one of the German books of this time that also appeared in English. Le Corbusier's *Vers une architecture*, translated into English in 1927, is really his own vision for a new architecture and is not about the work and ideas of his colleagues. In addition, many of the central texts of this period are not readily accessible. They are usually found in special collections of only the best libraries. It is not surprising, therefore, that the historically important *International Style* or Giedion's *Space, Time, and Architecture*, 1941, still form the basis for understanding Modernism.

The Background to the Debate in Germany: The Structure and Politics of Education As a Competitive System

During the 1920s Germany became the center of Modernism in architecture. The creation of the Bauhaus in 1919; the Werkbund Ausstellung "Die Wohnung" (a housing exposition held at Weissenhof in Stuttgart) in 1927 (with an international group of architects that included Mies, Le Corbusier, and Oud); and the meeting of CIAM II (Congrès Internationaux d'Architecture Moderne) in 1929 in Frankfurt are only a few of the more publicized events. Germany's centrality in the architectural avant-garde is not entirely due to the presumed liberalism of the Weimar Republic, with which the revolutionary tendencies of the decade are often equated.

The prelude to Germany (and Central Europe) becoming the international focus of modernist theory and debate must be sought, at least in part, in the exceptionally competitive and pluralistic educational system established in the course of the nineteenth century and fully in place by the end of the century.[46]

This was not the case in France. The Académie Royale de Peinture et de Sculpture and the Académie Royale d'Architecture (which merged in the nineteenth century to become the Ecole des Beaux-Arts) had been centralized under Louis XIV in order to preempt the power of the guilds.[47] Similarly, the Ecole Polytechnique, founded in the late eighteenth century, followed in the tradition of the older Ecole des Ponts et Chaussées (School of bridges and roadways). Although both the Ecole des Beaux-Arts and the Ecole Polytechnique underwent considerable restructuring over the years, neither was decentralized until after the student protests of 1968.

The difference in Germany was not the quality of the schools as such but the structural variation determined by the country's political history. In Germany, for instance, the struggle for control between the older guild system and the newer academies was not changed by the fiat of a powerful monarch as it had been in France. Debates about the respective merit of each continued into the early 1920s and the beginning years of the Bauhaus, when the school vacillated between being a lodge for artisans and an elite academy turning out designers for industry.

More importantly, because Germany consisted of a large number of independent principalities, the growth and development of architectural education differed from region to region. In the late eighteenth century, for instance, Prussia experimented with architectural instruction carried out in an art academy, but apparently because of an overemphasis on rules of taste and purely ceremonial expression, a separate school of architecture was founded in 1799, the Bauakademie in Berlin. Here construction and civic planning were given greater importance. The Berlin Bauakademie was united with the Gewerbeakademie (Crafts academy) in 1879 to form the Technische Hochschule (Polytechnic school). In the course of the nineteenth century separate polytechnic schools, rather than architecture departments attached to art academies, became the most prestigious schools of architecture, although those within art academies continued into the twentieth century. A polytechnic school was founded in Karlsruhe in 1825, in Dresden in 1838, in Stuttgart in 1840, in Hannover in 1862, in Darmstadt in 1864, in Munich in 1865, and in Aachen in 1870. Still others were founded after Germany's unification in 1871.[48]

Even after unification, polytechnic schools remained extraordinarily varied. Local traditions, once established, were not readily surrendered. Furthermore, member states were not treated equally. The larger southern states, such as the kingdoms of Württemberg and Bavaria, had exacted special privileges not extended to other states. At any rate, the control of civil liberties, the police, and education belonged to the separate states, not the federal government. Despite Prussia's attempt in the 1880s to establish educational standards for polytechnic schools in the Reich, it is not surprising that schools continued to differ in their pedagogical emphases, nor that those in the southern states, which had had a strong anti-Prussian history before 1871, were the most liberal institutions. Both the Technische Hochschule in Stuttgart and that in Munich, for example, were less pedantic in their education than the Berlin polytechnic school, which emphasized memorization and extremely long examinations. The schools in Karlsruhe, Darmstadt, and Dresden were more middle-of-the-road, somewhere between Berlin's conservative institution and the more liberal ones in Stuttgart and Munich.[49]

The most important unifying factor among the various polytechnic schools was of course the German language, allowing professors and students to move from one school to another. Gropius, for instance, attended both the Berlin and the Munich Technische Hochschule. For this reason students and teachers were kept aware of pedagogical differences. Where students were unable to influence curricula, they could certainly vote with their feet. Add to this matrix the polytechnic schools in German-speaking countries — among them, those in Vienna, Prague, Graz, Brno, and Zurich — and one can see the obvious potential for a lively competition.

At the same time, Germany, like most other countries, continued to rely on the older apprenticeship system. But unlike other countries, it also had a *Bauschule* (building school) or *Baugewerksschule* (building trade school); in 1957 such institutions were given the more impressive name *Ingenieurschulen für Bauwesen* (engineering schools for the construction trade). The polytechnic school was the most academically structured of these options, requiring graduation from a *Gymnasium,* the higher secondary school attended only by those who plan to go on to a university. A diploma from a polytechnic school was also the prerequisite for administrative jobs with the governmental bureaucracy. In this respect, the German polytechnic school was comparable to attending the Ecole des Beaux-Arts or Ecole Polytechnique in France.

The *Bauschule,* on the other hand, required only previous work as an apprentice. In Germany compulsory education ends at age fourteen with education in a *Volksschule.* For most of those entering an apprenticeship system, however, education continues in a "trade school" where classroom attendance is combined with on-the-job training. The *Bauschule* was close in conception to the trade schools set up for apprentices in other fields. Courses were usually given during the winter months when there was little construction, and summers were spent as an apprentice. The *Bauschule,* therefore, combined academic and apprenticeship training. It was in effect a part-time academy that retained the advantages of practical experience. The Munich Bauschule, the oldest, was founded in 1820, and the Weimar Bauschule was founded by Goethe in 1828.

By the early twentieth century, architectural education had attained a hierarchic configuration with the greatest prestige residing in the most academic training. Nonetheless, it was entirely possible for architecture students to avail themselves of all three systems — polytechnic school, *Bauschule*, or apprenticeship — really four systems if one includes the architecture departments in art academies. Thus the picture became even more complex and competitive. Taut, for example, studied at a *Bauschule*, then was apprenticed to several architects, and thereafter attended selected courses at the Berlin Technische Hochschule. Given the diversity of schools within the Reich — as well as the ability of students to attend several schools of the same academic rank in different states and to participate in the various hierarchic levels of architectural training — it becomes extremely difficult for the historian to make succinct generalizations about architectural education in Germany. One can only speculate that its basic structural complexity exposed young architects to a variety of competing approaches and philosophies, which in turn may account for the intensive debates surrounding architecture in the early twentieth century. The political change after 1918 would not have made an immediate impact, because the structure of these competing and interrelated pedagogical systems did not change drastically. Moreover, the modernists of the 1920s were all educated before 1918, at a time when these varied educational systems were all in place.

A comparison of two influential architects and mentors, Behrens and Theodor Fischer, can perhaps explain why certain architects became important teachers for the generation that came into prominence in the 1920s and how these teachers were affected by their own varied regional and educational backgrounds. Today, Behrens is still unfortunately seen as a "protomodernist" to whom Gropius, Mies, and Le Corbusier were all apprenticed. As Stanford Anderson has pointed out, this definition of Behrens is a kind of "back-formation" introduced by such historians as Nikolaus Pevsner and Hitchcock;[50] they saw Behrens through the work of his pupils and decided that he was the originator of modern industrial forms. A better case can be made, however, for viewing Behrens as an influential, if somewhat conservative, architect who received important commissions from German industry as well as from the Reich. His case is also interesting for demonstrating the shift from aristocratic to industrial, corporate patronage of crafts and architecture — symptomatic of Germany's late industrialization, which was burgeoning in the early twentieth century and transforming the country into one of Europe's foremost manufacturing centers.

Behrens's education as an architect was of the most unconventional sort, even in the context of the German pedagogical system. After receiving his training as a painter, he worked in Munich, where in 1897 he became one of the cofounders of the Vereinigte Werkstätten für Kunst im Handwerk (United workshops for art in craft), one of the several reformist arts and crafts associations that took their cue from the English Arts and Crafts Movement. In 1899 Behrens was one of seven artists invited by Grand Duke Ernst Ludwig of Hesse to become a member of the Darmstadt Artists' Colony. Because Ernst Ludwig was Queen Victoria's grandson, he had made many trips to England, where he had come in direct contact with the English Arts and Crafts Movement, and he had commissioned M. H. Baillie Scott and C. R. Ashbee to design rooms for him in Darmstadt. The Darmstadt Artists' Colony was the only one of such turn-of-the-century ventures to be organized by an aristocratic patron, as opposed to the artists themselves. On the Mathildenhöhe, a hill overlooking the city, Ernst Ludwig wanted to establish a "New Athens" in order to compete with nearby, more established cultural centers. The artists were paid a salary and were expected to produce a *Volkskultur*. Their communal studio building, designed by the Austrian Joseph Maria Olbrich (the only architect in residence), was initially called the Arbeitshaus (house of work) and later the Ernst-Ludwig-Haus. The location of such an exclusive colony on the Mathildenhöhe — above both city and palace, inverting the traditional hierarchy — vividly revealed the grand duke's high regard for the arts. It was an arrangement that remains, nevertheless, intrinsically hierarchic. It simply placed the artist at the top of the pyramid in place of the ruler.

If Ernst Ludwig expected a trickle-down effect from his New Athens, the architecture and crafts exhibited on the Mathildenhöhe never fostered a *Volkskultur*. On the contrary, some contemporary critics saw only an expression of luxury in the form of a *Gesamtkunstwerk*. In 1901, the year of the Mathildenhöhe's first exhibition, a deficit of 300,000 *Marks* was incurred by the Artists' Colony; this huge amount indicates that the artists were living like princes in the grand duke's not-so-rich Hesse.[51] Similarly, the Wiener Werkstätte went through a series of near-bankruptcies and bailouts by wealthy patrons.[52] This is not to question the beauty of many designs made by the Darmstadt group or the Wiener Werkstätte but rather their ability to bring their reforms to a wider audience as they intended. If they had studied the English Arts and Crafts development more diligently, they might have also discovered that William Morris had already encountered the problem of crafts production as something only the well-to-do could afford.

Despite the Artists' Colony's shortcomings, Behrens's contact with this group was important for his subsequent career change. At Darmstadt, Behrens was the only artist who was allowed to design his own house; all other buildings were designed by Olbrich. Without even an architectural apprenticeship, Behrens made the transition from painting and arts and crafts to architecture. He left Darmstadt in 1903 to take over the directorship of the Kunstgewerbeschule (Arts and crafts school) in Düsseldorf. During his Düsseldorf period Behrens met the wealthy, young Karl Ernst Osthaus, who quickly replaced Grand Duke Ernst Ludwig as a more "modern" patron of the arts and architecture. Osthaus came from a banking and industrialist family and at the age of twenty-two had inherited 65 million *Marks*. He established the Folkwang Museum in Hagen, an exhibition space for contemporary art with an interior designed by Henry van de Velde. Between 1904 and 1912 Behrens designed eight projects for Osthaus, including a plan of 1907 for Hagen-Eppenhausen, a garden suburb. Osthaus also became closely associated with the Werkbund and in 1909 helped to create the Deutsches Museum für Kunst im Handel und Gewerbe (German museum for art in trade and craft), in effect a Werkbund museum for traveling exhibitions. With Osthaus's patronage Hagen became a new cultural center, significantly in the middle of the industrial Ruhr district. In 1907 Behrens was named the chief architect and designer of the AEG, then Germany's foremost manufacturer of electrical products, which had its headquarters in Berlin. His factories for the AEG and his designs of the company's electric products were, if not frank industrial expressions, symbolic expressions of industrial might.

It was during this period that Gropius, Mies, and Le Corbusier were apprenticed to Behrens (not all at the same time). Each arrived with a different background, rather characteristic of any group of architects in Germany at the time. Gropius had the most formal education with four years of schooling at two different polytechnic schools. Mies had gone through several apprenticeships before joining Behrens, and Le Corbusier had attended an arts and crafts school at La Chaux-de-Fonds in the Swiss Jura, where he had initially learned to engrave watches. He arrived in Berlin, however, after an apprenticeship with Auguste and Gustave Perret in Paris. Behrens was not much their senior in terms of actual building experience, yet all chose to work for this "artist-architect" who had an ability to evoke powerful images. Le Corbusier in his report on German crafts and architecture, published in Switzerland in 1912, writes that Behrens's AEG Turbine Factory was referred to as a "cathedral of labor," suggesting perhaps the reason for Behrens's rapid progression from high art at the Mathildenhöhe to industrial image-making in Berlin.[53] Behne would later take issue with Behrens as a modernist.

Though less well known today, even among architectural historians, Fischer had a greater reputation as an architect and teacher than Behrens before 1914. Le Corbusier first set out for Munich hoping to work for Fischer, and only when Fischer did not have a place for him in his office did he venture on to Berlin in 1910 (with recommendations and letters of introduction from Fischer). During this period Le Corbusier also met with Hermann Muthesius, Osthaus, Bruno Paul, Wolf Dohrn, and Heinrich Tessenow, all among the more recognized figures of the early Werkbund.[54] Le Corbusier may have preferred to work with Fischer because he dealt with issues of city planning and was much better and more conventionally trained as an architect than Behrens. Fischer had been a student at the Munich Technische Hochschule and served an apprenticeship under Paul Wallot, the architect of the Reichstag in Berlin. In 1893 Fischer established himself as a practicing architect in Munich. He moved to Stuttgart in 1901 when he received an offer to teach at the Technische Hochschule there. He returned to Munich in 1909 and taught at the Munich Technische Hochschule until 1928. Among his many students and apprentices were Taut, Mendelsohn, Dominikus Böhm, Häring, Oud, Ernst May, Alois Welzenbacher, Fred Forbát, Martin Elsässer, and Paul Bonatz. His Swiss student Peter Meyer wrote in the 1930s that more than two hundred Swiss architects received their training with Fischer. Fritz Schumacher, professor of architecture at the Dreseden Technische Hochschule and the keynote speaker at the first Werkbund meeting in Munich in 1907, referred to him as the real teacher of a whole generation of architects. The historians of the Neues Bauen in the 1920s — Behrendt and Gustav Adolf Platz — still spoke of him as a great teacher. In 1932 he was one of the few to protest the closing of the Dessau Bauhaus — not because he was especially sympathetic to its pedagogy but because he believed on principle that an experimental school should be allowed to continue.

Throughout his career Fischer concerned himself with architectural education and was disturbed by its academic trend. He insisted on greater emphasis on learning through practical experience. One of his mottoes reveals his openness to his students' ideas: "I do not have a fixed conviction. I like to hear the opinion of the next generation in order to measure myself against it."[55] He also encouraged his students to follow their own interests and inclinations in order to gain confidence about their work, and he advised them to look for examples not in books but in their surroundings.

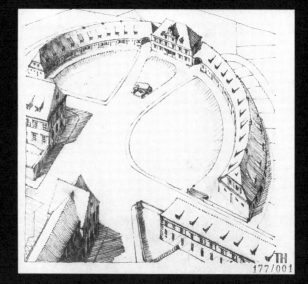

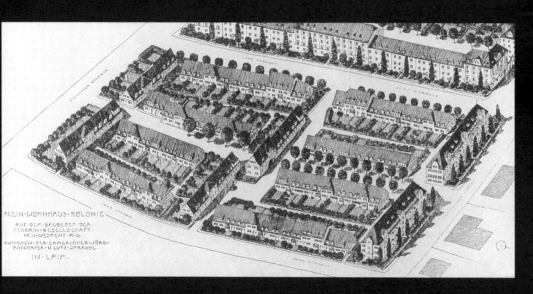

Fig. 1. Theodor Fischer, Bird's-eye view of a housing project in Gmindersdorf, near Reutlingen, 1903–1915. Munich, Architektursammlung, Technische Universität München.

Fig. 2. Theodor Fischer, Bird's-eye view of a housing project in Munich-Laim, 1910–1911. Munich, Architektursammlung, Technische Universität München. Photo: Courtesy Dipl. Ing. Klaus Kinold.

Fischer, whose own architecture was referred to as "South German" because of its modest regionalism, was particularly concerned with questions of urbanism and housing. His work has occasionally been associated with the artistic planning principles and the emphasis on picturesque urban views of Camillo Sitte as reflected in the latter's *Der Städte-Bau nach seinen künstlerischen Grundsätzen* (City planning according to artistic principles), 1889. While Sitte had not dealt with the social and economic issues of planning, his approach was based more on developing principles of psychological perception rather than on romantic, aestheticized imagery. Like Sitte, Fischer sought a practical aesthetics that was based on empirical studies and anthropological constants.[56]

Appointed as the director of Munich's municipal expansion office in 1893, Fischer had considerable influence on the development of new construction. Just as Sitte before him, he was critical of monumental, freestanding structures and preferred instead building sequences that maintain an urban texture and form a continuous enclosure. In addition to private commissions he built five schools and three bridges for the municipal government during his early Munich period. He received a large number of commissions for institutional buildings, such as museums and theaters. Among his larger projects were the Stadttheater in Heilbronn (1902–1913); the Universität in Jena (1905–1908), for which Taut produced one of the renderings; the reinforced concrete Garnisonskirche in Ulm (1908–1910); the Hessisches Landesmuseum in Kassel (1907–1913); the Museum in Wiesbaden (1911–1920); and the Kunstgebäude in Stuttgart (1909–1913), the last probably his most superbly sited public building.

Fischer completed two houses for Tessenow's garden city of Hellerau near Dresden (1909–1910) and a school project that remained unexecuted. His numerous housing projects include the factory town of Gmindersdorf, near Reutlingen (1903–1915; fig. 1), as well as housing in Munich-Laim (1910–1911; fig. 2). In his Alte Heide housing estate in Munich (1918–1930), executed for workers by a cooperative housing association in response to the postwar housing shortages, he turned to the severe scheme of a *Zeilenbau* (housing set in parallel rows) arrangement in order to rationalize as many small apartments as possible. It was quite unusual within the context of his previous work. His earlier projects influenced the housing of Taut, May, and Oud. Alte Heide, on the other hand, prefigures the rigidly rationalized *Zeilenbau* projects of the late 1920s, ostensibly produced to deal with the increasing housing shortage and worsening economy.

23

Like the work of Behrens and Josef Hoffmann, Fischer's approach became more conservative stylistically and therefore less influential by the 1920s. Most of his students cannot be called mainstream modernists, but several became pivotal figures in the Expressionist Movement in architecture after World War I, and many turned to social issues of housing. But some, like Elsässer and Bonatz, remained traditionalists. Bonatz, who had become Fischer's successor at the Stuttgart Technische Hochschule and who later became a National Socialist, railed against Fischer as a "wrecker of order." In the end Fischer regretted the increasing stylistic and political conservatism of the "Stuttgart School" even though it had originally been inspired by his work.

In 1907 both Behrens and Fischer became founding members of the German Werkbund, the association of architects and industrial firms that (according to modernist histories) left behind the retrospective ideals of the Arts and Crafts Movement and looked instead to progressivist notions of art and industry.[57] Fischer became the first president of the Werkbund in 1907, and he designed the main hall for the German Werkbund exhibition in Cologne in 1914 (fig. 3). Fischer's low-slung, Renaissance-inspired structure was flanked on either side by the templelike buildings by Behrens and Hoffmann. This group of Werkbund pavilions reveals the relative power of these traditionalists vis-à-vis the younger generation of Gropius and Taut, whose Werkbund buildings were assigned comparatively marginal sites. Although Fischer occupied a central position in the early Werkbund, he soon withdrew from its ideological struggles and came to believe that "this organization for the raising of the production standard" should have been dissolved after a few years.[58.]

Julius Posener in his text of 1964, *Anfänge des Funktionalismus* (The beginnings of functionalism), has already shown that most of the founding firms — such as the Deutsche Werkstätten für Handwerkskunst Dresden, Vereinigte Werkstätten für Kunst im Handwerk München, the Wiener Werkstätte, and several publishers — were more closely tied to the crafts than to modern industry, even though the intention of some of the members was certainly to move in the direction of design for industrial production.[59] The group had contemplated holding its first meeting in Nuremberg, site of Richard Wagner's *Meistersinger,* in part to emphasize a relationship to medieval guilds rather than to industry. In the end the first meeting was held in Munich, home of the Werkbund's first president, Fischer.

24

Fig. 3. Theodor Fischer, Main hall, German Werkbund exhibition, Cologne, 1914. Munich,
Architektursammlung, Technische Universität München.

In addition to architects such as Behrens and Fischer, the Werkbund included among its founding members an architect who all historians will agree was conservative both aesthetically and politically, Paul Schultze-Naumburg. Hermann Muthesius, who might also be included among the conservatives, was instrumental in the creation of the Werkbund as well, but for political reasons he had stayed in the background during its first meeting, so as not to jeopardize its foundation. As a bureaucrat of the Prussian Ministry of Trade in Berlin, Muthesius had criticized the imitation of styles in art and industry in a speech he made in early 1907; this in turn had provoked angry reactions and appeals to Kaiser Wilhelm for his dismissal from the Fachverband für die wirtschaftlichen Interessen des Kunstgewerbes (Trade association to further the economic interests of the art industries).[60]

Because of the Werkbund's extraordinarily varied makeup and the broad range of backgrounds among its members, by 1914 (that is, the year of its first major exhibition in Cologne), it was already split into hostile factions of arts-and-crafts individualists and progressive rationalists, as well as liberal and conservative camps. It was referred to at the time as an association of the most intimate enemies.[61]

Despite the Werkbund's lack of a clear direction, it became an important extra-academic transmitter of architectural ideas through its extensive membership, publications, and exhibitions. Stanislaus von Moos has shown that Le Corbusier appropriated some of the ideas and images he used in *Vers une architecture* (first published in *L'esprit nouveau*) from prewar Werkbund publications.[62] The Werkbund in its very makeup and heterogeneity was a reflection of the complex German educational scene in the early twentieth century. The debate at the Werkbund meeting of 1914 was in fact a political one, but it also hinged in part on a misunderstanding of the word *Typisierung* (standardization), prefiguring arguments and differences of opinion in the 1920s. Modernism as both practice and ideology was not a uniform concept, but it changed in the course of the 1920s and was constantly challenged from within and without the movement. The Werkbund, to which Behne belonged by 1913, illustrates perfectly the numerous academic and quasi-academic prewar institutions that fostered public discussion of the social implications of architecture and design.

Behne, in addition to his association with the Werkbund and his eventual critique of its goals, was a loyal supporter of the *Volkshochschule* Movement: a crucial but not well known aspect of nineteenth-century German educational reform. The *Volkshochschule* in Germany evolved in the second half of the nineteenth century and was based on Scandinavian models. It did not fall within the complex system of professional architectural education but added yet another layer to the already pluralistic professional educational possibilities. *Volkshochschule* teaching was like a mixture of American adult education and the courses taught to workers and new immigrants under Jane Addams at Chicago's Hull House and many later settlement houses in the early twentieth century.[63] It might further be compared to the turn-of-the-century art education movement in Germany, inspired by Alfred Lichtwark, who was appointed the director of the Hamburg Kunsthalle in 1886. Lichtwark directed his efforts especially toward the art education of young people. *Volkshochschule* lectures did not require entrance examinations, nor did they lead to diplomas (they were not set up for high school equivalency degrees as some such programs are in the United States). Courses, lectures, and study trips were meant to further the education of the public at large. Behne taught from the beginning until the end of his career within this open-ended, unstructured, and completely nonhierarchic educational program. Behne's central role in the Expressionist Arbeitsrat für Kunst (Work council on the arts) immediately after the war may also explain the group's concern in its manifestos with art education outside of established institutions.

Questions about the place of architecture and design that had arisen before the war against the background of a socially complex education system were not resolved after the war. In his well-known opening manifesto of 1919 for the Bauhaus (which was initially a state school, then a municipal school, and finally a private academy), Gropius insisted that only crafts can be taught, not art. He used the medieval guilds as his model of instruction. In 1922–1923 the Bauhaus curriculum began to address the design of industrial prototypes, but at the same time it hardly moved beyond a machine aesthetic; and only from 1928 to 1930, under Hannes Meyer's directorship, did Bauhaus instruction concern itself expressly with functionalism. Under Mies's directorship (1930–1933), the Bauhaus changed focus yet again toward straightforward architectural training without regard for the integration of the arts, which had been the mainstay of early Bauhaus teaching. Today, however, the Bauhaus is known for its "Bauhaus style" and "Bauhaus functionalism." Gropius later insisted that there was no such thing as a Bauhaus style. He was only partly correct. There were in fact several Bauhaus styles, suggesting an eclectic amalgam of several modernisms.

Behne's relationship with Gropius and the Bauhaus was an uneasy one. As early as 1923 Behne criticized Gropius and the first Bauhaus exhibition for its superficial use of several styles at the same time.

When Gropius had a chance to design a new building for the Bauhaus in Dessau, he was asked by his patron, the mayor of that city, to include space for the local crafts school. Thus, he could have brought together in a real sense traditional crafts training with Bauhaus instruction, but by the mid-1920s his pedagogical paradigm had become more technocentric. The two schools remained entirely separate entities within the new building, each with its own entry. Old hierarchies in the actual relationship between the avant-garde school and the municipal crafts school were disguised in the modern-looking plan of the building: it appears as if it has no center, but Gropius's office was in the bridge that both connected and separated the two schools.

Behne, Critic of Modernisms

Even before the end of the war, in 1917, Behne wrote a critique of the Werkbund that questioned its nationalist economic goals. He wrote that the Werkbund's attempt to bring art to bourgeois, commercial, and political life would lead only to sentimentality. He considered "artless" utensils far preferable to designed ones. He further questioned the "art-into-life" beliefs of the Jugendstil and of the Darmstadt Artists' Colony (which continued to form an underpinning of the Werkbund's principles), as well as the Werkbund's emphasis on economic competition. The introduction of aesthetics to the everyday object does not bring about an improvement in quality, he went on to argue, but turns it into kitsch. Somewhat perversely he stated that he preferred kitsch to the imposition of "art" on ordinary objects. He concluded (and here his argument is revealed as proto-Expressionist) that art should always remain a separate enterprise.[64] His belief suggested the bifurcation of art and the everyday, so common in Expressionism and probably best known in Gropius's assertion that art cannot be taught.

In 1920 Behne criticized the Werkbund again in the pages of *Sozialistische Monatshefte*. Once more he complained about its obsession with everything artistic, from "artistic norms" to "artistic advertisements." He hoped that the new members on its executive committee (twenty altogether, including Gropius, Osthaus, Taut, Bernhard Pankok, César Klein, and Poelzig as director) would bring about a change. He also conceded that the Werkbund was correct in rejecting Scheffler's "Ein Arbeitsprogramm für den Deutschen Werkbund" (A working program for the German Werkbund), which had insisted on a boycott of all foreign products.[65]

After the war Behne became closely associated with the Arbeitsrat für Kunst, which was founded in 1918, initially under Taut's leadership, and taken over a year later by Gropius. The Arbeitsrat consisted of a group of architects, critics, and artists and was modeled on the Arbeiterräte of the German Revolution of 1918. It sponsored publications, exhibitions, discussions, and circulars that raised questions about art education, public architecture, and the role of institutions in a postrevolutionary society. Behne became the business manager of the Arbeitsrat in 1919 and wrote the texts of several of its publications.[66] Although the Arbeitsrat maintained the Expressionist interest in mysticism, utopianism, and art as a transfiguring enterprise, it also became concerned with bringing art to a wider public by sponsoring exhibitions in the taverns of Berlin's working quarters. In March 1919 the Arbeitsrat followed a suggestion made by Taut and Behne and proposed a joint venture with the Werkbund to help with the reconstruction of northern France.[67] This idea for helping war-torn France is a succinct example of the groups' activist pacifism and especially of Taut's constructive utopianism. Behne, however, was not hopeful about the success of this effort. He was afraid that if German architects were sent to France, the French might wrongly assume that the Germans believed that the French did not have qualified architects of their own. The Werkbund, in any case, voted the project down.

By early 1921 when the artists of the Berlin Dada group had begun to intensify their critique of Expressionism for its emphasis on individualism and for not producing art that appealed to the worker,[68] the Arbeitsrat had already disbanded. As it became clear that the Arbeitsrat's expectations for a new society were far from the political reality, a disillusionment and withdrawal from the intense utopianism of the immediate postwar years took hold among its former members. As for the Dada effort to create a public art, it was no more successful than that of the Expressionists. Nevertheless, Dada's use of collages containing elements taken from the mass media, while not necessarily any clearer to the public than the Expressionists' use of folk art or children's art, proved to be an immensely fruitful artistic direction and prefigured the other "modernisms" of the later 1920s. Like the Expressionists, Dada artists believed that art could be used to revitalize society, a recurrent theme in early twentieth-century German art.

In an article in *Die Weltbühne* in 1926, entitled "An den Verein kommunistischer Kunstmaler" (To the Union of communist painters), Behne engaged in a direct confrontation with John Heartfield on the issue of political art.[69] The debate was occasioned by an earlier comment Behne had made about an exhibition organized by his friend Otto Nagel, a communist painter, in a store in the working-class district in Berlin-Wedding. Heartfield, then representing the official position of the KPD, insisted that the masses first have to be seized emotionally before art can be discussed. Behne, on the other hand, believed that the best art would, in the end, produce the best political art. The work on view was intended to show the suffering of the working class. Behne thought that the working class needed no instruction about its suffering and believed that this kind of art was regressive because it used the same means as bourgeois art. During a lecture Behne gave at the exhibition, workers demanded that pictures by Otto Dix showing proletarian women be removed. Their realism was found offensive. The KPD's attitude, Behne thought, was not unlike that expressed by the National Socialists, and he concluded that if one wants to "seize" the masses, one had better understand their psychology. Behne repeated similar ideas in an unpublished essay of 1932, "Sozialistische Kunst" (Socialist art).[70] He praised as successful the paintings of the German section of the *International Exhibition of Socialist Art* in Amsterdam in 1920, as well as the *Frauen in Not* (Women in distress) exhibition, organized by himself and Nagel in 1931; the latter was again held in the working-class district of Wedding.[71] The great irony in this debate was that although John Heartfield was an outstanding artist, the KPD vacillated in its support of his work.

In 1921 Behne also became the German correspondent for the English periodical *The Studio*. In 1920 he made a trip to Holland, probably in connection with the *International Exhibition of Socialist Art,* where he met Theo van Doesburg, Hendrik Berlage, H. Th. Wijdeveld, and Oud.[72] At the same time he was preparing a book on Dutch architecture, *Holländische Baukunst in der Gegenwart* (Contemporary Dutch architecture), which was published in 1922.[73] An excerpt from this book was published in *De Stijl*.

As the various modern art movements were becoming increasingly international in the early 1920s, Behne also made contact with architects and artists from other countries. Through his contact with László Moholy-Nagy, Behne had even tried to get Oud a commission for a house in Berlin. Moholy-Nagy had seen an article by Behne on Oud's work and through him Oud received the commission for a Mrs. Kallenbach. Oud came to visit Berlin to see the site, but the project fell through in 1922.[74] It was also Behne who first introduced Moholy-Nagy to Gropius.[75] In 1920 Gropius met van Doesburg at the house of Taut during van Doesburg's trip to prose-lytize De Stijl.[76] It is revealing that the two figures who in 1922–1923 were instrumental in directing the Bauhaus away from its Expressionist begin-nings — Moholy-Nagy and van Doesburg — were not known to Gropius before Taut and Behne introduced them to him. Thus the key figures of the Expressionist Arbeitsrat played a direct role in bringing about the change toward international Modernism, particularly the incorporation of De Stijl and Constructivism, in the Bauhaus after 1922.

During the early 1920s Behne, as well as Taut, was among the founding members of the Gesellschaft der Freunde des neuen Russland (Society of friends of the new Russia). Behne thereafter occasionally wrote articles for *Neues Russland*, the society's publication. In 1923, because of his association with this group, he was invited by the Soviet government to visit Petrograd and Moscow. In 1923 he also wrote one of his most insightful reviews of the first public exhibition at the Bauhaus:

> The exhibition suffers, I believe, because it takes place at a time when the Bauhaus is in a period of change. The new attitude toward linkage with technol-ogy, that is, standardization, is already recognizable, but does not yet appear with any consistency at all. The small-mindedness of handicrafts is also present and confuses the work, and even turns pure machine form into crafts.... The rejected decorative principle...celebrates triumphs in other places...why did this happen? In order to show that the new, the so-called Constructivist forms have been mastered.... The [model] house "Am Horn" stands among all these difficulties as somewhat uninteresting and unknowing. It is half-luxurious, half-primitive; half-ideal, half-time-bound; half-crafts, half-industrial; half-stan-dardization, half-idyll. It is in no sense pure and convincing, but again an aes-thetic, papery affair.

Behne held Gropius responsible for this attitude, because he found the same problems within the *Internationale Architektur* exhibition that was organized solely by Gropius as part of the larger Bauhaus exhibition. Behne felt that Gropius sought to disguise his uncertainty with an abrupt one-sidedness. Because of Gropius's "pseudoradical" attitude, *sachlich* tendencies, accord-ing to Behne, were simply presented as yet another "direction." Behne con-cluded that the future of the Bauhaus would depend on whether Gropius could find his way to an absolute *Sachlichkeit:* "This would allow him to take up all inspirations openly and without prejudice and competitiveness and to incorporate them together with his assistants. This would protect him from dipping into surface features here and there (in five projects Gropius changed his style of representation five times)."[77]

The same year that Behne wrote this cogent analysis of Bauhaus styles, he assembled material for his most important book, *Der moderne Zweckbau.* He apparently completed the text in 1923. When he could not find a publisher, he asked Gropius in 1924 to hold back his publication of *Internationale Architektur*, but Gropius refused. The latter was in fact surprised that as a result Behne considered him uncollegial and responded that there was room for more than one publication, even if many of the illustrated buildings were similar. Gropius must have known, however, that a book published under the auspices of the Bauhaus would have a greater impact on public perception. As noted earlier, Behne encountered further difficulties in assembling the material for his book because of the projected Bauhaus book series. Specifically, Oud no longer wanted to supply Behne with a copy of a lecture because he preferred to have it published by the Bauhaus.[78] Behne must have found all this extraordinarily ironic. In May of 1923, before the Bauhaus exhibition, Gropius had written to Behne requesting his assistance in the planning of the *Internationale Architektur* exhibition. In the same letter, however, Gropius announced that he could not give photographs of the Bauhaus to Behne because he was already planning a "special publication" that "obligated" him not to release illustrations beforehand.[79] While asking for Behne's help with his own project, Gropius (even before Behne's critical review of the *Internationale Architektur* exhibition) was unwilling to share information. Behne was probably less concerned about any similarity between his and Gropius's books than the prospect of having his serious analysis of Modernism overshadowed by the reputation of Bauhaus publications, a fear that was entirely justified.

In 1928, two years after *Der moderne Zweckbau* eventually appeared and shortly before Hannes Meyer replaced Gropius as the director of the Bauhaus, Behne wrote an appreciative article on Meyer's school in Bernau, near Berlin (fig. 4). In a letter Meyer had informed Behne of his deep interest in the cooperative movement in Scandinavia and its influence on his own work.[80] In 1929 Behne edited the periodical *Neues Berlin* with Martin Wagner, an early advocate of cooperative housing associations and later the socialist chief city planner for Berlin.

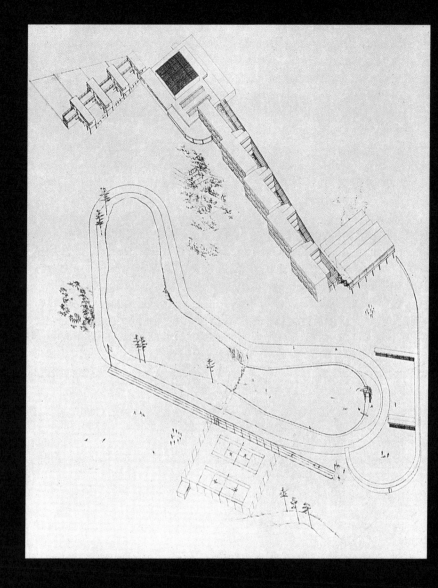

Fig. 4. Hannes Meyer, Axonometric view of the Bundesschule des Allgemeinen Deutschen
Gewerkschaftsbundes (ADGB), Bernau, 1928. Dessau, Stiftung Bauhaus Dessau, inv. no. I

Behne was forbidden to teach by the Nazis as early as 1933. This was due to his membership on the executive committee of PEN, the international literary organization, which had been founded in 1921 to fight for freedom of speech and humanitarian rights, and against racism. PEN had expressed fears about the threat of Nazi rule.[81] After his dismissal as a faculty member from the Humboldt-Hochschule and as a docent at the Städtische Berliner Volkshochschule, Behne published a number of politically neutral books on art historical subjects. Six weeks after the war ended he gave a lecture at the opening of the Volkshochschule Berlin-Wilmersdorf, titled "Entartete Kunst" (Degenerate art). It was about the artists who had been forced to emigrate under the Nazis. This lecture was published as a book in 1947. Behne died in 1948.

That he was forbidden to teach after 1933 does not, in itself, tell us precisely what Behne's political convictions were. After all, Emil Nolde, who was sympathetic to the Nazis, was forbidden to paint. On the one hand, Behne did not leave Germany, as did Taut, Mendelsohn, Gropius, Martin Wagner, and many others. On the other hand, Mies, who eventually did emigrate, did so only after he had tried unsuccessfully to work for the Nazis.

What is clear from Behne's writings, at least up until 1933, is that his incisive criticism was rarely held back. Together with his more specialized texts on art and architecture, he pursued his lifelong concern for wider public education through popular books on illustrators such as Heinrich Zille, who was known for his humorous and satirical drawings of the Berlin proletariat.[82] Behne also wrote critical essays about the pedagogical function of museums and their acquisitions policies.

Behne's analyses always have historical, contextual interest, but many of his critiques have not lost their power and meaning for the present-day reader. As Fritz Neumeyer wrote in *The Artless Word: Mies van der Rohe on the Building Art,* 1991:

> The most explicit critique of Mies's theme was formulated by Adolf Behne in his work *Der moderne Zweckbau....* It ranked among the most important publications up to then dealing with the New Building and has retained its significance as key work on the discussion of the theory of architecture. Behne's merit was that he had undertaken a summary of all the various impulses that originated in the years from 1900 to 1923 and arranged them in their contextual sequence, whereby he stressed the various concepts of rationalism and functionalism, illuminating their respective dogmas and prejudices.[83]

Der moderne Zweckbau

Despite its title, *Der moderne Zweckbau* is not a narrow interpretation of functionalism of the sort ascribed to Hannes Meyer by Hitchcock and Johnson, nor of the sort that postmodernists assume defines Modernism. From the outset Behne makes his approach abundantly clear. He defines the original need for building traditionally, that is, as a protective device against climate, animals, and enemies. The first building, he writes, fulfilled specific needs and had a purely functional character. In this sense buildings are essentially like tools. But from the beginning of human culture, he continues, there has been an urge toward playfulness, coupled with the need to be practical. He writes that primitive man was not strictly utilitarian as this double urge is verified in tools that are also beautiful and ornamented. The house is no exception: a house is as much a toy as a tool. What does change over time, in his opinion, is the balance between these two impulses, between function and form. In times when formalism has become paramount and tyrannical, it is necessary to stress function. Design, no matter what the current emphasis, should always aim for an equilibrium between these two competing factors.

Thus Behne did not insist on the primacy of function as such but considered it from a larger historical context that requires periodic adjustment. It could be an adjustment that moved toward function or form, but Behne perceived his own time to be so overwhelmed by formalism that he thought emphasis should be placed on functionalism. One might argue at this point that Behne was simply employing a larger picture of architecture in order to give contemporary functionalism historical legitimacy. His extensive explanation of the drawbacks of the functionalist position in later segments of the book, however, reveals that he was not a mere advocate of functionalism.

His linking the production of tools to the design of architecture is, of course, hardly new. With the rise of archaeology and anthropology in the late eighteenth and early nineteenth centuries, an interest in relating all human artifacts became increasingly pronounced. This new concern eventually came to include a consideration of crafts in any developmental process. Gottfried Semper's writings, especially his incomplete text on style, are probably the best-known instances of such an inclusive approach.[84] By the late nineteenth century Semper's influence could be seen in the art historical theories of Cornelius Gurlitt, as well as in Alois Riegl's *Altorientalische Teppiche* (Old oriental carpets), 1891.[85] Riegl had been keeper of textiles at

35

the Österreichisches Museum für angewandte Kunst (Austrian museum of applied arts) and thus was well aware of the importance of crafts in explaining cultural production. This allowed him to move beyond the standard notion of a "high period" of Roman art in his book *Die spätrömische Kunstindustrie* (Late Roman art industry), 1901. Using late Roman crafts production as his model, he not only directed art historical studies away from a specific high period but included what used to be called the "minor arts."

The incorporation of tools and crafts in theoretical considerations of art and architecture was not only affected by new fields of research such as anthropology but also by the changing value systems of the nineteenth century, which now stressed the everyday, bourgeois values of an essentially postaristocratic society. More importantly, while tools and crafts in an increasingly industrialized society became the foci of discussion because they were affected by industrial production, production in itself (because it had moved from the artisanal workshop to the factory) must also have assumed a larger role in the conception of arguments about developmental theories. Significantly, Riegl's book was about Roman *Kunstindustrie* (art industry).

Behne's balancing of form and function, although it seems a highly conceptual binary device, does not take on a hierarchic order. The notion of building as both a "toy" and a "tool," no matter what the current imbalance, does not imply any cultural progression or regression. He writes that a great gulf opened up in architecture between formal and functional approaches because form and function were separated. Thus, while employing these two apparently opposing concepts, Behne objects merely to their segregation. The balance between formal and functional building, Behne argues, has undergone a sea change in the last decade with the realization that a functional building can be formally pleasing and that formal buildings in themselves are not necessarily beautiful. Then he goes on to examine the current condition:

> Attitudes really had changed fundamentally. Architectural form was seen as a danger, and fulfillment of function was seen almost as a guarantee for the genesis of a good building. Whereas before people believed that artists had to be very clever in order to produce good buildings despite function...that is, buildings were again being seen much more as tools.
>
> Functional architectural concepts replaced formal ones. Functional buildings used to be specifically defined by their use, a link between the free creations of architects and the bare utilitarian structures of engineers and

technicians. Now every building became a functional building, that is, was tackled on the basis of its type and function. Fulfillment of purpose became one of the means of architectural design as it had been ever since Otto Wagner in 1895 wrote in *Baukunst unserer Zeit*: "Something impractical cannot be beautiful."[86]

Although Behne is not an advocate of functionalism, his occasional tangents on nineteenth-century historicism do reveal some of the prejudices of a modernist. Yet his belief that function and form must be balanced allows him to be critical of an overemphasis on function, and—unlike Pevsner or Giedion in their early writings—he does not see current trends as the only course for modern architecture. His model presumes that the present focus on functionalism would, at some point in the future, have to be adjusted in favor of formalism. In this sense Behne's *Der moderne Zweckbau* is about a modernist theory that contains within it the possibility of postmodernism.

The progression of his discussion spreads splendidly in ever-widening circles throughout the chapters of the book. After his analogy of tools and toys to architecture in the introduction, he moves from chapter 1, "No Longer a Facade but a House," to chapter 2, "No Longer a House but Shaped Space," and to chapter 3, "No Longer Shaped Space but Designed Reality." Here he brings us back to the larger social context of architecture.

In addition to singling out Otto Wagner in his opening chapter, he also speaks of Berlage's Amsterdam Stock Exchange and the demand for a *sachlich* development of architecture in Berlage's collected lectures *Grundlagen und Entwicklung der Architektur* (Foundations and development of architecture), 1908.[87] He also commends Alfred Messel's Wertheim Department Store in Berlin, which, on first view, he believes to be the most revolutionary work of these three architects (figs. 5, 6). On further reflection, however, he finds that the fulfillment of function in Messel's building is not absolutely *sachlich*. The department store's emphatic piers, which appear to be the most "structural" of its elements, reveal their intrinsically decorative nature in the way they merge with an overhanging roof line. Behne sees Taut's competition design of 1910 for the store's expansion as much more consistent (fig. 7), and he agrees with Le Corbusier's comment that German modern architecture frequently looks like "elevator-shaft architecture."[88]

Behne includes the country house in his broad conception of functional building, because he writes that in the houses of Frank Lloyd Wright (which he assumes to be country houses), the plan was freed of formalist rigidity and was used for a free balancing of space based "on the most careful inclusion

Fig. 5. Alfred Messel, View of the Wertheim Department Store from Leipzigerstraße, Berlin, 1904. From Gustav Adolf Platz, *Die Baukunst der neuesten Zeit* (Berlin: Propyläen, 1927), 230. Photo: Courtesy Verlag Ullstein GmbH, Berlin.

Fig. 6. Alfred Messel, Detail of the Wertheim Department Store from Rosenthalerstraße, Berlin, 1904. From Deutscher Werkbund, *Die Kunst in Industrie und Handel, Jahrbuch des Deutschen Werkbundes* (Jena: E. Diederichs, 1913), 65.

Fig. 7. Bruno Taut, Competition design for expansion of the Wertheim Department Store showing view from the street, 1910. From Kurt Junghanns, *Bruno Taut: 1880–1938* (Berlin: Henschelverlag Kunst und Gesellschaft, 1983), fig. 24. Photo: Courtesy Professor Dr. phil. habil. Heinrich Taut, Lehnitz.

of all requirements of comfort, quiet, and clear design. There is no longer any trace of symmetry or an axis, simply walls succinctly marking and accompanying the most comfortable traffic patterns for all the rooms. The accommodation to living functions goes so far that each piece of furniture has its specific place in the floor plan."[89] For Behne, Wright's plans "set space in motion as asymmetric as life itself." The description of Wright's interiors and furniture as accommodating living functions may have resulted from Behne's personal sympathy with this arrangement, but it may also have been based on his lack of direct experience with Wright's houses. Even though their plans are indeed fluid and asymmetrical, there is another sort of stasis and control in assigning every piece of furniture and built-in elements a fixed place, and this makes Wright's interiors actually quite inflexible. For Behne, as for Le Corbusier, the plan, rather than the elevation, has the most important value for contemporary architecture (Hitchcock and Johnson also state that functionalism had its strongest influence on the plan).

Behne then moves on to a discussion of industrial buildings, which he, like other modernists, believes are the most impressive in the United States. He quotes extensively from Henry Ford's *Autobiography*, which had just appeared as a best-seller in a German translation in 1923. The popularity of Ford's book was but an indication of the cult of *Amerikanismus* that swept Germany in the mid-1920s.[90] Ford's description of factory buildings seemed to combine the toughness of the demanding industrialist with Taylorism and an almost surreal emphasis on the Protestant work ethic and cleanliness. It is, in fact, a succinct example of the devolution from the Protestant work ethic to capitalism that Weber had described so convincingly in his *Protestant Ethic and the Spirit of Capitalism* of 1920. Behne quotes Ford thus: "Our machines.... are scientifically arranged, not only in the sequence of operations, but so as to give every man and every machine every square inch that he requires and, if possible, not a square inch...more than he requires.... The dark corners which invite expectoration are painted white. One cannot have morale without cleanliness."[91] Behne also cited Ford's opinion on art: "We need artists who master industrial relationships. We need masters of industrial methods," and "We will not put up elaborate buildings as monuments to our success. The interest on the investment and the cost of their upkeep would only serve to add uselessly to the cost of our products — so these monuments of success are apt to end as tombs."[92] Although Behne may not have agreed with Ford in general, by using this (and the architecture of Behrens for the AEG in particular) as his introduction to the design of German factories, he is able to highlight Behrens's aesthetic interpretation of form, which Behne earlier had criticized as exhibiting too much pathos.[93] Henry Ford's phrase "monuments of success are apt to end as tombs" is thus left in place as a signpost to Behne's interpretation of Behrens's turbine factory.

Behrens, in Behne's opinion, defines the machine as a pseudoaesthetic form. On the other hand, he regarded van de Velde as the first representative of a romantic machine cult, in which function is expressed as "dramatic" form. Behne detects van de Velde's continuing influence with younger architects, such as Mendelsohn. In Mendelsohn's work the decorative self-satisfaction of Hermann Finsterlin's organic projects is transformed into an engineerlike tension and energy. The attenuated character of Mendelsohn's Einstein Tower borders on anthropomorphism and is "dramatic" in the sense of van de Velde's work. Behne agrees with the Dutch architect J. F. Staal that the tower is more memorial than workshop. However, he finds Mendelsohn's Luckenwalde Hat Factory more *sachlich* with a purposeful organization of its production spaces.

Behne then further defines his concept of the functional plan, which he had touched upon in discussing the work of Wright. He describes orthogonal space not as a functional form but as a mechanical one. Organic life is not determined by the right angle. He gives as examples designs by Häring and Hans Scharoun, which on first sight are reminiscent of Finsterlin but have none of that painter's romantic willfulness. He also concedes that only an approximate, rather than absolute, adaptation to the natural fluidity of movement is possible.

He makes his expanded notion of functionalism even clearer when he goes on to insist that although the functionalist can be extremely practical, he is not to be confused with the utilitarian. Whereas the solutions of functionalists and utilitarians on some occasions may be related, their attitudes toward the problem of function are quite different:

> Functionalists are concerned with solving a problem of general significance to our culture. The utilitarian only asks: "What is the most practical way for me to act in this case?" But the functionalist asks: "How do I act most correctly in principle?" Their attitude inclines toward philosophy and has a metaphysical basis.... There is no question but that the functionalists, even the most [*sachlich*] ones, could more readily be classified as romantics than as rationalists.[94]

Behne's functionalism at its most extreme would turn the building into a pure tool and negate form (play) entirely. Would such an ultimate functionalism not lead to a dead end? He responds that the functionalist is right only as long as he is concerned with the individual room. Invoking his earlier description of the organic functionalist plan, he writes that it is correct that orthogonal space is not economical, that the curve describes functional space with greater precision. But when we group together several such "functional" rooms there is a loss of space because of poor tessellation. Häring's device of widening and narrowing corridors to accommodate the amount of traffic they bear, for instance, is based on the example of organic arteries. A building in this sense, however, is not analogous to a living organism that always performs the same function. Häring's undulating corridors assume that they will always carry the same distribution of traffic over the life of a building. Behne argues that this type of organic solution, which appears functional as a specific response at a certain moment in time, may also be too individualistic in a larger built context. Thus, from a social point of view, orthogonal space may in fact be more functional because it is more neutral when we consider a series of rooms or a group of buildings over time. He concludes that the deciding factor must be the general attitude of society.

Behne's argument for a neutral architecture in the public realm resembles the ideas of Loos. Although Behne mentions Loos only in passing in his text, he does list several of his books and essays in a footnote and in his recommended bibliography. But in an earlier article in *Frühlicht* of 1921–1922, Behne had specifically pointed to Loos's centrality in the demands for a *sachlich* architecture.[95]

Behne is at the same time always insistent that *Sachlichkeit* and the question of a functional architecture must be used to serve people. Staying close to postwar Expressionist beliefs, he therefore rejects outright technocentric justifications or machine metaphors. He writes that Le Corbusier's concept of a "machine for living" is acceptable if we view the machine as a prototype for a full-fledged human achievement. Le Corbusier's phrase will be misunderstood, according to Behne, if it is applied as a stylistic notion, that is, if it is used in the name of a falsely understood Constructivism that assumes that buildings and furniture must look smooth, cold, and polished, like machines. If it is misconceived, we will only arrive at a new subcategory of the Jugendstil, that is, a new taste or a new fashion that is nothing but a new pseudo-Constructivist machine formalism.

Behne further defines the differences between functionalism, rationalism, and utilitarianism:

> When the functionalist refers to the machine, he sees it as the moving tool, the perfect approximation to an organism.
>
> When the utilitarian refers to the machine, he sees it as an economic principle of saving work, power, and time.
>
> When the rationalist refers to the machine, he sees it as the representative and patron of standardization and typification.[96]

His description of the functionalist as someone who interprets the machine as an organic model is not much different from Greenough's mid-nineteenth-century functionalism. He does not suggest that functionalism is preferable to rationalism but instead describes the pitfalls of both these positions: the rationalist, who is concerned first of all with general principles (he places Le Corbusier in this category), must guard against becoming a rigid formalist. The functionalist, who is concerned with the specific principle, must be careful not to fall into the trap of individually expressed functions.

In his summary of German architecture in the context of European developments, Behne writes that Germany "is somewhat inclined to devote itself to an extreme that changes fairly frequently and then gives way to the opposite extreme — the consequence of an inner uncertainty."[97] He sees Russia (the East) and France (the West) as countervailing forces to Germany's persistent individualism: "It is a feature common to the East and West that . . . they proceed from the collective. But the collective is fundamentally different here and there: France has a structurally articulated society, Russia is dominated by the masses." Behne, using a social interpretation of internationalism, calls for a fusion of these tendencies. He quotes from Heinrich Mann to support such a linkage: "We are in the middle and it is our task to link East and West; one does not shut off nature. In the future we will be the republic in which representation of class and parliamentarianism are interlinked."[98]

Behne finds that recent Dutch architecture is also a good model: it exhibits a political realism and confidence that save it from the extremes of German architecture. He concludes the book with quotations from van Doesburg and Oud and an illustration of Vladimir Tatlin's *Monument to the Third International*. In *Der moderne Zweckbau* Behne does not allude to the conflict in Dutch architecture between the Amsterdam School and De Stijl, although

44

he had mentioned it in his book *Holländische Baukunst in der Gegenwart*, 1922. This may have been due to his acquaintance with van Doesburg and Oud, or more likely to the fact that by 1923 the Expressionist Amsterdam School had waned in importance in the face of van Doesburg's concerted efforts to proselytize De Stijl. Behne's change in emphasis also reflects the shift in Germany from Expressionism to the Neue Sachlichkeit between 1920 and 1923.

In general, however, his definition of architectural problems as moving between form and function, and between East and West in the cultural realm, resorts to a dualistic conception. In fact, he recommends a book by the German sociologist Alfred Vierkandt, *Dualismus im modernen Weltbild* (Dualism in the modern world picture), published in 1923. Vierkandt's methodology was phenomenological, not inductive. In this, he followed Simmel's sociology of human interaction. Vierkandt also invoked the treatment of community and society as irreducible phenomena in the sense of Ferdinand Toennies's *Gemeinschaft und Gesellschaft* (Community and society), 1887.[99] In Behne's use of this dualism one is also reminded of Wölfflin's reliance on a more formalist dualistic model in his first book, *Renaissance und Barock*, 1888. In *Der moderne Zweckbau* the dualistic paradigm is never reduced to a set of rules, however, since Behne investigates the differences between form and function only in order to draw them together without ever assuming the possiblity of a complete balance.

Within Behne's own writings this book was prefigured in his short essay "Architekten," which appeared in *Frühlicht*, a periodical edited by Taut from 1920 to 1922.[100] *Frühlicht* was initially an extension of and a voice for the Expressionist Gläserne Kette (Glass chain) group and was first published as an appendix to the periodical *Stadtbaukunst alter und neuer Zeit* (Art of city planning of past and new times). From the fall of 1921 until the summer of 1922, it was published as an independent journal in Magdeburg, where Taut had been appointed that city's chief planner. During its Magdeburg phase, when Behne's essay was published, the magazine had shifted away from the utopian Expressionism of the postwar years and increasingly covered issues of architecture and city planning. The period between 1920 and the stabilization of the runaway inflation at the end of 1923 (after which architectural construction resumed a normal level) is, therefore, a transitional period between Expressionism and what is commonly called the Neue Sachlichkeit.[101] *Frühlicht*'s articles during 1922 dealt primarily with urban issues but also included an essay by Kurt Schwitters and articles about Russian architecture, among them one on Tatlin's *Monument to the Third International*.

45

Behne's "Architekten" rejects what he calls Expressionism's "understandable utopianism" and is directed instead toward an internationalism that became important after 1919, possibly under the influence of the Third (Communist) International or the revival of the Second International by more moderate Socialists also in 1919. In this essay he also mentions the publication of Mendelsohn's work in *Wendingen* and a lecture he gave in Holland. Loos, Oud, and Le Corbusier are all cited in terms of their demands for a *sachlich* architecture. He quotes from Le Corbusier in *L'esprit nouveau*—as he was later to do in *Der moderne Zweckbau*—on the primacy of the plan in modern architecture, the banishment of all decoration, as well as the idiosyncratic.

He believes that the new architecture is collective and supraindividual. Behne's anti-individualism also clearly sets this essay apart from his own earlier Expressionism. The idea of the "supraindividual" seems to be indebted to van Doesburg's critique of Expressionism and his stress on apparently rational forms. What Behne does not address—whereas he exposes many forms of pseudofunctionalism and pseudorationalism—is De Stijl's own mystical, Platonic component.[102] De Stijl represents an ideology of the objective that effectively disguises its spiritual and transcendent beliefs.

Behne ends his essay by pointing to the transition from belief to action. He singles out in particular the work of the German cooperative housing associations that are helping to introduce rationalization and social concerns to the building industry. Quoting Martin Wagner, who headed one of these cooperative societies, he details the resistance of the larger building industry to change in conventional building methods.[103] He asserts that those forms belonging to the tradition of handicrafts will change in any case (and here he uses an economic argument that had been employed by Loos earlier) because they are becoming a luxury. Oud, who had distanced himself from De Stijl in 1922, became an important architect of social housing in Holland, which in turn provided a model for German housing. The cooperative building societies in Germany, which were generally set up by unions, benefited in the 1920s from funds that were collected as taxes on speculative building.

As already noted, in *Holländische Baukunst in der Gegenwart*, 1922, Behne mentions the tension between the Amsterdam School and De Stijl but writes that he prefers the impersonal and *sachlich* architecture of Rotterdam.[104] In another essay of 1922, "Kunst, Handwerk, Technik" (Art, craft, technology), he makes comparable statements about technology vis-à-vis crafts and satirizes Gropius's opening manifesto for the Bauhaus:

46

Depersonalization, which is in logical terms a process of objectivization, will bring not a creative revival of the crafts and folk art but rather a new and technical concept of labor. It is sufficient to glance at the important new European art, such as that of Léger, Malevich, Archipenko, Schlemmer, Baumeister, Tatlin, Mondrian, van Doesburg. Does it still have any inner connections to craft? It is antimanual, and instead intellectually constructive and technical. The phase of expressionism still cherished the cult of the crafts, but today, when the young European art has at last achieved a unison with the time and location of its creativity, the infatuation with the crafts (which, as the Dutch architect Oud rightly declares, blossoms at times when the delight in singular forms flourishes) is finished.

Architects, sculptors, painters...all of us must return to the crafts??? — No, we must move forward toward the demanding service of the intellect![105]

As in his Expressionist writings, Behne is openly polemical, but now he has become an advocate for De Stijl. In his critique of the Werkbund in 1917 he had still argued that the aesthetic aura of art kept it from being applied meaningfully to the common, everyday object, and in his Expressionist *Die Wiederkehr der Kunst* (The return of art), 1919, he had proclaimed art as the only true reality. He now questions the essential unity of the arts, as he will later question the idea of *Gesamtkunstwerk,* which had been an underpinning of design theory from Jugendstil to Expressionism and the early Bauhaus. By 1927 in an essay titled "Von der Sachlichkeit," he refers to the ideal of a *Gesamtkunstwerk* as a fata morgana.[106]

In 1924 he wrote a brief article, "Funktion und Form," in *Sozialistische Monatshefte.* It is basically his introduction to *Der moderne Zweckbau* and uses his toy and tool analogy to form and function.[107] He may have published this when he realized that Gropius would neither share his illustrations nor delay the publication of *Internationale Architektur.*

The Terms of the Debate

Behne's frequent use of *Sachlichkeit* and *Zweck* in his book raises questions concerning the meaning these terms had for him and whether his usage remained the same in the 1920s. Also of interest is the relationship between his understanding of these words and that of earlier and later writers. *Zweck* means purpose or function, while *Sachlichkeit,* although sometimes translated as function, literally means "thingness." *Sachlichkeit* is more properly translated as "the simple, practical, straightforward solution to a problem," as "matter-of-factness" and occasionally as "objectivity." *Sachlichkeit* simultaneously suggests the world of real objects and that of a conceptual rationalism. The philosophical allusions of *Sachlichkeit* in fact become more prevalent in the avant-garde books of the later 1920s and displace to some degree the term's "simple, practical" overtones. Because of its complexity and also because of its very particular associations with German culture, we have retained the German in this text and the translation. Sometimes Behne also uses the terms *Funktion* and *funktionell*. On many occasions he uses *Zweck, Sachlichkeit*, and *Funktion* interchangeably or as a series. But in his larger argument, as explained earlier, he draws a clear distinction between functionalism, rationalism, and utilitarianism.

As Harry Mallgrave has shown in his introduction to Otto Wagner's *Modern Architecture* and elsewhere, the architect Richard Streiter used the term *Sachlichkeit* as early as 1896 to define realist tendencies that had been a part of the German debate for nearly a decade.[108] Streiter raised the term in conjunction with *Zweckmäßigkeit* and *Funktion*, establishing a linked meaning of these concepts from the beginning. Yet, the precise meaning of *Sachlichkeit* was not altogether clearly defined. Streiter, for instance, used the word to describe the vernacular architecture of the Bavarian Gabriel von Seidl. The following year Lichtwark invoked the term in relation to the design of Messel's Wertheim Department Store in Berlin. This new linguistic preference within German theory for *Sachlichkeit* over the older term *Realismus* is made fully transparent in 1899 when Lichtwark, in the course of republishing an essay of 1897, changed its title from "Realistische Architektur" to "Sachliche Baukunst."[109]

Stanford Anderson has examined the use of such concepts in the early twentieth century. He writes that Muthesius did not advocate the pure *Sachlichkeit* of machines but rather a *sachliche Kunst*, an approach in which aesthetics seems to be paramount. Anderson has summed up a turn-of-the-century definition as follows:

> It was commonplace to recognize the engineering achievements of the nineteenth century, from tools or instruments to the great bridges and railroad sheds. Whether the critics saw these works as exemplary achievements or, resignedly, as the representative objects of a materialist epoch, they could agree that such works and the processes that produced them were marked by ratio-

nality, functionalism, and *Zweckmäßigkeit*. Muthesius subsumed such qualities under the term "pure" *Sachlichkeit*. . . .

Sachlichkeit is, then, a convenient umbrella term that invokes simplicity, a rational and straightforward attention to needs as well as to materials and processes.[110]

Anderson cautions at the same time that *Sachlichkeit* cannot be understood completely by such a generalization. Variations of meaning existed in the work of Otto Wagner and Behrens, who — Anderson believes — employed a symbolic functionalism.[111]

Behne and the Neue Sachlichkeit

Since there was already a degree of variation in the way *Sachlichkeit* was used at the turn of the century, we should not expect that the term ever assumed a completely uniform connotation. The Neues Bauen in general and the references in architectural texts to *Sachlichkeit* have understandably been associated with the Neue Sachlichkeit, a name first popularized by Hartlaub in May 1923 when he used it in a circular announcing an exhibition at the Mannheim Kunsthalle that took place in 1925. In a letter to Alfred Barr of July 1929 Hartlaub explained that the term applied to the new realism with a socialist flavor.[112] In 1923 in a review of the Bauhaus exhibition Giedion also mentioned the *"neue Gegenständlichkeit"* (new objectivity) that is everywhere in evidence in painting.[113] *Gegenstand* refers to a concrete object and is the same as the Russian *veshch,* which formed part of the Constructivist debate. A *Sache,* by contrast, is a more general fact or thing with abstract connotations.

The art historian Fritz Schmalenbach, who during the 1930s was at work on a book on the Neue Sachlichkeit, noted in an essay of 1940 that Wölfflin in his *Kunstgeschichtliche Grundbegriffe* (Principles of art history) and August Grisebach in *Die Baukunst im 19. und 20. Jahrhundert,* both of 1915, had used the term *neue Sachlichkeit* in passing. Schmalenbach, however, believed that Hartlaub's use of *Sachlichkeit* should be traced back to its architectural origins in the writings of Muthesius, Lichtwark, and Loos.[114]

The use of *neue* in Neue Sachlichkeit, according to Hartlaub in a letter to Schmalenbach, was intended to position the artists in his exhibition against the "old bourgeois naturalism of the Düsseldorf Academy."[115] As early as

49

1920 Hartlaub began to criticize Expressionist art for its utopianism and argued for a more *sachlich* Expressionism. In this conjunction of *sachlich* with Expressionism we find a similarity to Behne's use of *Sachlichkeit,* that is, at least in the early 1920s; the combination was used to suggest a transition away from Expressionism without implying a complete rupture with Expressionism. Even Giedion, who later formed an intense dislike toward Expressionism, wrote in 1923 that the *"neue Gegenständlichkeit . . . has absorbed the results of Expressionism."*[116] Dennis Crockett in his dissertation, "Die 'Neue Sachlichkeit': Post-Expressionism in Germany, 1919–1925," which contains a more detailed discussion of these issues and a thorough overview of the transitional nature of Neue Sachlichkeit in painting, has also pointed out that for Hartlaub himself the Neue Sachlichkeit exhibition was not about *all* of German art at the time—it did not include abstract art, for instance, nor did it cover, in Hartlaub's opinion, all of realist art. He never regarded it as a counterdevelopment to Expressionism but rather as only one tendency in an evolution away from Expressionism. Hartlaub wrote that the "new art was already contained in the old" and "retains much of the visionary quality of the older art."[117] In 1929 Hartlaub noted in his aforementioned letter to Barr that

> the expression ought really to apply as a label to the new realism bearing a socialist flavour. It was related to the general contemporary feeling in Germany of resignation and cynicism after a period of exuberant hopes (which had found an outlet in expressionism). Cynicism and resignation are the negative side of the *Neue Sachlichkeit,* the positive side expresses itself in the enthusiasm for the immediate reality as a result of a desire to take things entirely objectively on a material basis without immediately investing them with ideal implications.[118]

Schmalenbach, however, in his essay of 1940 did not agree with Hartlaub's specific understanding of the term: "In reality, it was not the 'objectivity' of the new painting which the term was intended in the first place and above all to formulate, but something more universal underlying this objectivity, and of which it was the expression, a revolution in the general mental attitude of the times, a general new *Sachlichkeit* of thought and feeling." He also wrote that it constituted a "radical rejection of all emotional bias, a deliberately cultivated unsentimentality.[119] Most later historians defined Neue Sachlichkeit in terms of its "sobriety" and "resignation" but usually in opposition to Expressionism. Marxist historians in particular saw it as the victory of capitalism, *Amerikanismus,* and Fordism — see, for example, Helmut Lethen, *Neue Sachlichkeit, 1924–1932,* 1970 — or as an instance of a reactionary culture produced during the period of economic stabilization — as in Jost Hermand's study of *Neue Sachlichkeit,* 1977.[120]

At any rate, the label from the outset, even Hartlaub's own early designation, was somewhat tenuous because the title of the exhibition itself changed as it traveled throughout Germany. Also, Hartlaub's terminology initially competed with Franz Roh's preferred term *Magischer Realismus* (Magic Realism), which was influenced by Italian metaphysical painting. Occasionally historians have categorized two constituent wings of Neue Sachlichkeit, a left and a right: respectively, those artists who fall under Hartlaub's notion of realism with a socialist flavor, and those who fall under Roh's concept of Magic Realism.[121] In the second half of the decade Neue Sachlichkeit became a popular label without the distinctions Hartlaub had conceived; it was viewed as one example of the several coexisting modernisms. Schmalenbach clearly preferred to use the term in its later, generalized, more all-encompassing sense.

As noted above, in his letter to Alfred Barr of 1929, Hartlaub discussed the positive aspect of Neue Sachlichkeit as an enthusiasm for immediate reality, whereas its negative side was its cynicism and resignation. Hartlaub also explained that "this healthy disillusionment finds its clearest expression in Germany in architecture. In the last analysis this battle cry is today much misused and it is high time to withdraw it from currency."[122] Thus Hartlaub, who had coined the label in 1923, believed the term to have become meaningless by 1929. Of course, one does not have to agree with Hartlaub's complete rejection of Neue Sachlichkeit. His complaint about its misuse, however, tells us a great deal about its volatility over a brief six-year period. Behne, as early as 1926, had referred with a sense of irony to the *"gebildete Spiessertum's"* (cultured philistines') enthusiastic embrace of a vulgarized version of Neue Sachlichkeit.[123] Most interesting for a discussion of Behne's *Der moderne Zweckbau* is Hartlaub's subtle understanding of a multifarious, layered Modernism. To the degree that Hartlaub does not accept Neue Sachlichkeit as a unified, comprehensive term, he seems to be in accord with Behne's definition of several directions present in 1923.

Even more important for understanding the use of *Sachlichkeit* within the architectural debates of the 1920s is Schmalenbach's suggestion that the label *Neue Sachlichkeit* had its origins in architectural texts written before the war. This is supported by Hartlaub's belief, expressed in 1929, that Neue

Sachlichkeit finds its "clearest expression" in German architecture. If the polemics at this stage have become too circular—those in the arts look to architecture for justification, and those in architecture look to the arts for an explanation—we can at least gain some insight from the intensity and back-and-forth of definitions that surround the controversies of the Neue Sachlichkeit. We realize that it was by no means a static concept; it was in fact continually redefined. The same is true for Behne's notion of *Sachlichkeit* and his attitude toward Neue Sachlichkeit: meanings and emphases changed in his writings in the course of the 1920s.

In *Die Wiederkehr der Kunst*, 1919, Behne had elevated the study of folk art even above the study of Albrecht Dürer or any high art. He wrote in characteristic Expressionist fashion that "we must rid ourselves of the rule of technology. Folk art dies where technique appears."[124] He also complained about Behrens's use of *Sachlichkeit* as if it could be employed as a template. In Behne's essay "Architekten," 1921–1922, where he frequently refers to *Sachlichkeit*, his outright rejection of naturalism still has much in common with the Expressionists' opposition to it, rather than with a resurgent realism of the *Neue Sachlichkeit*. He writes that art is a complete product of the human spirit and in this sense is antithetical to naturalism. He speaks of a tension between the natural and artistic, and he recommends replacing naturalism with Oud's belief in man's spiritual equality with nature. And using one of De Stijl's curious technospiritual metaphors, Behne concluded by exalting the "spiritual freedom of the machine."[125]

When he wrote *Der moderne Zweckbau*, however, Behne seems to have been more or less in agreement with Hartlaub, even though he uses the term *naturalism*, rather than *realism*, as was more common in painting:

Academic and historical styles have been abandoned and the concept of the facade has been disposed of. Yet the "house" is still standing. Success is achieved by returning to purpose in an architectural development that has its precise counterpart in painting of the period, which likewise disposed of academic and historical styles. Its medium is naturalism, which in the development of painting always allows a new freedom from prejudice, quite analogous to the significance that a return to function had for building. "Naturalism in architecture is functional fitness" (Karl Scheffler: *Messel*, p. 14).[126]

In *Der moderne Zweckbau* Behne did not satisfactorily explain why *Zweck, Funktion,* and *Sachlichkeit* are often used to form a constellation of words that seem to stand for slightly different aspects of Modernism, or why *Zweckbau* is used in the title, and not *Funktion* or *Sachlichkeit*. Perhaps these were evolving concepts at the time. In his later writings, however, his definition becomes clearer and the word *Sachlichkeit* begins to dominate other usages, probably in response to the increasingly widespread use of the term *Neue Sachlichkeit*. In one of his books intended for a mass audience, *Eine Stunde Architektur* (One hour of architecture), 1928, he is more explicit regarding the meaning of these terms: "*Zweckmäßigkeit* is only our minimum expectation. We conceive function in a more thoroughgoing way. The architect must not only fulfill given traditional functions, he must also establish new and higher functions. For this reason we shall prefer to speak of *Sachlichkeit*.... Therefore, fulfillment of function is for us not an end-in-itself but a means to get closer to life.... Reality as a medium of work must be conquered."[127]

In 1927 Behne expanded his definition of *Sachlichkeit* in *Neues Wohnen — Neues Bauen*, and *Zweck* no longer appears as often as it had in 1923. He writes that *Sachlichkeit* does not imply, as most assume, dryness, sobriety, or a solution from a purely mathematical point of view. *Sachlichkeit* simply means that the solution is adjusted to the *Sache*. He then goes on to explain what a *Sache* is: "Each *Sache* is a nodal point, a crossing point of relations between human being and human being.... To work *sachlich* means therefore to work socially in each discipline. To build *sachlich* means to build socially."[128] Behne's explanation of *Sachlichkeit* as a primarily social enterprise is similar to Simmel and Weber's notion of social action, and it aligns him in fact completely with Hartlaub's explanation of Neue Sachlichkeit. At the same time, his warning that it has nothing to do with a mathematical outlook, as most assume, indicates that by 1927 a mechanistic and technocentric understanding of the term had probably become prevalent.

In *Neues Wohnen — Neues Bauen* Behne further addresses some of the social issues that he had begun to explore in his earlier *Frühlicht* article in which he had praised Martin Wagner and the cooperative housing associations as a "transition to action" (fig. 8). He regards the housing shortage as the most pressing question in architecture, but goes on to say that housing is a political issue from the outset because it cannot be dealt with without also confronting the ownership of land (fig. 9). As in his and others' Expressionist writings, the idea of the "new man" is still used. This is why he refers in the title of the book to dwelling before building.[129] In his Expressionist writings he had stressed the harmonious, unifying elements of folk art and

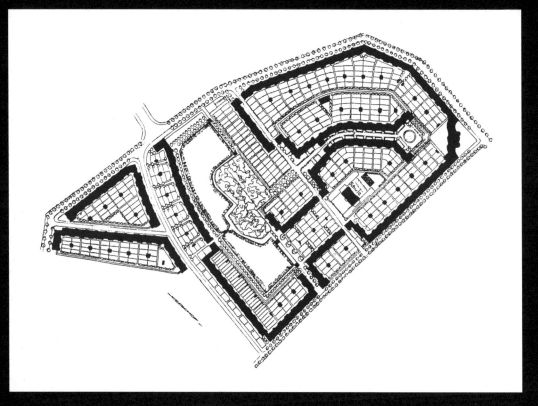

Fig. 8. Martin Wagner, Site plan for Lindenhof housing project, Berlin-Schöneberg, 1919.
From Ludovica Scarpa, *Martin Wagner und Berlin* (Braunschweig: Vieweg, 1986), 173, fig. 4
Photo: Courtesy Friedrich Vieweg & Sohn, Verlagsgesellschaft mbH, Wiesbaden.

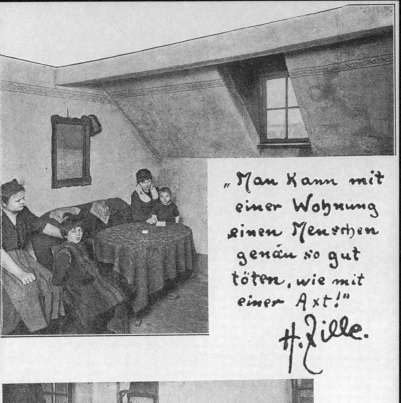

„Man kann mit einer Wohnung einen Menschen genäu so gut töten, wie mit einer Axt!"

H. Zille.

the Gothic cathedral; the retrospective element of Expressionism here, however, has given way to an international socialism, which had been merely a subtext in Expressionism's anarchist inheritance. This shift in Behne's attitude completely parallels changes seen in Taut's work and writings.

Behne explains in greater detail in *Neues Wohnen — Neues Bauen* what he means by building "socially." He cites, among other examples such housing complexes as the Siedlung Reichsverband für Kriegsbeschädigte in Berlin-Friedrichsfeld, 1925–1926, for which concrete panels were cast on the site and put in place with the help of cranes on tracks — a method adopted from Holland and further refined by Ernst May in Frankfurt. Yet Behne sees standardization only as the *precondition* for social building.[130]

In a chapter called "Diktatur oder Sachlichkeit" (Dictatorship or *Sachlichkeit*) he writes that *Sachlichkeit* can help to limit the dictatorship of the architect from above and the dictatorship of the tenant from below. He also points out that while some housing may look welcoming when new, it will look cramped once occupied because the tenants cannot afford new furniture. Often tenants themselves will add a petit bourgeois feeling to the interior by adding valances or antimacassars. But he also sees a tendency in modern architecture toward dictatorship if the building looks too much like a prison, and here he cites some of the housing by Oud. Whereas in his earlier writing he had been apologetic for the plain, apparently "uninteresting" look of Oud's work, he is now more critical, perhaps because Oud had refused to provide him with materials for *Der moderne Zweckbau*. Be that as it may, Behne maintains that if ornament is absent, the tenant feels his habitation looks like a penal institution and may automatically feel debased to the level of the proletariat because ornament is associated with the houses of the rich. He concludes that the architect has a tendency toward dictatorship in his attitude toward tenants and that tenants are partly right if they expect that architects are to serve them. At the same time he suggests that the tenant must be educated to become a "ruling type" just like the architect. His call for mutual education is rather characteristic of his trust in public education.[131]

In place of the Gothic cathedral of his Expressionist writings, Behne now turns to the image of a medieval knight encased in cumbersome armor as a metaphor for the general resistance to the concept of a social *Sachlichkeit*. In addition, he uses the walled city and its moat as an analogy for excluding *Sachlichkeit* in urban issues. He describes the *Mietskaserne* (literally, rental barracks) as the last castle, an example of an isolated, defensive space.[132] Though the normal five-story apartment block with forty to sixty families is a proper planning unit, it is in his opinion not an economic unit because ownership may change every twenty meters. There may also be a rigorous exploitation of the terrain, but this is not a *"sachliche, funktional zweckmäßige* solution."* The knight in armor, he writes, has been placed at the disposal of high capitalism (figs. 10, 11).[133]

In his "Von der Sachlichkeit," 1927, an introduction to a book on the work of Max Taut, Behne writes that a building can have many functional requirements and that *Sachlichkeit* is really the disciplined thought required to weigh them against each other. Here he also launches a very early critique of the *Zeilenbau,* the placement of parallel rows of buildings running north and south without regard to the site or street configuration. Behne regards the *Zeilenbau* method as too dogmatic because hygiene has been allowed to become the sole determining factor of architecture. This solution, he believes, is completely *unsachlich* and, in the end, formalistic. Behne and Bruno Taut among the modernists (fig. 12) — in contrast to Gropius, May, and Hannes Meyer — criticized the *Zeilenbau,* which was used as a planning scheme with increasing frequency in the late 1920s. Behne in an essay of 1930 would find fault with Gropius's Dammerstock Siedlung for this reason. Martin Wagner, associated with both Behne and Bruno Taut, also objected to the *Existenzminimum,* or minimum housing standard, as defined at CIAM II in Frankfurt, even though he strongly supported a rationalized system of production throughout the 1920s.[134]

In *Neues Wohnen — Neues Bauen* Behne summarizes his argument with the statement that the greatest work of art results from the creation of a "maximum of human respect for the most."[135] This assertion in effect seems to be simply a slight reformulation of Jeremy Bentham's eighteenth-century utilitarianism, which held that the greatest happiness of the greatest number is the self-evident, fundamental principle of morality. Just as utilitarianism later came to be understood as a purely pragmatic, economic concept — Behne himself uses it in its debased form in *Der moderne Zweckbau* — so the social implication of Behne's notion of *Sachlichkeit,* shared by Hartlaub's concept of Neue Sachlichkeit, was made blander and more uniform in its popularized form.

In his *Eine Stunde Architektur,* 1928, Behne maintained his basically antimechanistic notion of *Sachlichkeit* by writing that fantasy need not be left behind.[136] Contrasting the image of the armored knight as a metaphor for regression, he introduces the saint as the prophet of *Sachlichkeit:* "Function is the real saint in art history. It helped people to be free."[137] The cover of

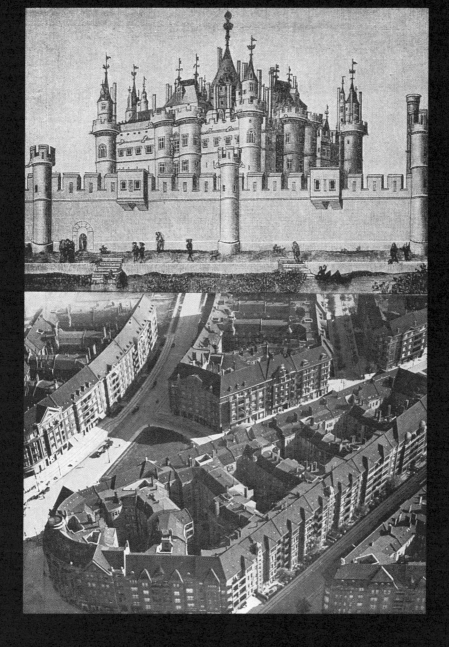

Fig. 10. Adolf Behne, Collage showing a knight and a modern man in combat. From Adolf Behne, *Neues Wohnen — Neues Bauen* (Leipzig: Hesse & Becker, 1927), 8.

Fig. 11. Adolf Behne, Collage contrasting a miniature from the Book of Hours of the Duc de Berry with an aerial view of speculative houses in southwestern Berlin. From Adolf Behne, *Eine Stunde Architektur* (Stuttgart: Akademischer Verlag Dr. Fritz Wedekind, 1928), 8. Photo: Courtesy Karl Krämer Fachbuchhandlung und Verlag, Stuttgart.

Fig. 12. Martin Wagner and Bruno Taut, View from Fritz-Reuter Allee into the "horseshoe building" of the Gehag Housing Association, Berlin-Britz, 1925–1926. From Kurt Junghanns, *Bruno Taut: 1880–1938* (Berlin: Henschelverlag Kunst und Gesellschaft, 1983), fig. 163. Photo: Courtesy Professor Dr. phil. habil. Heinrich Taut, Lehnitz.

the book (fig. 13) shows a collage by Max Fischer of Dürer's *Saint Jerome in His Study,* superimposed on the roof terrace of Le Corbusier's double house at the Weissenhof Siedlung (Le Corbusier's double house and a general view of Weissenhof are also contrasted with the walled castle in the book's illustrations). Saint Jerome, the scholar-monk on whose translation of the Bible the Latin Vulgate was based, has been brought out of his study into the open air of a *Siedlung* (housing development). The mysticism with which the Middle Ages was often invested in Expressionism has now simply become a shorthand device for revealing the "new man" at the center of *Sachlichkeit.*

Behne's *Blick über die Grenze: Baukunst des Auslandes* (View across the border: Architecture of foreign countries), published in 1925 in association with the Werkbund, contains the same internationalism and many of the same ideas expressed the following year in *Der moderne Zweckbau.* Like his "Funktion und Form" article of 1924, this may have been an attempt on his part to stake out his position vis-à-vis Gropius's *Internationale Architektur.* In *Blick über die Grenze* Behne expands upon his critique of German culture as moving from one extreme to the other and on its position between East and West. He writes that countries with a strong identifiable culture tend to be evolutionary and rarely succumb to dictators. He then makes one of his politically most insightful statements: "Germany . . . lacks a common culture and would be easy prey for a dictator, if it did not have a chronic shortage of strong authoritarians [*Willensmensch*]. No country has a harder time making unequivocal decisions. It swings between mistrust and belief, between democracy and dictatorship; between union with and isolation from Europe, between East and West, between yesterday and tomorrow."[138] Although critical in his assessment, Behne is not sufficiently prescient in believing that there is a shortage of authoritarian figures. By 1925, however, he is less sanguine than he had been in 1923 when he quoted Heinrich Mann on the need for a union between East and West. Still using his dualistic paradigm, he describes Russia as Europe's dynamic pole (speaking about Futurism and Constructivism) in whose revolutionary setting time becomes defined as experience. On the other hand, France to him represents a static pole in which time becomes a measure defined by tradition. More interestingly, he asks whether politics is not always the determining factor and writes that in Italy and Russia political methods have become dictatorial because both Bolshevists and Fascists are antidemocratic.

Just because it was conceived as early as 1923 *Der moderne Zweckbau* does not in every respect prefigure topics that became important in the later

1920s. After all, much of what is today considered modern architecture had not yet been built. Behne is, nevertheless, more comprehensive than Hitchcock and Johnson when it comes, for example, to Russian architecture. He is one of the few authors who during this period included the work of a female architect, Alexandra Exter's Isvestia Pavilion (1923). Chronologically, Behne's work might be compared with Mendelsohn's lecture "Dynamik und Funktion," delivered in Amsterdam in 1923, in which Mendelsohn noted:

> Whereas the grasping, pulling, and tearing activities of the machine are purely utilitarian functions, and function as conceived of in construction demonstrates only mathematical inevitability, function in architecture can only mean spatial and formal dependence on the givens derived from the program, the material and the construction. Therefore it seems impossible to me to somehow want to transfer the purposeful function of machines to the space, or the technological organization to the organism of architecture.... The machine, previously the obedient handyman of deadly exploitation, becomes a constructive element of a new living organism.... Thus the machine simultaneously becomes a symbol of decay as well as an element of a newly ordered life.[139]

In general, Mendelsohn's concern with expression and the representation of dynamic tension clearly differentiates this practicing architect-polemicist from the more analytical considerations of Behne, who grouped Mendelsohn with the romantic functionalists.[140]

Behne continued to be concerned about the belated publication of *Der moderne Zweckbau,* even after its appearance in 1926. In *Neues Wohnen — Neues Bauen,* 1927, he lists *Der moderne Zweckbau* both in the text and in the bibliography as having been published in 1925, probably a deliberate predating that was inadvertently picked up in a bibliography of Behne's writings by the Werkbund Archiv in 1972 and in some other publications.[141] At the same time, Behne, while listing Gropius's *Internationale Architektur* in his bibliography, does not give it a date. His initial conflict with Gropius over the publication of their respective books was clearly not forgotten. Behne today, however, has the last word: in the republication of his book in the Ullstein Bauwelt Fundamente series in 1964, the date of its conception and writing, not of its publication, appears prominently on the cover.

Gropius and Behne were often on opposite sides of the architectural debate in the late 1920s, but they also never stopped communicating with each other. In October of 1934 Gropius sent a letter to Behne, who by that

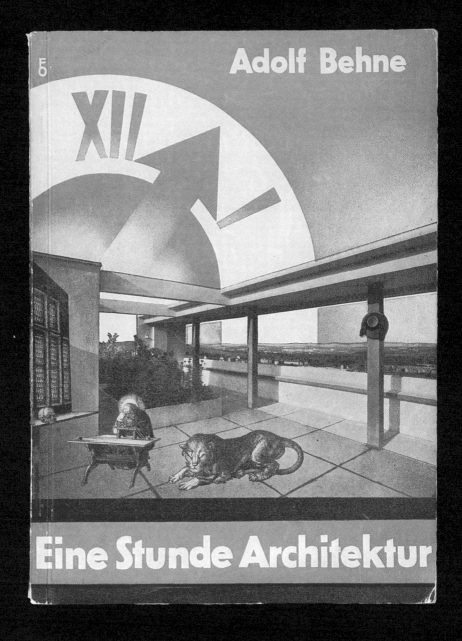

Fig. 13. Max Fischer, Collage of Albrecht Dürer's Saint Jerome and Le Corbusier's roof
garden at Stuttgart-Weissenhof. From Adolf Behne, *Eine Stunde Architektur* (Stuttgart:
Akademischer Verlag Dr. Fritz Wedekind, 1928), cover. Photo: Courtesy Karl Krämer
Fachbuchhandlung und Verlag, Stuttgart.

time had been dismissed from his teaching position at the Humboldt-Hochschule, as well as at the Städtische Berliner Volkshochschule (his *Sieg der Farbe* was confiscated as a degenerate text), and was taking a rest cure at a sanatorium because he suffered from tuberculosis. Gropius wrote that he hoped that Behne was not too depressed and remarked that sometimes such an involuntary break is useful in sorting out those events that are truly meaningful: "You are not really missing anything here. The conditions are so terribly distasteful, because an unparalleled irresolution reigns. Even in the camp of those in power opinions swing from one extreme to the other. The cultural area, which we think we know especially well, seems grotesque, and no one, even responsible people with whom I spoke in the ministry of propaganda and in the *Reichskulturkammer,* know where the trip is headed."[142] Behne's supposition of 1925—that Germany would be an easy prey for a dictator but lacked authoritarian figures—had turned out to be overly optimistic.

Sachlichkeit in the Publications of Other Modernists

None of the later books by Behne's friends and colleagues carried the detailed precision of *Der moderne Zweckbau.* They tended to rely more on their illustrations than had Behne's book. In *Internationale Architektur* Gropius freely admitted the existence of individual and national characteristics in current architecture, but despite this he discerned certain unifying characteristics, in effect the "international architecture" that had been the subject of his Bauhaus exhibition of 1923. He saw the common characteristics as a manifestation of a shared *Gestaltungswille,* or creative will. Any notion of *Sachlichkeit* that he perceived as yet another aspect of the new mode was subsumed under this idealistic concept of a creative will.[143] In his *Internationale neue Baukunst,* first published in 1927 under the auspices of the Werkbund, Hilberseimer finds a unity in contemporary architecture much as Gropius had, in the existence of a "creative will" rather than a style: "The creative will of the architect dominates everything . . . [The new architecture is the] expression of spiritual permeation. . . . It is not based on a stylistic conception."[144] Neither Gropius nor Hilberseimer defines the new architecture as a style or in mechanistic terms. However, their reliance on the idea of a creative will seems to be indebted to Schopenhauer or Riegl's idea of *Kunstwollen. Sachlichkeit* here seems to be an extension of the creative will and not, as in Behne's explanation, a social issue. Bruno Taut's definition of functional architecture in his book *Modern Architecture*, 1929, does address social and ethical questions, although in a less subtle way than Behne. By the 1930s, however, Taut would criticize his own earlier definition as too reductive.[145]

German writers were, of course, not unique in presenting Modernism as more than a technocentric polemic. Alberto Sartoris's *Gli elementi dell'architettura funzionale* (Elements of a functional architecture), first published in 1932, defined functional architecture in terms of paired opposites. He saw contemporary building characterized by both logic and lyricism, the practical and the aesthetic, both matter and spirit.[146]

There were also noteworthy exceptions to this modulated analysis of contemporary architecture. Behrendt's *Der Sieg des neuen Baustils*, 1927, published in conjunction with the Stuttgart Werkbund Exhibition, emphasized the style of the new architecture: its simple forms, flat planes, and absence of ornament. Behrendt regarded this as a proper expression of contemporary life, which he equated with machines, cars, and airplanes in the uninflected manner of early Futurism.[147] And Giedion, for example, in his *Bauen in Frankreich, Bauen in Eisen, Bauen in Eisenbeton* (Building in France, Building in Iron, Building in Ferroconcrete), 1928, based his methodology (as he would later in *Space, Time, and Architecture*) almost entirely on a materialistic premise, the development of "new" materials like iron and concrete, and the expectation of a yet-to-be-invented, even newer material for the twentieth century. In his review of the Bauhaus exhibition of 1923 he had already set out a similarly deterministic viewpoint. He wrote that while each material imposes absolute requirements, the "*Stilwille*" (style will) of our time will select instinctively those materials that are most adapted to its psyche, such as glass, concrete, and iron. He adds further that above this automatic response to ideal form is the machine.[148] Giedion's curious combination of idealism (*Stilwille*) with materialism is, of course, what prevailed as the standard reading of architectural history into the mid-twentieth century.

More moderate books published in the second half of the 1920s do not differ substantially from those of the avant-garde in a broad and usually non-mechanistic interpretation of functionalism. Gustav Platz in *Die Baukunst der neuesten Zeit* (Architecture of the most recent time), 1927, saw current architecture as existing between two poles: between the social, collective problems of the period and an unbridled activity of individual impulses.

Like Behne before him, Platz distinguished between functionalism and utilitarianism. Function for Platz could even be a "spiritual, artistic agent."[149]

Another one of these moderate books is *Berliner Architektur der Nachkriegszeit* (Berlin architecture of the postwar period), 1928, edited by E. M. Hajos and L. Zahn. And although its subject was more circumscribed, it had a perceptive introductory text by Edwin Redslob. Redslob, an art historian, later became (with the Werkbund's urging) *Reichskunstwart,* or overseer of all federal art projects. He defined modern architecture as follows: "Creation, not imitation should be the appropriate expression of our day. For the architect this means an end to the repetition of old styles . . . , but at the same time [creation] also mitigates against copying of engineering motifs, something the fashion of the day has decreed as a substitute for the despised imitation of styles."[150] Not unlike Behne, Redslob regarded both approaches as potentially dangerous. He called the imitation of older styles a "decorative formalism" produced by the "romanticizers of history"; the copying of engineering motifs he referred to as "functional formalism" practiced by the "romanticizers of technology."

What makes it impossible to associate the general notion of *Sachlichkeit* exclusively with Modernism in Germany is that conservatives claimed it as well. The most influential among these was undoubtedly Schultze-Naumburg, who since the start of the century had produced a series of books under the general title *Kulturarbeiten* (Cultural works). These dealt largely with anonymous urban, rural, and garden architecture. Schultze-Naumburg's didactic books were intended for a general public, and they were indeed widely read. In addition to texts they also contained pictorial contrasts of good and bad architecture, or examples and counterexamples, as he called them. In almost all of his comparisons older buildings are seen as preferable to more recent ones. Further, his categorical good and bad contrasts made his books a simple, efficient, and popular teaching tool.[151]

In his book *Kunst und Rasse* (Art and race), 1928, Schultze-Naumburg turned to a racial explanation of visual expression. The best art, he claimed, was always produced by pure, unmixed races. He did not insist on the supremacy of the Aryan race as some other writers had. Instead, he blamed what he regarded as the current low state of the arts on a greater mixture of formerly discrete racial types, a racial hodgepodge that he felt was made possible by modern technology, especially by the new faster modes of transportation. Behne castigated *Kunst und Rasse* in a review of 1929. He wrote that aside from its racism, it was patently absurd art history, because

Schultze-Naumburg assumed a clear analogy between pictorial figural representations and the way the human body actually looks.[152]

Most interestingly, Schultze-Naumburg criticized modern buildings not because they were too abstract nor because they had no ornament, but because he linked them with the debased expressions of an industrialized society. For this reason he disliked buildings from the late nineteenth century as much as current architecture. He made this point over and over in another one of his books of the late 1920s, *Das Gesicht des deutschen Hauses* (The face of the German house), 1929, which was really a sequel to *Kunst und Rasse*, but one that dealt exclusively with architecture.[153] Schultze-Naumburg, for instance, contrasted an old rural town, which for him expressed coherence, with modern architecture that displayed what he regarded as the incoherence of the machine age. Schultze-Naumburg's good-and-bad juxtapositions do not have quite the moralizing conviction of Augustus Welby Pugin's *Contrasts* of 1836. Nevertheless, as in Pugin, there is in all of Schultze-Naumburg's writings a high degree of nostalgia for a less confusing past. Both men reacted against industrialization and urbanization. While the Industrial Revolution had occurred in England over a long period of time, in Germany it was telescoped into a few decades of the late nineteenth century, producing disturbingly rapid social changes that, in the words of the historian Golo Mann, "could be compared to an explosion."[154] What Schultze-Naumburg seemed to look for in preindustrial architecture was the security of calm simplicity and also, surprisingly, *Sachlichkeit*. In the preface to *Das Gesicht des deutschen Hauses* he wrote that his object with the earlier *Kulturarbeiten* had been to call attention to the then little-noticed, simple, bourgeois architecture before 1800. In fact, Schultze-Naumburg's selections are almost analogous to those of Paul Mebes in his influential *Um 1800* (Around 1800) of 1908.[155] It represents, in effect, a Biedermeier revival of sorts with parallel implications of a withdrawal from the contemporary world and its social upheavals into a more comfortable realm of older conventions.

Although Schultze-Naumburg objected to the Werkbund's Weissenhof Siedlung—illustrated by him without proper identification (all counterexamples are condemned in his books to eternal anonymity)—he rejected not its severity, abstract quality, or even modern "style." What he disliked was the absence of pitched roofs. While Schultze-Naumburg had been an early member of the Werkbund, by 1925 he had distanced himself from its activities. For Schultze-Naumburg the pitched roof was the primordial

Figs. 14a. Bruno Taut, Photograph of the SS *Australia* as modern architecture. From Bruno Taut, *Modern Architecture* (New York: Albert & Charles Boni, 1929), 6. Photo: Courtesy Professor Dr. phil. habil. Heinrich Taut, Lehnitz.

Fig. 14b. Bruno Taut, Appropriation of the SS *Australia* (see fig. 14a) for a caricature of the modern house. From Bruno Taut, *Modern Architecture* (New York: Albert & Charles Boni, 1929), 7. Photo: Courtesy Professor Dr. phil. habil. Heinrich Taut, Lehnitz.

element of the house. He wrote that to omit it would be like having a face without a nose (a rather awkward physiognomic analogy). His general objection, symptomatic of contemporary conservative reactions to Modernism, is part and parcel of a racial theory of physiognomic expression. But at the same time he also couched his critique in a rational argument. He wrote that the flat roof may be quite suitable for a Mediterranean setting, where it can be regarded as an indigenous ethnic expression, but he found it totally inappropriate in the North, where it lacks tradition and is impractical. He complained that the new architecture pretends to be *sachlich* but is nothing of the sort. Although his argument was rife with inconsistencies, he and other traditionalists claimed *Sachlichkeit* for themselves. Possibly because of the inflammatory quality of Schultze-Naumburg's writings, the flat roof of modern architecture became a major issue of the architectural debate in Germany.[156] This was surely an instance of the negative side of the intense architectural polemics in Germany in the early twentieth century.

To summarize attitudes in Germany in the 1920s, questions of functionalism ranged from the nuanced discussion of Behne, to the more simplistic idealizing interpretation of Gropius and Hilberseimer, to the reductive utilitarian-pragmatic explanation of Schultze-Naumburg, in whose writing *Sachlichkeit* is a cover for ethnic appropriateness. The functionalism ascribed by Hitchcock and Johnson to Hannes Meyer was hardly symptomatic of the whole conceptual development and complexities of this issue in German theory.

Taut's *Modern Architecture*, used by David Watkin to criticize the modernist notion of functionalism, contains the following passage: "The outward characteristics of the new construction — flat roofs, huge sheets of glass...horizontal ribbon windows with pillars...were finally reduced to the level of a kind of sport, as has happened and is still happening to the admirable ancient styles.... In the same way, the 'modern' style has been imitating itself"(figs, 14a, b).[157] Thus three years before Hitchcock and Johnson elevated contemporary aesthetic tendencies to stylistic principles, Taut had already satirized them as fashionable clichés. Like Taut, his friend Behne had demonstrated even earlier that the definition of a modern *style* should not be of central concern. By investigating the ideologies behind the various approaches to functionalism in the early 1920s, he uncovered at the same time the eclecticism and pluralism of early Modernism.

Notes

References of the type "*The Modern Functional Building* [00]" direct the reader to the appropriate page of the translation of Behne's text that appears in this volume. Unless otherwise indicated, all translations given in the introduction are mine.

1. Adolf Behne, *Der moderne Zweckbau* (Munich: Drei Masken-Verlag, 1926).

2. Walter Gropius, *Internationale Architektur*, Bauhausbücher 1 (Munich: Albert Langen, 1925); Ludwig Hilberseimer, *Internationale neue Baukunst* (Stuttgart: Hoffmann, 1927); Walter Curt Behrendt, *Der Sieg des neuen Baustils* (Stuttgart: Akademischer Verlag Fr. Wedekind, 1927); Bruno Taut, *Die neue Baukunst in Europa und Amerika* (Stuttgart: Hoffmann, 1929), published in English as *Modern Architecture* (London: Studio; New York: Albert & Charles Boni, 1929). Although Taut does not say so in his foreword, the English publication of his book was presumably made possible through Behne's contacts with the journal *Studio*, for which he was a correspondent.

3. Henry-Russell Hitchcock, *Modern Architecture: Romanticism and Reintegration* (New York: Payson & Clark, 1929); Henry-Russell Hitchcock and Philip Johnson, *The International Style: Architecture since 1922* (New York: Norton, 1932).

4. The Getty Research Institute is currently preparing a translation of Behrendt's book as part of its Text & Documents series.

5. Helen Searing, "The Dutch Scene: Black and White and Red All Over," *Art Journal* 43 (summer 1983): 170–77, esp. n. 1.

6. Karl Scheffler, *Moderne Baukunst* (Berlin: Bard, 1907).

7. Akademie der Künste, *Arbeitsrat für Kunst Berlin, 1918–1921*, exh. cat. (Berlin: Akademie der Künste, 1980), 124 n.

8. Bruno Taut, *Die neue Wohnung: Die Frau als Schöpferin* (Leipzig: Klinkhardt & Biermann, 1924).

9. Adolf Behne, *Neues Wohnen — Neues Bauen*, Prometheus-Bücher (Leipzig: Hesse & Becker, 1927); Bruno Taut, *Bauen — Der neue Wohnbau* (Leipzig & Berlin: Klinkhardt & Biermann, 1927). In *Neues Bauen, 1918–1933: Moderne Architektur in der Weimarer Republik* (Munich: Moos, 1975), Norbert Huse writes that the term *Neues Bauen* stresses the act of building, whereas the use of *modern* places more value on the end product. He does not deal with the possible origins of *Neues Bauen*. Interestingly, in the section of his book titled "Form und Zweck: Häring und Behne" (n.p.), Huse describes Behne's *Der moderne Zweckbau* fairly but fails to point out that while Behne dealt with Häring's organic functionalism, he rejected it because it was not workable in a larger social context.

10. Walter Curt Behrendt, *Modern Building: Its Nature, Problems, and Forms* (New York: Harcourt, 1937).

11. Alan Colquhoun in a symposium held at Columbia University School of Architecture on 22 September 1993 on the occasion of the publication of Joan Ockman's book, *Architecture Culture, 1943–1968,* Columbia Books of Architecture (New York: Rizzoli, 1993).

12. See below, pp. 49–52.

13. For biographical information see Adolf Behne, "Lebenslauf," in *Der Inkrustationsstil in Toscana* (Berlin: Ebering, 1912), last page; Janos Frecot, ed., "Bibliographische Berichte: Adolf Behne," in Janos Frecot and Diethart Kerbs, eds., *Werkbund Archiv* 1 (1972), 81–83; "Adolf Behne," in Akademie der Künste (see note 7), 127–28; and the entry "Adolf Behne" in *Wer Ist's,* 9th ed. (Berlin: Degener, 1928). According to Frecot, Behne's literary estate, which through the intervention of Hans Scharoun was meant to go to the Akademie der Künste, Berlin, is presumed lost. See also Haila Ochs's preface in Adolf Behne, *Architekturkritik in der Zeit und über die Zeit hinaus: Texte 1913–1946,* ed. Haila Ochs (Basel: Birkhäuser, 1994), 7–15. Behne's wife, who in *Wer Ist's* was listed as the former Elfriede Schäfer, is referred to by Ochs as Elfriede Schneider (see p. 9).

14. Iain Boyd Whyte, *Bruno Taut and the Architecture of Activism* (Cambridge: Cambridge Univ. Press, 1982), 12.

15. Joan Campbell, *The German Werkbund: The Politics of Reform in the Applied Arts* (Princeton: Princeton Univ. Press, 1978), 17–18.

16. During the 1920s Behne was responsible for a column titled "Kultur" in *Sozialistische Monatshefte;* this position was later assumed by Ludwig Hilberseimer. See also Adolf Behne, "Museen als Volksbilgungsstätten," *Die Tat* 6 (1914–1915): 63–71; idem, "Das moderne Museum," *Sozialistische Monatshefte* 34 (1928): 42–45; idem, "Das gerahmte Bild im Museum," *Das Tagebuch* 11 (1930): 1438–39. "Das reproduktive Zeitalter," *Marsyas* 3 (November/December 1917): 219–26. This relationship between Behne and Benjamin is suggested by Arnd Bohm in "Artful Reproduction: Benjamin's Appropriation of Adolf Behne's 'Das reproduktive Zeitalter' in the *Kunstwerk*-Essay," *The Germanic Review* 68/4 (1993): 146–55.

17. Adolf Behne, "Reklame als Bilder-Rätsel," *Das Tagebuch* 5 (1924): 844–48. Behne had similarly written about fashion as a subject that does not benefit from the imposition of aesthetics in "Mode," *Sozialistische Monatshefte* 27 (1921): 373–74.

18. Adolf Behne, "Der Film als Kunstwerk," *Sozialistische Monatshefte* 27 (1921): 1116–18; idem, "Der Film als Pädagoge," *Das neue Frankfurt* 2 (1928): 203–5.

19. Adolf Behne, "Expressionistische Architektur," *Der Sturm* 5, nos. 19–20 (January 1915): 175.

20. Adolf Behne, "Der Hass der Neutralen," *Die Tat* 7 (July 1915): 340–41. For initially euphoric responses to World War 1 from Max Weber, Thomas Mann, and others, see A. J.

Ryder, *Twentieth-Century Germany: From Bismarck to Brandt* (New York: Columbia Univ. Press, 1973), 148 ff.

21. Whyte (see note 14), 11 ff., 40, 173 ff.

22. Ryder (see note 20), 27.

23. Magdalena Bushart, *Der Geist der Gotik und die Expressionistische Kunst* (Munich: S. Schreiber, 1990). Issues concerning nationalism and internationalism are also discussed in Rose-Carol Washton Long, "National or International? Berlin Critics and the Question of Expressionism," in Thomas W. Gaehtgens, ed., *Künstlerischer Austausch: Artistic Exchange,* Akten des xxviii. Internationalen Kongresses für Kunstgeschichte, Berlin, 15.–20. Juli 1992 (Berlin: Akademie Verlag, 1993): 521–33.

24. For Walter Benjamin see Paul Mattick, Jr., "Lost in Translation," review of *The Correspondence of Walter Benjamin, The Nation* (31 October 1994): 497–501.

25. Lukács's and Bloch's essays on Expressionism appear in English in "The Left and the Debate over Expressionism in the Thirties," in Rose-Carol Washton Long, ed., *German Expressionism: Documents from the End of the Wilhelmine Empire to the Rise of National Socialism* (New York: G. K. Hall, 1993), 312–27. For a further discussion of this issue, see also Fredric Jameson, ed., *Aesthetics and Politics,* trans. Ronald Taylor (London: NLB, 1977).

26. Manfredo Tafuri and Francesco Dal Co, *Modern Architecture,* trans. Robert Erich Wolf (New York: Harry N. Abrams, 1979), 162, 193. Tafuri and Dal Co refer to Expressionism as displaying a "dogged continuity with the late romantic experiments that had flourished in Germany at the turn of the century" while at the same time praising Lukács's "rigorism" and Socialist Realism.

27. Behne's three lectures were published as *Die Kunst Asiens* (Berlin: Verlag des Zentralbildungsausschusses der Sozialdemokratischen Partei Deutschlands, 1914). See also Adolf Behne, "Arbeitsdarstellungen in der Kunst," *Die neue Zeit: Wochenschrift der deutschen Sozialdemokratie* 31 (1914): 129–33.

28. Adolf Behne, *Oranienburg: Ein Beispiel für Stadtbetrachtungen,* Flugschrift des Dürerbundes 171 (Munich: Georg Callwey, 1917), and idem, "Ist das Schwäche?" *Sozialistische Monatshefte* 23 (1917): 1285–88.

29. Gordon A. Craig, *Germany 1866–1945* (New York: Oxford Univ. Press, 1980), 384, 386. Behne's party membership is documented in Long (see note 25), 202.

30. Ryder (see note 20), 171.

31. Detlev J. K. Peukert, *The Weimar Republik: The Crisis of Classical Modernity* (New York: Hill & Wang, 1987), 32, 151–52.

32. Adolf Behne, "Unsere moralische Krisis," *Sozialistische Monatshefte* 25 (1919): 34–38.

33. Adolf Behne, *Die Überfahrt am Schreckenstein: Eine Einführung in die Kunst* (Berlin: Arbeiter-Jugend Verlag, 1925); and idem, *Von Kunst zur Gestaltung: Eine Einführung in die moderne Kunst* (Berlin: Arbeiter-Jugend Verlag, 1925).

34. Whyte sees Behne as the leader in the transition from Expressionism to functionalism in 1921; Whyte (see note 14), 220.

35. Edward Robert de Zurko, *Origins of Functionalist Theory* (New York: Columbia Univ. Press, 1957), ix.

36. David Watkin, *Morality and Architecture* (Oxford: Clarendon, 1977), 40.

37. De Zurko (see note 35), 8.

38. Horatio Greenough, *Form and Function: Remarks on Art, Design, and Architecture,* ed. Harold A. Small (Berkeley: Univ. of California Press, 1969), 57–59.

39. Hugh Dalziel Duncan, *Culture and Democracy* (New York: Bedminster, 1965), 287. On the shift from a transcendental idealism to the pragmatic realism of the Chicago School, see Lauren S. Weingarden, *Louis H. Sullivan: The Banks* (Cambridge: MIT Press, 1987), 15.

40. Hitchcock and Johnson (see note 3), 35.

41. Lewis Mumford, "Function and Expression in Architecture," *Architectural Record* 110 (November 1951): 106–12; reprinted in idem, *Architecture As a Home for Man,* ed. Jeanne M. Davern (New York: Architectural Record Books, 1975), 154–60.

42. Joseph Hudnut, "The Post-Modern House," *Architectural Record* 97 (May 1945): 70–75; Hudnut's essay is reprinted in Ockman (see note 11), 71–76. The essay was also published in revised form in Lewis Mumford, *Roots of Contemporary Architecture* (New York: Reinhold, 1952), 306–16.

43. Heinrich Klotz, *Moderne und Postmoderne: Architektur der Gegenwart* (Braunschweig: Vieweg, 1984); and idem, *The History of Postmodern Architecture* (Cambridge: MIT Press, 1988), 8 ff., 24–25.

44. Alan Colquhoun, *Essays in Architectural Criticism: Modern Architecture and Historical Change,* intro. Kenneth Frampton, Oppositions Books (Cambridge: MIT Press, 1981), 12. Another assessment of two contrasting forms of functionalism can be found in Kenneth Frampton, "The Humanist v. the Utilitarian Ideal," *Architectural Design* 38 (March 1968): 134–36.

45. Stanford Anderson, "The Fiction of Function," *Assemblage* 2 (February 1987): 21.

46. I first presented a slightly different version of this discussion as a lecture, "The Politics of Architectural Training," in the session "The Rise of Modernism and the German Empire, 1871–1918," chaired by Françoise Forster-Hahn, College Art Association annual meeting, Houston, 11 February 1988.

47. The historical background to the Ecole des Beaux-Arts is discussed briefly in Richard Chafee, "The Teaching of Architecture at the Ecole des Beaux-Arts," in Arthur Drexler, ed., *The Architecture of the Ecole des Beaux-Arts* (New York: Museum of Modern Art, 1975), 61 ff.

48. Ronald Wiedenhoeft, "The Curricula in Architecture in the Technische Hochschulen in the German-Speaking Lands, 1880–1920" (unpublished paper, Columbia Univ.,

1967). Wiedenhoeft not only deals with the formation of polytechnic schools but also with the change of curricula and calls for reform that came from architects within these institutions (Theodor Fischer among them). Possibly because there were so many polytechnic schools, each with a slightly different curriculum, a full-fledged comparative study of their role has not been published. When it comes to gathering information, the centralized Ecole des Beaux-Arts presents historians with a distinct advantage. The sheer plurality of the German educational system has discouraged a comprehensive study.

49. Wiedenhoeft (see note 48).

50. Stanford Anderson, "Peter Behrens and the New Architecture of Germany, 1900–1917" (Ph.D. diss., Columbia Univ., 1970); and idem, "Peter Behrens' Changing Concept," *Architectural Design* 39 (February 1969): 72–78.

51. Annette Wolde, "Der ökonomische Hintergrund der Künstlerkolonie," in *Ein Dokument deutscher Kunst: Darmstadt, 1901–1976*, exh. cat., vol. 5 (Darmstadt: E. Roether, 1976), 49–55.

52. Werner Schweiger, *Wiener Werkstätte: Design in Vienna, 1903–1932* (New York: Abbeville, 1984), 73, 96, 125–26.

53. Stanislaus von Moos, *Le Corbusier: Elements of a Synthesis* (Cambridge: MIT Press, 1979), 12–13. See also Charles-Edouard Jeanneret, *Etude sur le mouvement d'art décoratif en Allemagne* (La Chaux-de-Fonds: L'Ecole d'Art de La Chaux-de-Fonds, 1912).

54. Von Moos reports on Le Corbusier's contacts with Muthesius, Tessenow, and other members of the Werkbund; see von Moos (note 53), 12. I am indebted to Francesco Passanti for first pointing out to me in 1985 that Le Corbusier had written to Fischer to secure a place in his studio. Also, in *Theodor Fischer: Architekt und Städtebauer* (Berlin: Ernst & Sohn, 1988), Winfried Nerdinger discusses Le Corbusier's attempt to work in Fischer's office (p. 90); on Fischer as a teacher, see particularly Nerdinger's chapter 5, "Erziehung zum Können — Der Lehrer und seine Schüler," 86 ff. Gabriele Schickel deals more specifically with German architectural education and with Fischer and Behrens as contrasting teachers. She claims, however, that it was not possible to study modern architecture in Germany until Gropius established architectural education at the Bauhaus in 1927, suggesting that her notion of Modernism is rather circumscribed. See Gabriele Schickel, "Theodor Fischer als Lehrer der Avantgarde," in Vittorio Magnago Lampugnani and Romana Schneider, eds., *Reform und Tradition: Moderne Architektur in Deutschland 1900 bis 1950* (Stuttgart: Hatje, 1992), 55 ff.

55. Nerdinger (see note 54), 88.

56. Nerdinger (see note 54), 24. For the extensive influence of Sitte in Germany, see George Collins and Christiane C. Collins, eds., *Camillo Sitte: The Birth of Modern City Planning* (New York: Rizzoli, 1986).

57. Behrens's work for the AEG is cited as an instance of a collaboration between a Werkbund architect and industry even in such a recent publication as that of Tilmann Buddensieg,

ed., *Berlin 1900–1933: Architecture and Design* (New York: Cooper-Hewitt Museum, 1987). In Buddensieg's earlier *Industriekultur: Peter Behrens and the AEG, 1907–1914* (Cambridge: MIT Press, 1984) the differences between the Werkbund and Behrens's work for the AEG are more carefully drawn. Behrens's work for the AEG did not come about through his association with the Werkbund. Because the Werkbund became part of a protomodernist myth, its initial ideals and membership are not always closely examined. Joan Campbell in her otherwise informative monograph on the Werkbund does not name all twelve architects or the twelve industrial firms that formed its original membership. Campbell's book is excellent on the institutional changes in the Werkbund and concerning its influence on museums and other art institutions, but it is not as thorough when it comes to the intellectual and political disagreements that were also part of its early history. See Campbell (note 15).

58. Nerdinger (see note 54), 13.

59. Julius Posener, *Anfänge des Funktionalismus: Von Arts and Crafts zum Deutschen Werkbund* (Berlin: Ullstein, 1964), 21–22. See also Sebastian Müller, *Kunst und Industrie: Ideologie und Organisation des Funktionalismus in der Architektur* (Munich: Hanser, 1974), 150 n. 48. The participants mentioned by Müller differ slightly from those mentioned by Posener.

60. Campbell (see note 15), 12 ff. In "The *Kunstgewerbe*, the *Werkbund*, and the Aesthetics of Culture in the Wilhelmine Period," *Journal of the Society of Architectural Historians* 53 (March 1994): 7–19, Mark Jarzombek attempts to correct the earlier progressivist interpretations but goes too far in making the Werkbund seem entirely conservative.

61. Richard Pommer and Christian F. Otto, *Weissenhof 1927 and the Modern Movement in Architecture* (Chicago: Univ. of Chicago Press, 1991), 5.

62. Von Moos (see note 53), 47; see also idem, "Standard und Elite: Le Corbusier, die Industrie und der *Esprit Nouveau*," in Tilmann Buddensieg and Henning Rogge, eds., *Die nützlichen Künste* (Berlin: Quadriga, 1981), 306–23; and, in greater detail, idem, "Industrie und Wahrnehmung," in *L'esprit nouveau: Le Corbusier und die Industrie, 1920–1925*, exh. cat. (Zurich: Museum für Gestaltung; Berlin: Wilhelm Ernst & Sohn, 1987), 12–25.

63. Dolores Hayden, *The Grand Domestic Revolution: A History of Feminist Designs for American Homes, Neighborhoods, and Cities* (Cambridge: MIT Press, 1981), 164–65. Gordon A. Craig also points to the eighteenth-century establishment of elementary schools in the German states, long before compulsory education was established in England and France in the late nineteenth century. He suspects that there is a direct connection between Germany's high literacy rate and the rapid growth of German industry after 1871; see Craig (note 29), 186–87.

64. Adolf Behne, "Kritik des Werkbundes," *Die Tat* 9 (1917): 430–38. This essay is reprinted in Frecot and Kerbs (see note 13), 118–28, together with responses by Fritz Hellwag (pp. 130–33) and Bruno Rauecker (pp. 134–37).

65. Adolf Behne, "Werkbund," *Sozialistische Monatshefte* 54 (26 January 1920): 68–69; and Karl Scheffler, "Ein Arbeitsprogramm für den Deutschen Werkbund," *Kunst und Künstler* 17 (1920): 43–52.

66. Akademie der Künste (see note 7). See also Long (note 25), 191–209 (chapter 3 on the Arbeitsrat für Kunst).

67. Akademie der Künste (see note 7), 108; and Campbell (see note 15), 125–26.

68. See the chapter on "Dada" in Long (note 25), 262–78.

69. Adolf Behne, "An den Verein kommunistischer Kunstmaler," *Die Weltbühne* 22 (1926): 460–61.

70. Adolf Behne, "Sozialistische Kunst," unpublished essay, circa 1932, printed in Frecot and Kerbs (see note 13), 142–47.

71. Adolf Behne, "Tempelhofer Feld und Wedding (Kunstausstellung Wedding)" *Weltbühne* 22 (1926): 346–48.

72. Iain Boyd Whyte, ed. and trans., *The Crystal Chain Letters* (Cambridge: MIT Press, 1985), 186 n. 1.

73. Adolf Behne, *Holländische Baukunst in der Gegenwart* (Berlin: Wasmuth, 1922). While he was preparing this book, he also published "Von holländischer Baukunst," *Feuer* (1920–1921): 279–92; and "Holländische Baukunst in der Gegenwart," *Wasmuths Monatshefte für Baukunst* 6 (1921–1922): 1–38.

74. Charlotte I. Loeb and Arthur L. Loeb, trans., *De Stijl: The Formative Years, 1917–1922* (Cambridge: MIT Press, 1982), 146–48.

75. Frank Whitford, *Bauhaus* (London: Thames & Hudson, 1984), 123.

76. H. L. C. Jaffe, *De Stijl, 1917–1931: Der niederländische Beitrag zur modernen Kunst* (Berlin: Ullstein, 1965), 182; and Walker Art Center, *De Stijl, 1917–1931: Visions of Utopia*, intro. H. L. C. Jaffe, exh. cat. (New York: Abbeville; Minneapolis: Walker Art Center, 1982), 230.

77. Adolf Behne, "Das Bauhaus Weimar," *Die Weltbühne* 19 (1923): 291–92; Behne published a review of the international architecture exhibition at the Bauhaus exhibition of 1923: "Die Internationale Architekten Ausstellung im Bauhaus zu Weimar," *Bauwelt* 14 (1923): 533. Here he cautioned against allowing geometries and the right angle to become a formal principle but generally commended the exhibited works by such architects as Le Corbusier, Robert Mallet-Stevens, Wright, Oud, Dudok, Wils, Taut, Scharoun, Adolf Rading, and Häring.

Behne in late 1919 and early 1920 had been among the Arbeitsrat members, who together with the Novembergruppe — Theodor Däubler, Raoul Hausmann, Ludwig Justi, Martin Wagner, and others — defended Gropius and the Bauhaus when it had come under attack in the *Vossische Zeitung* and the *Generalanzeiger für Sachsen-Weimar-Eisenach* for its program and for harboring too many foreigners; see Adolf Behne, "Weimar," *Sozialistische Monatshefte* (26 January 1920): 69. On 3 January 1923 Gropius also wrote a letter to Behne thanking him for trying to mediate the split between the Bauhaus and many artists that had been precipitated by van Doesburg. He also welcomed the suggestion of Behne to meet with Moholy-Nagy and Lissitzky to discuss these problems; see Frecot and Kerbs (note 13), 148–49.

Behne also reviewed Gropius's speech at the opening of the Bauhaus exhibition of 1923, "Bauhausresumee," *Sozialistische Monatshefte* 29 (1923): 542–45. Behne's review of the Bauhaus exhibition might be compared with Sigfried Giedion's "Bauhaus und Bauhauswoche zu Weimar," *Das Werk* 10 (1923): 232–34, which already betrays the materialist tendencies of *Space, Time, and Architecture.*

78. Ulrich Conrads, "Vor vierzig Jahren — Vorbemerkungen zum Neudruck 1964," in Adolf Behne, *Der moderne Zweckbau* (Berlin: Ullstein, 1964), 7. Conrads states that Behne's text was essentially completed in 1923, requiring only minor alterations for the publication in 1926.

79. Frecot and Kerbs (see note 13). The letter is dated 12 May 1923, 150.

80. Adolf Behne, "Die Gewerkschaftsschule in Bernau bei Berlin," *Zentralblatt der Bauverwaltung* 48 (1928): 397–402. See also a letter of Hannes Meyer to Behne dated 8 January 1928 in Frecot and Kerbs (note 13), 152–54.

81. Frecot and Kerbs (see note 13), 81.

82. Adolf Behne, *Heinrich Zille,* Graphiker der Gegenwart, vol. 12 (Berlin: Willy Weise, 1925); idem, ed., *Heinrich Zille* (Halle: Morgner, 1947); and idem, ed., *Heinrich Zille Studien* (Berlin: Neue Berlin, 1949).

83. Fritz Neumeyer, *The Artless Word: Mies van der Rohe on the Building Art* (Cambridge: MIT Press, 1991), 167–68.

84. Gottfried Semper, *The Four Elements of Architecture and Other Writings,* ed. Harry Francis Mallgrave (Cambridge: Cambridge Univ. Press, 1989).

85. Cornelius Gurlitt, "Göllers aesthetische Lehre," *Deutsche Bauzeitung* (17 December 1987), 602–4, 606–7; Alois Riegl, *Altorientalische Teppiche* (Leipzig: Weigel, 1891); and idem, *Die Spätrömische Kunstindustrie,* 2 vols. (Vienna: Staatsdruckerei, 1901–1923).

86. *The Modern Functional Building* [88–89]. Behne seems to have been aware only of Wagner's fourth edition of this book. For an analysis and publication history, see Otto Wagner, *Modern Architecture,* intro. Harry Francis Mallgrave (Santa Monica: The Getty Center for the History of Art and the Humanities, 1988).

87. These lectures and other texts by Berlage have recently been translated into English; see *Hendrik Petrus Berlage: Thoughts on Style, 1886–1909,* intro. Iain Boyd Whyte (Santa Monica: The Getty Center for the History of Art and the Humanities, 1996).

88. *The Modern Functional Building* [97].

89. *The Modern Functional Building* [37, 41].

90. Peukert (see note 31); see the section titled "'Americanism' Versus *Kulturkritik*," 178 ff.

91. *The Modern Functional Building* [104].

92. *The Modern Functional Building* [105].

93. Adolf Behne, "Romantiker, Pathetiker und Logiker im modernen Industriebau," *Preussische Jahrbücher* 154 (October 1913): 171–74. See also Anderson (note 45).

94. *The Modern Functional Building* [122–23].

95. Adolf Behne, "Architekten," *Frühlicht* 2 (1921–1922); this article was reprinted in Bruno Taut, *Frühlicht, 1920–1922* (Frankfurt am Main: Ullstein, 1963), 129. Behne's knowledge of nineteenth-century history seems occasionally episodic: Joseph Paxton's early version for the Crystal Palace is illustrated and captioned as an "industrial hall" built in 1854, and Adolf Loos is referred to as Theodor Loos.

96. *The Modern Functional Building* [130].

97. *The Modern Functional Building* [145–46].

98. *The Modern Functional Building* [142].

99. For a discussion of Vierkandt's methodology in relation to that of other sociologists, see Alfred Vierkandt, *Gesellschaftslehre* (New York: Arno Press, 1975). This is a reprint of the second revised edition (Stuttgart: Enke, 1928), 19–20. For a broader discussion of issues surrounding the concepts of community and society in German sociology that seem to have influenced Behne, see Harry Liebersohn, *Fate and Utopia in German Sociology, 1870–1923* (Cambridge: MIT Press, 1988).

100. Behne (see note 95).

101. For a discussion of the continuity between Expressionism and the Neue Sachlichkeit, see Rosemarie Haag Bletter, "Expressionism and the New Objectivity," *Art Journal* 43 (summer 1983): 108–20.

102. Loeb and Loeb (see note 74), 32.

103. For Martin Wagner and urban planning see Ludovica Scarpa, *Martin Wagner und Berlin,* trans. Heinz-Dieter Held (Braunschweig: Friedr. Vieweg & Sohn, 1986).

104. Behne (see note 73), 3. He had also alluded to the conflict in his earlier essay, "Von holländischer Baukunst" (see note 73), 292.

105. Adolf Behne, "Kunst, Handwerk, Technik," *Die neue Rundschau* 33 (1922): 1021–37. This article has been translated by Christiane Crasemann Collins in Francesco Dal Co, *Figures of Architecture and Thought: German Architecture Culture, 1880–1920* (New York: Rizzoli, 1990), 324–38.

106. Adolf Behne, *Die Wiederkehr der Kunst* (Leipzig: Kurt Wolff, 1919), 36ff. "Von der Sachlichkeit" appeared as an introduction to Max Taut, *Bauten und Pläne* (Berlin: Hübsch, 1927), and it has been reprinted in Adolf Behne, *Eine Stunde Architektur* (Berlin: Archibook-Verlag, 1984), 29.

107. Adolf Behne, "Funktion und Form," *Sozialistische Monatshefte* 30 (1924): 767–68.

108. Harry Francis Mallgrave in Wagner (see note 86), 4.

109. Harry Francis Mallgrave, "From Realism to *Sachlichkeit*: The Polemics of Architectural Modernity in the 1890s," in Harry Francis Mallgrave, ed., *Otto Wagner: Reflections on the Raiment of Modernity* (Santa Monica: The Getty Center for the History of Art and the Humanities, 1993), 304.

110. Stanford Anderson, "*Sachlichkeit* and Modernity, or Realist Architecture," in Mallgrave (see note 109), 340.

111. By contrast Müller (see note 59), 10–11, employing Karl Bötticher's notion of *Kunstform* and *Kernform* (art-form and core-form), writes that the two concepts become increasingly separate under the influence of industrial production in a capitalist society. He sees the work of Mies as a succinct instance in which *Kernform* has become self-sufficient. But one could, in fact, argue that in Mies's architecture both are present. At any rate, whereas Behne's form and function are not dissimilar to Bötticher's paradigm, and whereas Behne even refers to Bötticher's work in passing, Behne showed that these two concepts were already treated as segregated entities in the time of Schinkel.

112. Fritz Schmalenbach, "The Term 'Neue Sachlichkeit,'" *Art Bulletin* 22 (September 1940): 161–65; idem, *Die Malerei der Neuen Sachlichkeit* (Berlin: Mann, 1973). Hartlaub's letter appears in Alfred Barr, "Otto Dix," *The Arts* 4 (1931): 237.

113. Giedion (see note 77), 234.

114. Schmalenbach (see note 112).

115. Schmalenbach (see note 112), 163.

116. Giedion (see note 77), 234.

117. Dennis Crockett, "Die 'Neue Sachlichkeit': Post-Expressionism in Germany, 1919–1925" (Ph.D. diss., City Univ. of New York Graduate Center, 1993), 334. The full title for Hartlaub's exhibition was *Die Neue Sachlichkeit: Nachexpressionistiche Malerei* (Neue Sachlichkeit: German art since Expressionism). On the connection between Expressionism and the post-1923 period see also Bletter (note 101).

118. Barr (see note 112). As Crockett points out, Hartlaub recalled the date of the plan for the exhibition incorrectly in this letter as 1924 rather than 1923; (see note 117), 341. Hartlaub's letter to Barr forms the basis of an excellent synoptic discussion of the New Objectivity in Kenneth Frampton, *Modern Architecture: A Critical History* (New York: Oxford Univ. Press, 1980), 130 ff.

119. Schmalenbach (see note 112), 163–64.

120. Crockett (see note 117), 17–18; Helmut Lethen, *Neue Sachlichkeit, 1924–1932: Studien zur Literatur des 'Weissen Sozialismus'* (Stuttgart: Metzler, 1970); and Jost Hermand, "Unity within Diversity? The History of the Concept 'Neue Sachlichkeit,'" in K. Bullivant, ed., *Culture and Society in the Weimar Republic* (Manchester: Manchester Univ., 1977), 167.

121. Crockett (see note 117), 315.

122. Barr (see note 112), 237.

123. Behne (see note 69), 461.

124. Behne (see note 106), 111.

125. Behne (see note 95), 126–27.

126. *The Modern Functional Building* [100–101].

127. Adolf Behne, *Eine Stunde Architektur* (Stuttgart: Akademischer Verlag Dr. Fritz Wedekind, 1928). A slightly abridged version is reprinted in the 1984 edition of *Eine Stunde Architektur* (see note 106), 21–23. More recently, Theodor Adorno in a discussion of functionalism also used *Funktionalismus* and *Sachlichkeit* as interchangeable terms. See "Funktionalismus heute," in Theodor Adorno, *Ohne Leitbild: Parva Aesthetica* (Frankfurt: Suhrkamp, 1967), 104–27.

128. Behne (see note 9), 34.

129. Behne (see note 9), 6–12.

130. Behne (see note 9), 21–22.

131. Behne (see note 9), 29–33.

132. Behne (see note 9), 89.

133. Behne (see note 9), 92.

134. Adolf Behne's "Von der Sachlichkeit," is reprinted in *Eine Stunde Architektur, 1984* (see note 127). Adolf Behne, "Dammerstock," *Die Form* 5:6 (1930): 163–66; idem, "Dammerstock-Schlusswort," *Die Form* 5:18 (1930): 494. The "Dammerstock" article is reprinted in *Eine Stunde Architektur, 1984* (see note 127), 46 ff. For the critique of Dammerstock and *Zeilenbau,* see also Pommer and Otto (note 61), 148–49.

135. Behne (see note 9), 101.

136. Behne, 1984 (see note 127), 61. Julius Posener in *Hans Poelzig* (New York: Architectural History Foundation and MIT Press, 1992) considers this a rather curious definition of *Sachlichkeit* (see p. 158).

137. Behne, 1984 (see note 127), 61.

138. Adolf Behne, *Blick über die Grenze: Baukunst des Auslandes* (Berlin: Otto Stollberg, 1925), 4.

139. Erich Mendelsohn, "The International Consensus on the New Architectural Concept, or Dynamics and Function," in *Erich Mendelsohn: Complete Works of the Architect,* trans. Antje Fritsch (Princeton: Princeton Architectural Press, 1992), 31. An excerpt also appears in Ulrich Conrads, *Programs and Manifestoes on Twentieth-Century Architecture,* trans. Michael Bullock (Cambridge: MIT Press, 1970), 72–73. For an introduction to Mendelsohn's place in Expressionism see Rosemarie Haag Bletter, "Expressionist Architecture," in Long (note 25), 132–34.

140. Erich Mendelsohn, *Amerika* (Berlin: Mosse, 1925). Behne made use of some of Mendelsohn's photographs from this book without always acknowledging them — not only in *Der moderne Zweckbau* but also in *Blick über die Grenze* and *Neues Wohnen–Neues Bauen.*

141. Frecot and Kerbs (see note 13), 85–116. This Behne bibliography is invaluable, if not complete. However, some of the dates, in addition to that of *Der moderne Zweckbau* are wrong. *Die Wiederkehr der Kunst*, for instance, is cited with a date of 1920. Whyte, *The Crystal Chain Letters* (see note 72), presumably picked up the wrong dates for these two books from this bibliography. There are, in addition, a number of Behne's publications that are not listed in Frecot and Kerbs. Although Ochs includes a more complete bibliography (see note 13), she gives the date of *Der moderne Zweckbau* as 1925.

142. Frecot and Kerbs (see note 13), 155.

143. Gropius (see note 2), 5–6. I first presented an outline of the attitudes toward functionalism and Modernism manifest in German books of the 1920s as a lecture, "Neues Bauen versus Heimatstil: Objectivity for all Occasions," at a conference on "The International Style in Perspective," Graduate School of Design, Harvard University, 16–17 April 1982.

144. Hilberseimer (see note 2), 5.

145. Bruno Taut, *Architekturlehre*, ed. Tilmann Heinisch and Goerd Peschken (Hamburg: VSA, 1977), 119–54.

146. Alberto Sartoris, *Gli elementi dell'architettura funzionale: Sintesi panoramica dell'architettura moderna*, pref. Le Corbusier (Milan: Hoepli, 1932). A second edition was published in 1935.

147. Behrendt (see note 2), 20–22.

148. Sigfried Giedion, *Bauen in Frankreich, Bauen in Eisen, Bauen in Eisenbeton* (Leipzig: Klinkhardt & Biermann, 1928). A second edition was also published in 1928. This text has recently been translated into English; see Sigfried Giedion, *Building in France, Building in Iron, Building in Ferroconcrete*, intro. Sokratis Georgiadis (Santa Monica: The Getty Center for the History of Art and the Humanities, 1995). See also Giedion (note 77), 232.

149. Gustav Adolf Platz, *Die Baukunst der neuesten Zeit* (Berlin: Propyläen, 1927), 92, 112. For a similarly balanced approach see Peter Meyer, *Moderne Architektur und Tradition* (Zurich: H. Girsberger, 1927). A revised edition was published in 1928. Meyer had been one of Fischer's Swiss students.

150. E[lisabeth] M[aria] Hajos and L[eopold] Zahn, eds., *Berliner Architektur der Nachkriegszeit* (Berlin: Albertus, 1928), vii.

151. Paul Schultze-Naumburg, *Kulturarbeiten*, 9 vols. (Munich: Callwey, 1902–1917). Published under the auspices of *Der Kunstwart*, these books went through several printings before a revised edition began to appear in 1922. For a comparison of Schultze-Naumburg's early writings with the theories of the Werkbund, see Christian F. Otto, "Modern Environment and Historical Continuity: The Heimatschutz Discourse in Germany," *Art Journal* 43 (summer 1983): 148–57.

152. Paul Schultze-Naumburg, *Kunst und Rasse* (Munich: J. F. Lehmans, 1928), 108.

Behne's review, "Gibt es einen Weg aus der Wirrnis 'Deutscher' Kunstanschauungen?" appeared in *Deutsche Bauzeitung* 63 (1929): 750–51.

153. *Das Gesicht des deutschen Hauses* is volume 4 of the revised edition of *Kulturarbeiten* (Munich: Callwey, 1929). This book corresponds to volumes 1, 3, and 5 of the original edition. Many illustrations were reused, but the text is entirely new.

154. Golo Mann, *Deutsche Geschichte des 19. und 20. Jahrhunderts* (Frankfurt: S. Fischer, 1958), 397.

155. Paul Mebes, *Um 1800: Architektur und Handwerk im letzten Jahrhundert ihrer traditionellen Entwicklung*, 2 vols. (Munich: Bruckmann, 1908).

156. Schultze-Naumburg (see note 153), 128 ff. On the debate over the flat roof in Germany, see Richard Pommer, "The Flat Roof: A Modernist Controversy in Germany," *Art Journal* 43 (summer 1983): 158–69. On Schultze-Naumburg's changing relationship with the Werkbund, see Pommer and Otto (note 61), 142.

157. Taut (see note 2), 5–6.

THE MODERN FUNCTIONAL BUILDING

Dedicated to my wife[1]

Written November 1923

Foreword

Man's primordial reason for building is to protect himself against the cold, against animals, against enemies. He is driven by necessity; he would not build were it not for definite, compelling, urgent purposes. His early buildings are purely functional in character; they are in their nature essentially tools.

But when we study the earliest stages of human culture, we find that the instinctive joys of play cannot be separated from practical matters. Primitive man is not strictly utilitarian. He demonstrates his instinct for play even in his tools, which he makes smooth and beautiful beyond the demands of strict necessity, painting them or decorating them with ornaments.

The tool called "house" is no exception to this.

From the very beginning the house has been as much a toy as a tool. It is difficult to say how long a balance was maintained between the two poles.

In the course of history we only rarely find such a balance.

The play instinct led to interest in form. Without that instinct it would be impossible to understand why the tool called "house" must look good and be a certain shape. Thus our play instinct established certain laws of form, although they are subject to change from time to time.

The laws of form did change periodically. But if laws of form were unquestionably the secondary element in the origin of all building, they became the stronger, stricter, more rigid principle in the history of human building—stronger, stricter, and more rigid than mere fulfillment of utilitarian function. Formal considerations outweighed considerations of purpose.

Thus a return to purpose is always revolutionary in its effect. Forms that have become tyrannical are discarded in order to create—from the recollection of the original function, from as neutral a condition as possible—a rejuvenated, living, breathing form.

Its character as a tool makes the building relative. Its character as a toy makes it an absolute. The building must maintain a balance between these two tensions.

In the case of the last few centuries of European architectural history, one cannot speak of a balance. Form has predominated, and the purpose was entirely satisfied if the house functioned despite its form, that is, if form did not actually negate purpose.

The building that could arouse human interest in any way, that was more than a fence or a shed, was the building as form: the work of an artist. Its fulfillment of purpose was entirely immaterial.

Of course functional building existed alongside it—fences, sheds, log cabins, stables: the work of anyone at all.

A great gulf existed between formal and functional building because form and purpose were separated. Schinkel: "Two elements must be distinguished precisely: the one intended to work for practical necessity and the one that is meant only to express directly the pure idea. The former is slowly enhanced over the millennia to become an ideal, the latter has this end directly in sight."[2]

It turned out in practice that the functional building was not as bad aesthetically as one might have assumed from its alienation from form, and that the formal building was by no means as captivating as one might have anticipated from its superiority to any kind of lowly functionalism. Experience consistently confirmed that modern people of sound mind looked with disdain upon the formal buildings of their period, preferring functional structures: iron bridges, cranes, and machinery halls.

How was this possible?

Aesthetic sensibility had undergone a revolution. In the 1890s people had dutifully admired any dense ballast of form and almost equated art with finery, but with the turn of the century came a victorious breakthrough: appreciation of light, conciseness, and clarity. It opened people's eyes to the beauty of things suited to their purpose. Defying expectations, sensibilities refused to find beauty in the superfluous and willingly followed the logic of the functional.

There can be no doubt that the Jugendstil to a certain extent must be judged in light of this attitude. Today we are far removed from this period that so optimistically could invent its way past fundamental problems. But it cannot be overlooked that the Jugendstil introduced lighter forms, and the best early efforts of van de Velde, Endell, and Olbrich produced objects that aspired to austerity, energy, and tension of technical functions.[3]

Attitudes really had changed fundamentally. Architectural form was seen as a danger, and fulfillment of purpose was seen almost as a guarantee for creating a good building. Whereas before people believed that artists had to be very clever in order to produce good buildings despite function, now they thought that architects were much more likely to produce good buildings by liberating themselves from formal notions and setting their minds on fulfilling function, that is, buildings were again being seen much more as tools.

Functional architectural concepts replaced formal ones. Functional buildings used to be defined specifically by their use, a link between the free creations of architects and the bare utilitarian structures of engineers and technicians. Now every building became a functional building, that is, it was tackled on the basis of its type and function. Fulfillment of purpose became one of the means of architectural design as it had been ever since Otto Wagner in 1895 wrote in *Baukunst unserer Zeit* [The building-art of our time]: "Something impractical cannot be beautiful."[4]

In this book we intend to adhere mainly to the old concept of functional building, which has gained currency in describing a particular group of buildings. But we shall at the same time show how the new conception of architecture, more strongly established here than in other spheres of activity, left its novel mark on building in general.

I. No Longer a Facade but a House

In the last few decades of European architecture, Baroque design has congealed into an arid academicism. Among the very rare buildings of character are Franz Schwechten's Stettin and Anhalt railroad stations in Berlin (1878).[5]

The plan was dominated by facades overloaded with decorative motifs, Heidelberg castles with a "composition" irrelevant to their functional requirements. The most grotesque example: Ihne's Staatsbibliothek in Berlin, a concrete building that needs an artifical, complicated iron frame to support its sandstone Baroque facade, like a mask; or, by the same Ihne, the Kaiser-Friedrich-Museum, in whose plan the flight of stairs in the vestibule could be moved from one side to the other without having the slightest effect on the architecture of the building as a whole.[6]

At almost the same time a determined opposition, associated with the names of H. P. Berlage, Alfred Messel, and Otto Wagner, was successfully asserting itself in Holland, Germany, and Austria.[7] Buildings by these leading architects, which became benchmarks, are the Amsterdam Stock Exchange, the Wertheim Department Store in Berlin, and the buildings for the Vienna Stadtbahn. Work on the Amsterdam Stock Exchange started in 1897, the first phase of the Wertheim Building on Leipzigerstraße was completed in 1898, and the Vienna Stadtbahn dates from 1894 to 1897. The casino in Saint-Malo by the brothers Auguste and Gustave Perret, with a reinforced concrete vault that is very bold for its period, dates from the same time (1899/1900). But, as was so often also the case with the Perret brothers' later buildings, the architecture remained untouched by the constructional innovations.[8]

Berlage (b. 1856), Messel (b. 1853), and Otto Wagner (b. 1841) are the first generation of leaders in the fight for the renewal of architecture.*

---

* America's first modern architect, Arthur [Louis Henry] Sullivan, born 1856 in

91

Berlage, Messel, and Wagner were all trained during the period of academicism and eclecticism, and their own early works were eclectic. It suffices to name Berlage's fantastic plan for a mausoleum in which he actually intended to use all historical styles side by side (1889), Messel's Werder-Haus and his office building on Krausenstraße (Berlin, 1894/1895), and Otto Wagner's ideal design, "Artibus" (1880). This makes their historical achievement all the more important. They developed the first sound modern buildings in which form was no longer a finished, independent construct based on books and rules, with only very superficial connection with the

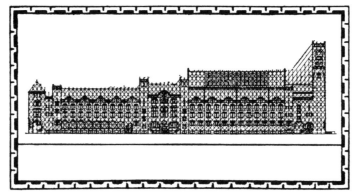

Berlage: Stock exchange elevation

object, but actually became an always new, young, and specific function of the project, or at least approached it. Berlage, Messel, and Wagner provided the new architecture with the gift of *Sachlichkeit*; they were the first who dared affirm consciously and consistently and to make into a positive design tool something that until then had been avoided and pushed aside: purpose.[9]

This development is particularly clear in the case of Berlage. His first competition sketch for the stock exchange, from 1895 — academic architecture in a Dutch Renaissance style, scarcely distinguishable from Cuypers's railroad station or his Rijksmuseum — has such a confused abundance of motifs that it looks like a small town.[10] In 1897 three designs rapidly developed into a modern stock exchange.

Boston, died 1924 in Chicago, belongs to the same generation. His Wainwright Building in St. Louis was the earliest skyscraper.

The first already shows an extraordinary degree of simplification.
A unified building emerges from the gables, towers, and onion domes; a
single roof runs from the entrance, stripped of its peculiar architecture,
right through to the last room. The confident strength of the quiet masses
replaces the uncertainty of many facades fitted over one another. The new
feature of the strong corner tower emphasizes the building's unshakable
strength. The second design shows no fundamental progress but translates
the first design's very arid institutional Gothic into a suppler, more personal
ecclesiastical Gothic. The third version almost completely replaces elements of historical style with a very energetic reassurance and an increasing respect for rectangularity, a tendency further strengthened in the
built version. Incidentally the small De Nederlanden office building in The
Hague, built in 1895 and much improved by remodeling in 1905, acted
as a harbinger for the work on the stock exchange.

In his book *Grundlagen und Entwicklung der Architektur* [The foundations
and development of architecture] (Berlin, 1908), based on lectures given in
Zurich in 1907, Berlage defines the path

> that we must now adopt, the path that will be available for the future, and that will
> lead us to a new art:
>
> 1. A geometric scheme should once again provide the basis of architectural com-
> position.
> 2. The characteristic forms of earlier styles should not be used.
> 3. Architectural forms should be developed in the spirit of *Sachlichkeit* (p. 100).[11]

The successive versions of the building Berlage put up in Amsterdam
more and more resembled a commercial conference center or office block.
The first design could equally well have been interpreted as a theater,
museum, railroad station, restaurant, palace, or town hall. The final building does not unmistakably say "stock exchange," but it no longer contains
misleading elements, with the possible exception of the tower. At least
it has a general physiognomy, and that is the main thing. A French critic
(*L'architecte*, 1924, p. 8) compares the creator of the Amsterdam Stock
Exchange with Vaudremer: "But Vaudremer did not have the honor of defi-
nitively leading the young generation down the path of a French national
architecture. Berlage has that honor in Dutch architecture."[12]

When Messel was building the Wertheim store on Leipzigerstraße in
Berlin, he found that his task offered the occasion for a really clear character.

He was in a position to create a new type, the department store, practically out of nothing. (The stages of his own work were the Werder-Haus, the house on Krausenstraße, the Wertheim store on Oranienstraße, the Wertheim store on Rosenthalerstraße.)

To his contemporaries the Wertheim store represented a more forceful and lucid sally against the tradition of form than any other building of its period. Here a desire to do complete justice to purpose and to resist aesthetic cliché was more successful than anywhere else. It was not Messel's ambition to build a beautiful facade behind which enough space could ultimately be found to accommodate the business of a department store but rather to provide an entirely distinct, concise form for the management of a department store, one arising from the most refined and alert sense of its quite particular and specific requirements and needs. Thus out of the requirement for maximum light and display window area, Messel designed for Leipzigerstraße a glass wall hung between slender stone piers; he designed open light wells that reveal the structure of the building as if in cross section.

Here a new type arose from the fulfillment of purpose. This building could be nothing other than a department store, a warehouse, an emporium, a gigantic department store.

Otto Wagner's contemporary buildings for the Vienna Stadtbahn are seemingly much less revolutionary (incidentally, in 1884, Wagner, too, produced a project for the Amsterdam Stock Exchange). A certain classicism persists but yet they are essentially modern. They have an austerity, clarity, and coolness that enable them to accommodate constructional parts remarkably well, even when highly traditional elements remain. Consistent with their building sequence: "The stations of the Stadtbahn show the gradual development of this utilitarian style. On the Gürtellinie, Wagner is still working freely with classical forms, predominantly with the Doric style; on the Wientallinie, the iron construction is formally emphasized in the great decorative arches of the outer halls; the Donaukanallinie represents another step forward: everything becomes simpler and more structural as iron arches are replaced by stanchions with braced girders" (Dagobert Frey).[13] Simple horizontals and verticals are retained almost throughout, placed strictly parallel to the always dominant track; and in their emotionless, distant coolness they absolutely produce the effect of "transport buildings." They remain perfectly within their sphere, whereas Messel's Wertheim Building contains a strongly alien artistic element, which was to appear increasingly in Messel's later work.

It is indeed curious that Messel, who at first showed the most revolutionary achievement among the three architects, did not continue along
the newly opened path, whereas both Berlage and Otto Wagner moved step
by step toward their goal. Berlage's route led from the stock exchange
to the Diamantbewerkersbond (1899), the De Nederlanden office building
in Rotterdam (1910), Müller & Co.'s office building in London (1914), and
the sketch for the Upper House in The Hague (1921). And Otto Wagner
created the Postsparkasse building in Vienna after 1903 at a time when
Messel had already returned to a traditional building style that in 1910 led
to his sketches for a Berlin museum, that is, to a style that once more
completely suppressed purpose in favor of a beautiful facade. In contrast,
Otto Wagner's development went as follows: Kirche Am Steinhof (1906),
Universitätsbibliotek (1910), block of flats in Vienna VII (1911), Lupusheil-
stätte [Sanatorium] (1913).

From Otto Wagner's *Baukunst unserer Zeit* (first edition, 1895):

Here it is appropriate to shout a loud and encouraging "forward" to the modern
creative architect and to warn him against an excessive and heartfelt devotion to
the old, so that he might regain a (however modest) self-confidence, without which
no great act whatsoever can arise.[14]

... If I were to summarize what has been said in this book and try to coin in a
few words what is essential, in order to show the young architect the shortest and
best way to the goal in any kind of work, these words and the sequence of their
application would run approximately as follows:

1. A scrupulously exact apprehension and complete fulfillment of the purpose
(down to the smallest detail);

2. A happy choice of the material of construction to be used (meaning one that
is readily available, easily workable, long-lasting, economical);

3. Simple and economic construction; and only considering these three main
points;

4. The form arising from these premises (it will flow from the pen as if of its
own accord and will always be easily understandable)."[15]

If we look more closely, we ought to recognize that the Wertheim
Building—to put it paradoxically—is more revolutionary than its architect,
yet not as revolutionary as it seems. This is because, despite the energy
and lack of prejudice with which it fulfills its purpose, it is not absolutely
sachlich. It quickly turned out to be a mistake to try to see the Wertheim

95

Building as the prototypical department store; for apart from Sehring's Tietz store at the other end of Leipzigerstraße, which adopted the glass surfaces on an even bigger scale, subsequent developments did not follow Messel's example.[16] Furthermore, outside Germany it had absolutely no effect at all. But even in Germany, beginning with Olbrich's Tietz store in Düsseldorf, we soon see walls once again gaining mass, the system of piers receding, and horizontals again reappearing, so that by the time we get to Emil Schaudt's Kaufhaus des Westens in Charlottenburg, there is nothing at all left of Messel's system. No doubt this development was affected by building codes that for fire protection required a solid wall at least one meter high between every two floors; thus, horizontal articulation was arrested, but the ultimate reasons went deeper than this.

Messel's facade seemed highly structural in its intention, but in the shadow of the roof and behind the capital-like ornamental headwork the piers are without much ado transformed into a harmless wall, thus revealing that the grandiloquent profile is merely decorative. The connection between roof and wall is very superficial, and the roof is a feeble, spaceless stopgap.

In a competition design of 1910 for an extension to Messel's building, Bruno Taut underlined Messel's principle with greater purity: his smooth piers are arched above to form the wall supporting the roof.[17] In his design for a Mittag department store in Magdeburg (1913), the same architect carried Messel's idea of verticality to its logical constructional solution by supporting the roof from above with concrete piers using a system of arches.

Messel's piers were not really the strong element that they first appeared but rather the weak element of his building. They were a consequence of the unclear thinking that led Messel to stack five ground floors on top of one another. The idea of increasing display space fivefold is—looking at the matter rationally—a mistake, as only the ground-floor windows are actually display windows. The upper rows of windows have little or no significance for advertising purposes; in fact, displays were very quickly removed from them and replaced with screenlike stands. Thus one did not even take full advantage of an additional light source. This is why we said that Messel's idea, directed solely at light and display space, was not entirely *sachlich*. It led him to stack five floors of display windows atop one another, and this in turn led to a verticality that brought piers into being as a stopgap measure; basically the piers are nothing more than the additive lifting above the street level, a fivefold raising of the street elevation—making Le Corbusier's remark that modern German architecture is frequently an "elevator-shaft architecture" absolutely accurate in the case of the Wertheim Building.[18] And it is also because of the internal inconsistency of these apparently so grandiloquent piers that the roof sits on them as it does: unrelated, thin, and random, like a makeshift roof. (Anyone wishing to adopt the terminology of Leo Frobenius in *Das unbekannte Afrika* could see verticalism as a continuing effect of Ethiopian-tellurian pile-frame architecture and horizontalism as a persisting element of Hamitic-chthonic building. It is incidentally also remarkable that Frobenius describes Hamitic social structure as horizontal layering [castes] and Ethiopian social structure as vertical layering [clans].)[19]

There is thus a great deal to criticize in this building of 1898, which when it was expanded, probably contrary to Messel's original conception, acquired multiple axes. And yet at the time it was of the greatest significance, although this was probably more psychological than strictly tectonic. The department store as a type did not develop in this direction, not in Germany, indeed not even in Berlin, and Messel himself recognized why in the way he terminated the building facing Leipzigerplatz. Here, warmly applauded by cultured people, he adopted an ecclesiastical note with a strong Gothic element, which led a Berlin critic to remark that the opening of a new department store in the Lustgarten (Raschdorff's cathedral) coincided with the consecration of a new cathedral on Leipzigerplatz.[20]

The ecclesiastical note had already been struck in the first building phase with the system of tall monumental piers. When foreshortened, they closed to form a solemn church wall. It rather gave the impression of a gigantic Gothic church converted into a store by installing intermediate ceilings and glass paneling. In the first building phase this tendency may have derived from an inner uncertainty, but in the section facing the square it became a conscious game with Gothicizing style elements.

All in all this building, apparently designed more radically in pursuit of purpose than any other of its period, is a very artificial construction, which is probably clearest when one compares it with, for instance, the architecture of the Louvre Department Store in Paris.

It cannot be said, however, that this establishes a new type—if there really is such a thing! The fact that a department store has become much larger has not changed the basis for the French architect. He thinks perhaps more conservatively but also genuinely more *sachlich*. He places large display windows where they are appropriate and have a purpose: on the ground floor. On the upper stories there are many windows arranged in regularly ordered rows. One story is placed above another: not as a repeated ground floor but as second, third, fourth, and fifth floor, i.e., with conscious emphasis on the horizontal, corresponding to reality. Finally the vaulted roof with its many skylights and chimneys makes the whole thing look like a warehouse, a gigantic storehouse accommodating a large number of things at the same time. In brief, the modern department store ultimately finds a mode of expression here where it was not being sought, an expression more genuine and purer than in Messel's work — simply because the tendency to grandiose stylization is absent, a tendency that inclined excessively toward art and thus led to a falsely ecclesiastical character, isolating the building from its neighbors, although its purpose is not particularly different from theirs. The Louvre Department Store remains entirely a part of the street, and precisely this is part of its truth. As the department store was built quite specifically in, on, and for the street, it is not allowed to be the most alien, conspicuous, and isolated building along the entire street, which was the case with Messel's store along Leipzigerstraße.

Messel's pointed, one-sided emphasis on a single function — display — made him untrue to the whole; the building lacked integration.

If we nevertheless assign Messel's building such an important place, it is because it had enormous psychological impact. He gave others the courage to break away from conventional schemes, to dare to create new types — even though his own attempt was far less happy and far less *sachlich* than it first appeared.

The modern country-house plan was also developed in the mid-1890s by the Chicago architect Frank Lloyd Wright, Sullivan's student.[21] Conventional terminology would not place the country house in the category of functional buildings, but the sensibility articulated in Wright's new floor plans is extraordinarily important as it is characterized by the liberation of the plan from formalist rigidity by returning to the functional element. This development begins somewhere between the plans for the Winslow House in River Forest (1893) and the Heller House in Chicago (1896) and reaches its peak in the plan for the Coonley House in Riverside (1908). Here Wright has given up fitting the rooms together in an ornamental scheme in favor of "free balancing in space" (Herre), based on the most careful inclusion of all requirements of comfort, quiet, and clear design.[22] There is no longer any trace of symmetry or axis, simply walls succinctly marking and accompanying the most comfortable traffic patterns for all the rooms. The accommodation to living functions goes so far that each piece of furniture has its specific place in the floor plan. This plan "unfolds." The house is not complicated by stairs ascending to the upstairs—a rudiment of medieval castle and masonry wall architecture. The plot of land has space enough to allow the building and almost all its rooms to develop directly at ground level.

In Wright's plans the rooms are not inserted next to one another but set in motion—as asymmetrically as life itself, strangely enough. Influenced by the Japanese, Wright already started building unusually flat roofs, mostly with wide overhangs. This means suppressing the picturesque and stressing constructional and cubic elements. It is logical that a house organized as freely balanced spaces should reject the roof as a hat that unites every-thing. Even the roof changes from a "motif" into a "function."

Wright's influence on European architecture was significant: in Germany (Peter Behrens, Gropius, Mendelsohn, Mies van der Rohe); in Holland (Oud [b. 1890], Jan Wils, van t'Hoff, Greve); in Switzerland (Le Corbusier); in Czechoslovakia (Obrtel, Krejcar, Tyl, Černy, Višek, Fragner, Feuerstein)—at first probably affecting the elevation more than the plan, which has only recently come to be fully understood.[23]

Compositionally, Wright's country houses are of the greatest significance because they consistently emphasize the horizontal. Their high-tension, nervy force, always contrasting ingeniously with concise verticals, actually makes the houses look as though they are a component of the street, although in their very idiosyncratic interpenetration of public and private space they almost never open to the roadside. Eschewing all ornament, which to our taste often plays a surprising role in the interior (recently increasing also on the exterior), he achieves the aesthetic composition of the house from the basic elements of accelerated horizontal movement, subtly and strikingly stopped verticals, and textured walls that never appear as supporting but always as supported parts. All visible parts are com-pletely conveyed as function: the precise relationship of open and closed areas produces the "building."

Every attentive observer senses the close connection with machine aes-thetics, completely new in the history of architecture. In an essay for the New York *Architectural Record* in 1908, Wright says:

> The machine cannot be removed from the world, it is here to stay. It is the fore-runner of the democracy that is the final goal of our hopes and dreams.
> There is no more important work before the architect now than to use this

modern tool to the greatest possible extent. But what does he do instead? He abuses this tool in reproducing forms born of other times, under distant skies, forms that today seem boring because one cannot avoid them anywhere; all of this happens with the help of the machine, whose main task it is to destroy just these forms.[24]

Berlage, Otto Wagner, and Alfred Messel (the latter with the reservations mentioned above) had successfully championed the cause of *Sachlichkeit*. But their *Sachlichkeit* was restricted primarily to resisting and avoiding *Unsachlichkeit*. Common sense, a feeling for cleanliness and its practice found acceptance, and fear of purpose ceased. But they still failed to address the task directly enough. They remained house builders. It may be that their commissions (stock exchange, office building, etc.) had something to do with this. At any rate, they did not approach the plan in a new way. Even Otto Wagner expressly stresses the importance of symmetry in the plan: "A simple, clear plan in most cases requires the symmetry of the work. In a symmetrical arrangement there is some measure of self-containment, completeness, balance; an impossibility of enlargement; even self-assurance. Gravity and dignity, the constant companions of architecture, also demand symmetry."[25]

Wright provided the first real breakthrough. Through a positive *Sachlichkeit,* he developed the country-house plan as something new and directly based on life, by returning to the most elementary functions of the inhabitants. This was the decisive turn from formal restraint to a commitment to life itself—in the confidence that a form appropriate to a healthy and orderly life will of necessity be beautiful—space newly conquered by purpose and function.

This attitude, when applied to the great tasks typical of the times, could lead to a new architecture.

And to an increasing extent in the first decade of the century, factory buildings and industrial problems represented just such tasks.

Academic and historical styles have been abandoned and the concept of the facade has been disposed of. Yet the "house" is still standing. Success is achieved by returning to purpose in an architectural development that has its precise counterpart in painting of the period, which likewise disposed of academic and historical styles. Its medium is naturalism, which in the development of painting always allows a new freedom from prejudice, quite analogous to the significance that a return to function had for building. "Naturalism in architecture is functional fitness" (Karl Scheffler: *Messel*, p. 14).[26]

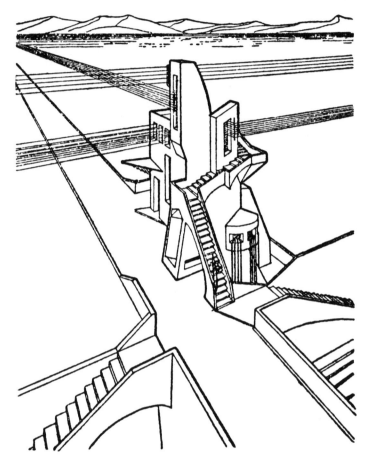

Virgilio Marchi, Rome: Telegraph station

II. No Longer a House
but Shaped Space

Industrial commissions had already produced surprising solutions in America. Walter Gropius put together an interesting selection in his essay "Die Entwicklung moderner Industriebaukunst" [The development of modern industrial architecture] in the German Werkbund yearbook of 1913.[27] The distinguishing feature of these American buildings (without exception the work of engineers, not architects) is their complete absence of compulsive ideas about form, their quite unprejudiced design, and their spatial realization of production and working processes. Take the grain silos for the Washbury-Crosby Company in Buffalo: a group of vertical tubes of different heights and widths, with bracing quite openly revealed—no hint of cladding, balancing, or refinement. Note also the contrast of angular elevator sections and connecting tracks extending horizontally, an absolutely asymmetrical and irregular plant that for this reason is so convincingly a legitimate and thrilling example of functional or dynamic building. It is a building that seizes upon tensions arising from the production process, and in working with them it actively articulates space without inhibitions or suppressions. It is completely analogous to the approach of Wright, who has had no industrial commissions himself with the exception of the Larkin Building in Buffalo. (The film studios [sic] in Olive Hill, California, also cannot be classified as such.) In order to show the strong effect of these works (an excellent compilation appeared in *Ingenieurbauten*, published by Ernst Wasmuth, Berlin, 1923) on the younger European architects, I quote a few sentences from the above-mentioned essay by Walter Gropius:

> In the motherland of industry, in America, large industrial plants have been built whose unknown majesty excels even that of our best German buildings in this genre. The grain silos in Canada and South America, the coal stores for the great railway lines, and the ultramodern factories for North American industries are almost comparable to the buildings of ancient Egypt in their monumental power. Their architectural features have such assurance that the purpose of the complex

is made unambiguously comprehensible to the observer with convincing force. The self-evident truth of these buildings does not come from their material superiority in extent and scale—this is certainly not where the reason for their monumental effect is to be found. It is much more that those who built them seem to have retained a natural sense for large-scale, concise forms in a way that is independent, healthy, and pure. There is a valuable lesson in all this for us. We should once and for all cease paying attention to historical yearnings and other misgivings of an intellectual nature, which are crippling modern European artistic creativity and obstructing artistic naïveté.[28]

Henry Ford's remarks on the subject of factory building are very typical:

One point that is absolutely essential to high capacity, as well as to humane production, is a clean, well-lighted and well-ventilated factory. Our machines are placed very close together—every foot of floor space in the factory carries, of course, the same overhead charge. The consumer must pay the extra overhead and the extra transportation involved in having machines even six inches farther apart than they have to be.... This brings our machines closer together than in probably any other factory in the world. To a stranger they may seem piled right on top of one another, but they are scientifically arranged, not only in the sequence of operations but so as to give every man and every machine every square inch that he requires and, if possible, not a square inch, and certainly not a square foot, more than he requires.... When we put up the older buildings, we did not understand so much about ventilation as we do today. In all the later buildings, the supporting columns are made hollow and through them the bad air is pumped out and the good air introduced. A nearly even temperature is kept everywhere the year round and, during daylight, there is nowhere the necessity for artificial light.... The dark corners which invite expectoration are painted white. One cannot have morale without cleanliness. We tolerate makeshift cleanliness no more than makeshift methods" (p. 113 ff.).[29]

Ford writes about his hospital: "Because of the arrangements it is easily possible for a nurse to care for seven patients who are not desperately ill. In the ordinary hospital the nurses must make many useless steps. More of their time is spent running around than caring for the patient. This hospital is designed to save steps" (p. 55).[30]

It will not take us too far away from the point at hand to quote the longer passage in which Ford formulates his attitude toward art:

104

We seemingly limit the creative functions to productions that may be hung on walls, or heard in concert halls, or otherwise displayed where idle and fastidious people gather to admire each other's culture. But if a man wants a field for vital creative work, let him come where he is dealing with higher laws than those of sound, or line, or colour; let him come where he may deal with the laws of personality. We need artists who master industrial relationships. We need masters of industrial methods. We need those who can mould the shapeless mass in political, social, industrial, and moral respects into a sound and shapely whole. We have limited the creative faculty much too much and have misused it for too trivial ends. We need men who can create the working design for all that is right and good and desirable (p. 104).[31]

Ford is also being entirely consistent with this when he says:

We will not put up elaborate buildings as monuments to our success. The interest on the investment and the cost of their upkeep would only serve to add uselessly to the cost of our products — so these monuments of success are apt to end as tombs. A great administration building may sometimes be necessary, although it arouses my suspicion that perhaps there is too much administration. We have never found a need for elaborate administration and would prefer to be advertised by our product, rather than where we make our product (p. 173).[32]

The first European to solve industrial tasks in the grand style was Peter Behrens (b. 1868), whom Emil Rathenau called to be artistic adviser to the AEG in 1907.[33]

Peter Behrens started his career as a painter in Munich, moved on to decorative and applied artwork at an early stage, and risked the leap to architecture in Darmstadt in 1901. The house in Darmstadt was followed by the Düsseldorf exhibition garden (1904), the Oldenburg exhibition pavilions (1905), a private house in Saarbrücken, some rooms for the Dresden Applied Arts exhibition [Kunstgewerbeausstellung] (1906), and the crematorium in Hagen, Westphalia (1907), all works then outstanding for their stereometric simplicity and conscious return to clear, cubic proportions. It is certainly not yet possible to talk about a real creation of space; there is more reduction than production, more graphics than architecture. But there was an unmistakable hint of a modern attitude in the work, a pleasure in concise, precise, and technical form — elements that make Rathenau's choice seem the happiest that could have been made at the time.

105

What had been happening in German industrial architecture until then?

Factories were thrown up here, as everywhere, in the rawest and cheapest way with, in fact, insulting contempt. Not even a minimum of design consideration was wasted on them, and if occasionally a bit of Gothic tracery or a Renaissance gable was added, the effect was all the more artificial. Factories with dark courtyards, narrow passages, blind windows, and low, dark rooms, more like prisons than places for productive work, repellent, stifling, joyless hammer mills mirrored perfectly the ever more terrible back premises of the urban tenements in which the majority of toilers in the factory had to live. No one has drawn the horrific misery of these buildings — with their hordes of subtenants, lodgers, transients, and illicit stills — more accurately and movingly than Heinrich Zille.[34]

This hopeless brutality, this contemptuous negation of all design consciousness was highly fitting for a period dominated by middle-class culture. Art was Raphael and Hans Makart, and what did a factory have to do with Raphael and Hans Makart?![35]

Peter Behrens's early work for the AEG was on a small scale. Arc lamps, fans, electrical cooking and heating equipment were designed simply, clearly, and logically, entirely without ornament. Behrens's great gift for creating new aesthetic values with the object itself was already beginning to show, and this was probably the first time in our age that things emerged that were typical rather than individual in form. Great emphasis was placed upon precise proportions and appropriate handling of materials. These works aroused general interest, for instance, at the Berlin shipbuilding exhibition of 1908. They were an early attempt at a clear and pure form for our times.

The AEG's most important buildings are the Huttenstraße Turbine Factory (1909), high-voltage factory (1910), small-motor factory (1911), assembly plant (1912) — all at Humboldt-Hain. Later came buildings for other industrial concerns, such as the administration building for the Mannesmann Factory in Düsseldorf (1911/1912), the Frankfurt Gasworks (1911/1912), the NAG [Nationale Automobil-Gesellschaft] Factory in Berlin-Oberschöneweide (1920), and more recently, the administration building for the Höchst Dye Factory.

We should not underestimate the contribution made by Peter Behrens in recognizing the historical meaning of the task that fell to him. Early on he correctly sensed that here was a job to do that had to be fundamental for the formation of a style for our times. From the start, Behrens had no

106

doubts that he had to adapt his work to typical solutions. The poorly imi-
tated, dissipated, ornate Baroque motifs jumbled together to suffocate,
inhibit, and dislocate any life there might have been in the original architectural rhythms were, with a new pride, replaced by the beauty of the pure
surface, of taut smoothness, of precise and concise outline, and of exact
edges—fitting things for an age in which the machine had started to orga-
nize a fundamentally new working process. Wright was unmistakably a
model for all this.

Here are some striking passages from an essay by Peter Behrens for the
AEG (*Plakat*, June 1920):

In questions of form for all industrial plants it is always a matter of creating character from the very nature of the things to be designed, to discover the type, just
as all past art is seen today to reveal sublime greatness by being typical of the
respective condition of the times. This means no less than that one must address
all the artistic and technical conditions that a plant imposes, support them,
indeed elevate them to a fundamental principle and let this principle become a
visible expression.

This applies first to the placement of the building. It has to follow the scale of
the production process. The location of railroad tracks is crucial to the siting of
the building. Staggering the buildings allows for the proper entry of rail tracks
through the gates of the factory buildings. At the same time spacious storage
yards should be provided, and this touches upon a city planning principle of great
aesthetic significance. It is precisely this staggering of buildings, necessary in
practical terms, that will give the plant an effective silhouette; and the necessary
layout of the yards fulfills a demand by a past master of city planning, Camillo
Sitte, who described a square enclosed by buildings as one of the most necessary
aspects of architectural effects.

Whenever the opportunity arises to compare plants designed from such a
purely practical point of view with others based on random factors or built in
stages, one is astonished to see how such different impressions can be created
with the same expenditure of construction and materials.

But the same is also true of a factory's interior layout. The spatial arrangement
grows out of the organization of the production process. Clear layout, ease of
interchange and forward movement of products, and unhampered mobility of tools,
machines, or trucks require open, uncluttered, well-lit halls. Workplaces should be
as well lit and spacious as possible. It is therefore recommended that staircases
and elevators be moved to the exterior; this will at the same time make the archi-

tectural effect more impressive, producing a long sequence of work spaces inside and on the outside rows of windows picturesquely enlivened by protruding stair-wells and elevator shafts towering above the roof. Since light is a prerequisite for good work, factory buildings should have large window openings; they should dominate, control the surface of the building, and lend support in their effect as windows. For this reason they should not seem like large holes in the wall but appear flush with the outer wall, giving the exterior a friendly appearance.[36]

At this point I should like to draw attention to an important essay by H. Lülwes, "Was muß beim Entwurf neuer Werke beachtet werden?" [What has to be considered in the design of new works?] (*Hawa-Nachrichten*, January 1922).[37]

If we compare Peter Behrens's achievements with American examples, the crucial difference is that Behrens is still intent on stylization, on artistic interpretation through form, whereas the Americans present the object completely bare. There is no doubt that Behrens was extraordinarily refreshed, broadened, and strengthened in his forms by an unprejudiced accommodation to the living process of industry, but in the end his behavior was not altogether without prejudice. He abandoned a number of conventions, gave up a great deal of rigidity and tradition, but he did not unquestioningly devote himself to the purpose, to function. Many concepts persisted for him, even the concept of a "house." And it is just this clinging to this notion of a house that compels him to stylize. For how could the small-motor factory on Voltastraße express itself as such—and Peter Behrens cared for "expression"—other than by applied forms (in this case strongly stressed piers) if the basic layout of the plan is not fully and unconditionally committed to the thing, and then of course it is no longer a "house."

A duality still remains in the case of Behrens: a good fulfillment of purpose and its integration into a normal body—wall, roof, window, etc. But because he wanted to destroy the normal house for the sake of a greater and more powerful concept, Peter Behrens's pathos was born, which unfortunately found many imitators. For example, Stoffregen's Delmenhorst Factory showed an inclination toward the vertical, perhaps still under the influence of Messel.[38]

It is now very interesting to see that the earliest of Behrens's AEG buildings makes the greatest and freest break with the conventional house type, and that his last industrial buildings (Oberschöneweide) are classical. There seems to be a certain analogy with Messel's development.

With the Turbine Hall in Huttenstraße there suddenly emerged an industrial building that was a new type, a new life: no longer a "house," no longer a shed, no longer convention, and no longer a cross between various historical types. For the first time in this country, industry built a workspace solely according to work requirements, not as a trivial stopgap but with self-confident strength, using the new materials iron, concrete, and glass. The new feature of this building was the stronger unification of a more massive body. The body built here to house the working process was an indivisible, unbroken whole: from socle to ridgeline its mass is informed with a will and a life; it stands like an improbable giant amid the childishly stuccoed tenement facades of the area. Decoration, ornament, and form were swept away. The building was itself form, it needed no forms. The shaping force was directed away from an obsolete concern with facade ballast and toward the body, toward fulfilling purpose, and toward exploiting the new materials. They had of course been used before (Perret), but with a few exceptions their style-forming possibilities had never been recognized.

In contrast to this, in the Frankfurt Gasworks we find once again the method of delimiting and dividing, and the reduction of the design to a few abstract forms ("sphere, cone, and cylinder"). In the NAG buildings in Oberschöneweide we definitely find the emphasis on classical form, the neutralization of function and purpose behind impenetrable calm, here consistently also forgoing any expression. The house reasserts itself.

We could establish a parallel between the Turbine Hall and the Wertheim Building with the following observation: the Turbine Hall, more than any other building by Behrens, is devoted to function. This makes it the most unusual, revolutionary, and influential of his buildings and at the same time, very analogous to the Wertheim Building, the one most isolated and alien in its surroundings, so that the juxtaposition of tenement buildings and the Turbine Hall borders on the grotesque. Just as the desired typology led the Wertheim Building toward the ecclesiastical, the Turbine Hall was driven toward the heroic. The hall arose in the style of a Cyclopean force, for which there was no basis. The assembly hall in Humboldt-Hain was essentially more sober, more *sachlich*, thus more honest and also more consistent, making better use of the materials.

All in all, Peter Behrens still "builds" factories. The same is true of Hans Poelzig, whose chemical plant for Milch & Co. in Lubin near Posen is probably the best and most *sachlich* of all "built" factories. Unfortunately the excellent Werder Mill design has not been executed. Poelzig's attitude

109

toward purpose was made surprisingly clear in a speech he delivered in Salzburg in 1921 explaining his Festspielhaus [theater] design (*Kunstblatt*, 1921, no. 3, p. 77 ff.):

> All purely technical considerations are an abomination to the artist from the start. Even if he knows that these purely technical matters cannot be avoided, that they have to be tackled, he also knows and continually feels that technology plays far too large a part in the life of the present age, and he will continue to struggle against its dominance. Technical and artistic intentions are and remain complete contrasts, and the artist knows only too well how German art expresses this confused, rowdy, deviate, utter and complete irrational charm.... He (the artist) thinks of nothing but the chance that he may plant this piece of land with the constructs of his imagination—to the extent they are at his disposal—and only then does he try to whittle down his constructs to the level on which present-day life moves.[39]

Purpose? "What a dreadful epithet for a work of art."
Result? The Salzburg Festspielhaus!
Elsewhere Poelzig says: "Art begins only where one is building for the good Lord" (*Neubau*, 10 January 1924). "For the good Lord"—in other words, for no one!

The Fagus factory in Alfeld an der Leine, built in phases by Walter Gropius (b. 1883) beginning in 1913 [1911], may be considered, along with his buildings for the Cologne Werkbund exhibition (1914), to be the first factory that was no longer built but "constructed" from iron, concrete, and glass. The following sentence from the essay mentioned above may serve to characterize Gropius's approach:

> A clear internal plan that also from the outside clearly expresses the layout simplifies the production process considerably. But it is by no means socially immaterial whether the modern factory worker does his work in a dreary, ugly, industrial barracks or in well-proportioned rooms. He will work with much greater pleasure on large collective projects if his workplace, designed by an artist, complies with the sense of beauty innate in all of us, one that has an enlivening effect on the monotony of mechanical work. Thus the increasing contentment will increase the working spirit and the business performance.[40]

(*Sept arts*, 15 February 1923 [Brussels], demands that the noise and racket of a large factory should also not be allowed to rage unchecked: "Doubtless, one will never arrive at some sweet harmony, but it is necessary to strive for a rational organization of all sonorous brutality.")[41]

It is clear from the Alfeld factory how much Gropius's study of American utilitarian buildings had a liberating effect—and just as clear that Gropius nevertheless subjects American directness to a certain aesthetic filtering. There is a sense of distant refinement, even caution, that detracts from the unconditional inner unity of the first phase of this important building. The way in which all false pathos is coolly avoided is very admirable, but a certain aesthetic urge deprives the work as a whole of its ultimate simplicity. This simplicity could almost be called complicated. It vacillates between object and form, between "America" and "Osterndorf." But there is no doubt that it is still the most modern, the most exemplary German factory of the prewar period, not perhaps as compelling or as direct as Poelzig's plant in Lubin but unquestionably bolder. Gropius's view coincides with Jean Cocteau's, for instance, who writes in *Le coq et l'arlequin:* "American machines and buildings resemble Greek art in the sense that utility confers on them a spareness and a grandeur stripped of the superfluous. But this is not art. The role of art consists in grasping the sense of the time and drawing upon the spectacle of this applied spareness to create an antidote to the beauty of the useless that encourages the superfluous."[42]

Fritz [Friedrich] Kaldenbach's Seeck [Sack] Factory in Dresden also deserves an honorable mention.[43]

Apart from a relatively unimportant factory for Vorster & Co. in Hagen, Westphalia, Henry van de Velde (b. 1863) has produced no industrial buildings. And yet his work is important for the further development of functional architecture because of its consistent emphasis on functional form. By including the element of movement in architecture, van de Velde gave the younger European generation courage to devote itself with real frankness and without classical prejudice to the force of technical and economic functions.

We have already talked about the element of "movement" in the case of Wright. For van de Velde it is an essentially different matter. The difference is between a sober, *sachlich* American and a romantic European; for there is a romantic in van de Velde as well as a rationalist.

Wright's "movement" is a more consistent and conscious conception of space (in plan) and a tighter relationship of tension between the parts of the building (in elevation). The building parts themselves are absolutely "expressionless"; they are immobile, technically determined, standardized, ready-made pieces. Movement works as a mechanical force from the outside. A human will, with the machine's help, has constructed the building from prefabricated parts, with all its angles and corners.

Van de Velde takes movement in a more literal sense, as a force plastically organizing the building from the inside. He arrives at curves and flourishes, at forms that could be true once only, i.e., they are valid in only one context. He arrives at expressive forms that speak. Human will, which is seen as limited, does not determine and fix the work, but the will of *Sachlichkeiten*, of purposes, of materials is itself translated into reality; thus the human being is more the mediator. Van de Velde injects an empathy into the function, and from there he arrives at a formal expression of movement that Wright definitely avoids. Van de Velde's conception parallels the Expressionist Movement, making its appearance somewhat later in painting.

Function—movement—expression as well—symbolism—romanticism—individualism—and finally anthropomorphism are logically very closely related, that is, van de Velde's influence was important and valuable but not completely harmless. It also contained a danger.

In Wright's conception the "house" type could continue to exist despite all innovations and improvements. Unequivocalness, clarity, and the assurance of edges delimited a space that the human will had conquered and arranged.

In van de Velde's conception these limits are easily blurred. The freely given forces of strong curves and flourishes could very well destroy the box and replace it with a free organism of a completely different nature—a small example: the Osthaus desk.

Van de Velde's houses (for Esche and Körner in Chemnitz; Hohenhof and Springmann in Hagen, Westphalia; Dürckheim and Henneberg in Weimar; and Schulenberg in Gera) do not show dissolution of the conventional "house" concept and they therefore do not show any dissolution (the one that comes closest is the house for Dr. Leuring, a physician in Scheveningen). The reason for this is that van de Velde is both a romantic and a constructor. As such, he only abandons the "house" type where there is a *sachlich* imperative, as in the Weimar Kunstschule or the Werkbund Theater in Cologne, which unfortunately has been pulled down for no obvious reason.

These last two buildings show how valuable van de Velde's view of move-ment can be regarding the renewal of the building mass—despite the many echoes of the Jugendstil still resounding here.

Of course if we want to see the ultimate consequence of a functionalism colored with a romantic and pantheistic tinge, then the best place to look is among Hermann Finsterlin's designs, the most radical dissolution of the "house" concept imaginable, approaching the forms of organic, growing nature.

> The formal type that is the last greatest genial invention of the terrestrial spirit— organic form—lies between the crystalline and the amorphous. My architecture also sprouts at this transition point. Inside the new house one will not only feel as though one is the occupant of a fabulous crystal druse, but like the internal resi-dent of an organism, wandering from organ to organ, a symbiont of giving and receiving within a fossil of a gigantic mother's body. A small fragment of the trans-posed set of boxes of world forms is to be found in the sequence of town, house, furniture, and vessel; growing out of one another like the gonads of an organism, these hollow creatures need no longer be displaced foreign bodies as they have been hitherto. Tell me, are you never irritated by the brutal scheme of your six walls and the injected material coffin of your thousand necessities? Has the mys-terious urge never crept over you to rearrange yourselves in accordance with the rhythm of your breathing souls? (*Frühlicht*, no. 2, p. 36).[44]

Finsterlin, who refers to his designs as "glacier crevice systems for the soul" [*Seelengletschermühlensysteme*], is an unabashed romantic. Van de Velde is not just a romantic but a rationalist at the same time. Neither van de Velde the romantic nor Finsterlin are backward-looking in their views— and the rationalist is emphatically a man of our times.

"Nothing is ugly in the world of technical inventions, machines, and the thousand everyday objects that serve purposes just as important as architecture and the applied arts. Yes, their forms so shaken by truth and boldness have elicited the greatest admiration from all those who were passionately waiting for a new beauty, the beauty of the future" (*Die drei Sünden wider die Schönheit* [The three sins against beauty], p. 41).[45]

> The thing that seems most to bother people who oppose these principles is the fact that they are just principles, that they moreover require an intellectual effort to which people are no longer accustomed.... Are we at the end of the world, or

have we wandered into the blind alley of the driest puritanism because we plead for a formal and simple rule of construction in which I have perhaps discovered the secret trait of our times. It is a rule that, after everything is examined and checked off, one only includes those things (no matter what field) that still seem reasonable, powerful, and capable of being followed up by things that are even more reasonable and powerful (*Innen-Dekoration*, November 1902).[46]

The bridge between van de Velde the romantic and van de Velde the rationalist is construction. In summing up his comments on the shape of his column in the Folkwang-Museum vestibule, van de Velde says: "Its form shows its soul or, to put it more precisely, its bones (*Innen-Dekoration*, October–November 1902).[47]

In searching for expressive form he found those forms arising from construction to be the most expressive; or rather, reason leads him to construction and feeling interprets construction.

Another passage characteristic of van de Velde is his commentary on the Folkwang-Museum:

I searched a long time for a solution to the banister, which was made significantly more difficult by the design of the steps. When I had found a way of attaching a wrought-iron baluster to every step (a shallow bracket is attached below the profile of the tread with a bolt, while the two outside stiles of this railing, resting on the tread, thrust upward in a horseshoe shape), it seemed so clear and simple to me that I was almost ashamed to have taken so long thinking about such a thing.[48]

The functional suppleness of his early rooms for Bing's L'Art Nouveau in Paris (1897), still thoroughly Jugendstil, already delighted one of the Goncourts, who in his review coined the apt word *yachting-style* (Osthaus, p. 18).[49]

Van de Velde's attitude toward technology and construction is thus aesthetic, just as his enthusiasm for machines is not incompatible with empathy. Van de Velde even sees machines in formal and aesthetic terms, for he bitterly rejects their consequences. Whereas Peter Behrens somewhat coolly defines machines as pseudo-aesthetic structures, van de Velde is the first representative of a romantic machine cult that has found many followers.

Machine: that means standardization, typification, collectivism—but van de Velde is a passionate individualist! At the Cologne Werkbund conference (1914) he led the "artists" group against Muthesius's proposals for types.

He declared: "The artist is in his innermost essence a fervent individualist; he will never of his own free will submit to a discipline that imposes a type upon him." The essay "Devant l'architecture" indicates a change. It is imbued with a profound understanding of the collective architectural task of our times and a fine confidence in the work of the younger generation in all countries (*Europe,* 15 July 1924).[50]

Van de Velde was less prone to notions of historical-monumental form than Behrens. He was drawn more to the idea of movement in every living thing and thus developed form determined by function, a dynamic form that he himself was fond of describing as "dramatic," that is, a less histori-cal form, an emergent form, with its character rooted in engineering and construction. It is revealing to compare a utensil by van de Velde with Peter Behrens's AEG lamps, for instance. Van de Velde tries to find the unifying thrust of movement through empathy and the fulfillment of the functions of standing, rising, gripping, carrying, etc. He frequently says of his forms: "I reveal their innermost nature, their soul." Peter Behrens, closer to Wright, contrasts simple stereometric forms. There temperament, here distance.

Van de Velde's marked influence on the younger generation of European architects is seen very clearly in Erich Mendelsohn's (b. 1887) Einstein Tower near Potsdam (1920/21). A certain hint of Olbrich (early Darmstadt exhibition buildings) can be traced in Mendelsohn. Early sketches for the Einstein Tower (the title page of the *Wendingen* issue [of 1919], for instance) show how very close Finsterlin was to him at the time as well. Compare, for example, Finsterlin's works on pages eleven or fourteen in this *Wendingen* issue to the drawing by Mendelsohn cited above. Finsterlin's decorative self-sufficiency is certainly transformed into an engineer-like energy and tension by Mendelsohn. Incidentally, it is very characteristic that the journal of the Amsterdam Movement in Holland, which inclines to romanticism (De Klerk [d. 1923], van der Meij, Kropholler, Wijdeveld, etc.), should devote special issues to these two Germans: Mendelsohn and Finsterlin.[51]

The desire for exaggerated characterization and expressive individuality brought Mendelsohn, with his Einstein Tower and also—less markedly—his Mosse Building (Berlin, 1921–1923), to an architecture that worked a great deal with movement and anthropomorphism, that really can be called "dra-matic" in van de Velde's sense, and that must definitely be placed within the Expressionist Movement. The entrance "draws us in," the walls "lead," the steps "sway," etc. (On the Mosse Building: "no passive spectator of the

rushing cars, of the traffic flowing to and fro, but it has become an assimi-
lating, contributing element of this motion.") The exhibition gallery built by
Richard Döcker for a Werkbund exhibition in Stuttgart (1921) was the product of a similar attitude, whereas certain early works by Hans and Wassili
Luckhardt had the special nuance of Novembergruppe Expressionism,
which they soon grew out of with their Norma Factory and Wender Garage.[52]
Döcker's gallery was only a transition as well.

The exaggerated character of the Einstein Tower places it within the
series Wertheim Building and Turbine Hall. In his critique of the tower, the
Dutch architect J. F. Staal remarked quite aptly that it was more a monument than a workshop: "It is the best German [building], it ranks among his
best individual works, but it is still German and still individual" (*Wendingen*,
October 1920).[53]

Some of Mendelsohn's industrial designs are more *sachlich* and more
objective, and now for the first time they show the benefit derived from all
the work. Disregarding, as always, American engineering buildings, it is only
here that the "house" type of vertical walls, roof, and windows is completely
overcome by the concept of shaped space. It is subdued from the inside,
not just concealed from the outside, by pathos and stylization. That which,
from the inside out, necessarily led to the break with the old type was the
consistent use of the iron truss. In his lecture "Problem einer neuen Baukunst" (1919) Mendelsohn stresses how a new chapter of architectural history started with the appearance of the iron truss: "From the columns and
marble beams of the Greek temple to the piers and stone vaulting of the
Gothic cathedral come the flexible trusses of iron halls. After the balance of
loads of antiquity and neutralization of structural loads of medieval times
comes the dynamic tension of ferroconcrete construction" (*Wasmuth's
Monatshefte,* 1924, p. 3).[54]

His model of 1919 for an optical factory is already convincing. Here and
in the Luckenwalde Hat Factory of 1921–1923 there develops from the most
expedient organization of the production process a tight, closely fitting,
spatial form, a form intended to follow and be appropriate to the functions
of the business, to the production sequence, like the parts of a machine.
Mendelsohn achieved an admirable simplicity and repose in his renovation
of the Wüstegiersdorf Textile Works (1922/23), and especially in his competition project (with Richard Neutra) for the Haifa business center (1923).[55]

Hans Scharoun — Insterburg: *Chicago Tribune* competition sketch

III. No Longer Shaped Space but Designed Reality

From this point forward, two trends in contemporary European architecture diverge fairly sharply; they can be called eastern and western. Both are aligned with *Sachlichkeit,* both like to make reference to machines, both want an expression of our time and our region, but they arrive at very different results. Otherwise, the boundaries are entirely fluid.

At the time of the Russian Revolution artists in Russia and Germany began to negate the concept of "art." They no longer wanted to be producers of luxuries, they wanted to fulfill a necessary function in the life process of society. They rejected decoration entirely, commited themselves to construction and artistic production, and opposed any sort of aesthetics or concern with form.

The Russian engineer Lapshin declared, for example: "There is no architecture as such and no separate architecture as such, there is only uniform, strictly scientific design.... So-called artistic matters still dominate building."[56] We have to come closer to the style of our times. (The demand for an independent "style for our times" is found already with Schinkel and has been echoed by every architect since. Schinkel says: "Why should we always want to build in the style of another period? Why should we not try to invent a style of our own!?") No artists were summoned to build the Palace of Labor in Moscow, but factory managers with great technical expertise were brought in. Lapshin is against treating building from an aesthetic point of view and suggests that it should become part of engineering.

The surest guiding principle to absolutely *sachlich,* necessary, extra-aesthetic design seemed to be adaptation to technical and economic functions, which with consistent work must in fact lead to the dissolution of the concept of form. Thus building would unconditionally become a tool.

Strict suitability to functions — what could the building gain by that?

When the parts of a building are arranged according to a sense of their use, when aesthetic space becomes living space — and this is the kind of order we call dynamic—the building throws off the fetters of the old, fossilized, static order, axes, symmetry, etc., and achieves a new starting point. A cramped, material, stable equilibrium (symmetry) gives way to a new, bolder equilibrium, delicately balanced in broad tensions (polarity) that correspond better to our essence, and with this comes a form that is entirely new and alive, free from constraints and stabilization.

And then, through this suitability to function, a building achieves a much broader and better inner unity: it becomes more organic by abandoning the old conventions and formalisms of representation, which inhibit the materialization of necessary form.

It is therefore no wonder that architects tried to exploit the possibilities of functionalism to the full. Building presumes the optimum functional articulation of the proposed living space; architecture is no more than a fixed and visible structure of the final organization of every movement, every occupation, every purpose and use of the building.* It is no small architectural achievement if all the paths through a building relate to each other clearly and coherently, absolutely free and open to every possible combination, and not just in a mechanical sense — "twelve doors in a long corridor"—but with the aim of achieving the finest and most ambitious organization and best possible construction. The architect can only grasp and carry out his truly artistic work, that is, the creative work, when he addresses questions of his client's attitude to life, way of living, business methods—something that of course he can only do with him, not without him or against him. For this reason "being a client" is not just buying a piece of land, some bricks, and an architect. The client must be an activity, whose taking possession of the acquired space is so definite, clear, rich, and organic that it can be transformed into the relationships of masonry walls, indeed relationships governed not by convention or mere custom but by necessity and a living sense.

---

* Von Crancin, Director of Building in Hessen, wrote in 1792: "There are still architects —at least this character is often ascribed to them—who arrange the symmetry of windows, doors, and other such parts of the building according to the beds and other things that they want to put in the rooms, or even according to the greater or lesser quantity of light needed in a room or chamber, or even according to the occupations to be pursued there" (Ehmig [Paul Ehmig, *Das deutsche Haus* (Berlin: Ernst Wasmuth Verlag, 1914)]).

It is the architect's task to balance spaces freely against each other, simply according to their *sachlich* functions, excluding anything arbitrary; only
then is it possible to have the ambition—from floors, circulation, size of
interior and exterior space, the best spatial sequence, the disposition to
light, to garden, to street, to traffic—of creating the final tectonic order of
all factors: the building. In this process all symmetrical axes, all drawing
board geometry, all floor plan ornaments must completely disappear; architecture becomes shaped reality (see also Richard Döcker, "Über Baukunst,"
Volkswohnung 5, no. 13).[57]

As an example of a logical form in this sense, let us take a plan and elevation for a farm being built by the Berlin architect Hugo Häring.[58] (Some
fine plans by Fritz Kaldenbach, who died young in 1918, show a transition
from formalism to functionalism, not via Wright but more via van de Velde
and Lauweriks.)[59] Häring finds a way of working with curves that is at first
reminiscent of Finsterlin's projects, and it is of course related to these as
well, but it is also fundamentally different because of the strict *Sachlichkeit*
of its curves, as opposed to Finsterlin's romantic arbitrariness. For similar
reasons Hans Scharoun of Insterburg comes to use the curve in plan and
elevation, and so occasionally does Adolf Rading of Breslau.[60]

Is there an internal logic for such use of the curve, one that has little to
do with the illustrative, symbolic use of van de Velde? Certainly!

The rectangular room and the straight line are not functional but
mechanical creations. If I were to work consistently from biological function,
then the rectangular room is nonsensical, for its four corners are unusable
dead space. If I were to outline the areas in a room that are actually used
and walked upon, then I would inevitably arrive at a curve.

The flow of organic life knows no right angles and no straight lines.
And as the functionalist always appeals to the flow of organic life as the
finest example of pure functionalism, his fondness for the curve is entirely
understandable. Straight lines will always resist the ultimate adaptation
to functional mobility and fluidity. They allow only a general, approximate
adaptation, nothing absolute. Thus the consistent functionalist has to take
curves rather than straight lines as his starting point, as Hans Scharoun
does when he writes: "Why does everything have to be straight, when
straightness only evolves from material values and our milieu!"

Scharoun's competition entry for a new post office in Bremen (rejected
in the first round) is a fine example of functional work. An officially pre-
pared floor plan combined counter hall, parcel room, and check office under

the same roof and behind a facade, for which the competition really only sought a style. Scharoun differentiates and articulates the mass. His work carried the typical motto: "Business—not official image!" Counter hall and parcel room can and should be flat. As a purely administrative building with no public traffic to speak of, the check office can be concentrated upward. The parcel room lies long and narrow next to the railway line. The counter hall evolves practically from a circular plan, and a building with a clear physiognomy emerges, articulated in height, width, and length, a building appropriate to the dynamic tensions of its functions—just as Häring's plan solves this problem in the most subtle, sensitive, and functional way for an agricultural enterprise.

Functional thinking, almost in the spirit of Roux's "evolutionary mechanics of animal organisms," is shown when Häring and Scharoun, working on office plans for Berlin (Friedrichstraße office building) and Königsberg (Börsenhof), choose to run corridors not as channels with a consistently regular cross section, independent of the volume of traffic flow, but as paths that are wider where many people have to use them and narrower at the end where fewer people need to use the doors.[61] Functional thinking is shown in Heinrich de Fries's plan for an office and large tenement building, similar to the planned Börsenhof in Königsberg, which is formed not around the individual office room as a cellular unit (as Peter Behrens had rightly done in his Düsseldorf Mannesmann building, in which the entire space belonged to one firm) but around the unit of the smallest possible group (for instance director's office, typing room, public room), whose internal traffic is not dependent upon the public corridor.[62] Here is what de Fries was aiming for: "Fusing maximum organizational usefulness and economy in the floor plan with the strongest possible rhythm of masses by dissolving hitherto customary surface facades." It seems to be carried out more consistently in his competition entry for the office building in Prinz-Albrecht-Gärten, Berlin (1924).

This consideration shows functionalists concerned with very practical matters. And yet it would be a mistake to see functionalists as utilitarians. Results produced by both groups overlap here and there, but they derive from quite different attitudes.

Functionalists are concerned with solving a problem of general significance to our culture. The utilitarian only asks: "What is the most practical way for me to act in this case?" But the functionalist asks: "How do I act most correctly in principle?" Their attitude inclines toward philosophy and has a metaphysical basis. Their thinking will be in sympathy with the thought processes of someone like Frobenius considering chthonic and tel-lurian architecture, and there is no question but that the functionalists, even the most *sachlich* ones, could more readily be classified as romantics than as rationalists.

The utilitarian who absolutely must derive all phenomena from the pur-pose in many cases achieves this only by wrongly equating "purpose" with "meaning," as, for example, when he asserts that ornaments in prehistoric caves also had their "purpose." They certainly have a "meaning" but not a "purpose." Even Lu Märten's *Resultate historisch-materialistischer Unter-suchungen* [Results of historical-materialist investigations] (nature and change of forms) only explains the general fact of existence, not the partic-ular way in which existence is manifested (Frankfurt am Main: Taifun-Verlag, 1924).[63]

The utilitarian subordinates himself to purposes in a commonsensical way that the citizen of today indeed knows and recognizes. He can, as a result, easily become a materialist.

The functionalist is clearly no less decisive in approving of purpose, but he does not see it as something complete, unalterable, rigidly prescribed; rather, it is a means to broaden and refine, intensify and sublimate, move and mold human beings. For him every satisfied purpose is an implement for creating new, more refined human beings. Residents in his building have everything at hand—the architect has the residents in hand—through purpose. The architect creates purpose as much as purpose creates the architect!

To be fully consistent the functionalist would make a building into a pure tool. He would necessarily arrive at a negation of form, as he could only completely achieve his ideal of absolute adaptation to the events in a space by means of movement.

Is consistent functionalism not a dead-end street?

It certainly leads to biological relativism,* which in the end not only dis-

---

* Viktor Engelhardt speaks of a biological influence in later philosophical positivism and of its relativistic consequences (*Weltanschauung und Technik* [Leipzig, 1922–1923], p. 40).

solves the conventions of decorative art forms (which would be an advantage) but of building itself. One can, as Jennings does, define an animal as a mere incident, but not a house. And why can one not do that?

An animal is a moving organism with its own limited, temporally measured life. Its forms are forms of being, identical with the individual, not utilitarian forms for the many. A snail shell, for example, is part of the body of an individual snail and cannot serve as a house—organically—for anyone else. It grows with the individual snail and dies with it. (When nature needs space for a number of creatures she organizes it on the basis of a mechanical principle that can be standardized: the mass tenement of the honeycomb.)

The built house neither grows nor dies. When the functionalist nevertheless compares it with an organism (in a cinema design Scharoun mentions its "maw," "stomach," "digestion," and "backside"), he is trying to express that it should be as appropriate in its parts and as logical and unified in its classification as a grown organism.

The objection to an ultimately consistent functionalism is the exaggerated and overstated individualization of its body, a potentially dangerous tendency for Germans. Take, for example, the Wertheim Building—Turbine Hall—Einstein Tower sequence. We stressed that a functional attitude is capable of furthering and enhancing the inner unity of a building to a very large extent, but we must now add that it makes it equally difficult for greater objective unity to emerge from several or many entities. Once more: Wertheim Building—Turbine Hall—Einstein Tower.

Are we really dealing with inevitabilities here?

If we consider nature's ideal functional constructions, then we recognize that the richer and more subtle a living creature's organization, the more distinctively it is individualized. In the same way it is quite logical that a perfectly good, tried and tested tool does not have an "environment," and it is quite immaterial where a machine is placed. Its elements and proportions relate only and exclusively to itself. Therefore if the guideline for shaping a building is only the optimal fulfillment of function, then concern for what has to be taken into consideration also ends at the four walls of that building.

Here one might raise the objection that individuals in organic nature do form a unit. Be that as it may, these individuals are, in any case, distinguished by the possibility afforded them of movement and change of place. Their unity is probably fundamentally based on this possibility, and this is the very thing that is denied the house on principle. A house stands firmly on its site, in permanent surroundings, and can only endure time, never create it.* This is important because all the efforts of functionalists to give the outside of their buildings the unity they so markedly exhibit on the inside necessarily lead to seizing the element of movement that has suggested itself since van de Velde—movement that of course can only be apparent, a surrogate of movement.

I am thinking, for example, of Hans Scharoun's conceptual sketch for the Chicago Tribune building (see page 117). To be sure, this work consciously embodies its environment. It considers "the articulated point connecting a low building to a tall one" and connecting the indifference of a frantically busy street to formal clarity. And it is typical that in doing this Scharoun arrives at concepts expressly concerned with movement: "(1) The front is fixed; (2) seeks a standpoint; (3) collects tension; (4) rises steeply; and (5) carries working platforms." You could describe a machine in operation like that. In fact Scharoun wants a tower block to be perceived as a "machine," not as "house or monument." Other functionalists as well like to refer to machines, which as moving tools are bound to attract their greatest attention.

Scharoun's work certainly reflects its environment, but the referential process remains one-sided. The building devours the environment and digests it for itself, so that some of its features appear in its functional accounting; but the result remains completely individualistic in principle, even where the work takes on a large collective form. Despite its relation to the street, the form remains unique and particular; indeed it may be that with this approach the assimilation of the environmental elements only reinforces the building's emphatic individuality. This is easily proved. Is it possible to make Scharoun's solution into a type? That is no more possible than it is for Bruno Taut's Chicago Tribune design, which may be impeccable in constructional-functional terms but, when taken as a type (and this is the yardstick for every modern building), would turn downtown Chicago into a Negro village [Negerdorf].

In German architecture we repeatedly find an inclination to a one-sided verticalism: individual elements exaggerated in character and usually exaggerated in form as well, not relating to each other, with nothing in common. Parallelism is the only bond. Our political attitude suggests itself here. From

---

* Note Theo van Doesburg's opposite view (De Stijl, nos. 6/7 [1924]).

this perspective we can understand the Bismarck Tower epidemic and the epidemic of ideal designs for skyscrapers. With an approach like this, the basis for every new building is always different and always new. "The systematic use of the vertical in Germany is a kind of mysticism — a mysticism in matters of physics is the poison of German architecture. A simple fact refutes all this: we live in a building floor by floor, horizontally layered, not vertically" (Le Corbusier in *L'esprit nouveau*).

From this point of view, whose essence is unconscious separation ("singularity") and a one-sided direction of creative forces inward ("introspection"), it is therefore to some extent difficult to imagine how we could arrive at the totality of a city. When Scharoun calls buildings like cinemas or theaters components of an urban development plan, one is skeptical as long as the riddle remains unsolved of how a whole can be formed from elements that do not desire this whole but only themselves.

An essay in the Flemish magazine *Het Overzicht* (September 1923) on "Stedenbouw" is interesting in this context. Although the author, Louis van der Swaelmen, does persistently speak the language of a functionalist — "It here concerns functions and organs" — in practical terms he opts for Le Nôtre and Haussmann.[64]

We said that the element of movement in architecture can never play more than a surrogate role, but it should be added here that there are attempts in Russia to turn actual movement (change of place) into an architectural device.

The most radical and earliest attempt is Tatlin's model for the *Monument to the Third International* in Moscow (1919/1920) (page 147).

The model is 20 m high. The building itself would be over 400 m high. [...] It consists of two cylinders and a pyramid of glass that turn at different speeds. Within these glass structures are the great halls for meetings, reunions, accords, etc. Then there are great plants for climate control: heating the assembly rooms in winter and cooling them in summer. These building units are surrounded by an iron spiral soaring into the sky.* [...] His monument has the same practical beauty as a crane or an industrial bridge. Tatlin says that he made the triangle the pre-

---

* Trotsky said of an essay by Lenin written in 1917 that it was like "a massive steel spiral surrounded by a solid ring, and that the spiral in the future would extend, expand

dominant form in order to express Renaissance statics. He expresses the dynamics of our time in a wonderful spiral. For his material he chose glass as well as
iron, already commonly in use for modern construction.[65]

(Here one should mention Bruno Taut's glass house at the Cologne Werkbund exhibition [1914], the first to try out the constructive and aesthetic
possibilities of building with glass [Elias Ehrenburg, *Frühlicht,* no. 3].)[66]
Bruno Taut's Iron Monument of 1913, height 30 m, can be considered the
orthogonal-static miniature ancestor of Tatlin's monument, and some
designs for exhibition towers by Wenzel August Hablik of Itzehoe (1918/19)
can be seen as intermediate links in the evolutionary chain.[67] Here the
dynamic elements of rotation and oblique position begin to appear.

Recently the less than satisfactory outcome of a competition for a Palace
of Labor in Mosow led to a discussion in the Russian press, stimulated by a
very bold essay by K. Selinski, entitled "Stil und Stahl," which ended with the
words: "Architects, engineers, adapt to the pace and meaning of history—
build movement."[68]

But it would be a mistake to believe that movement, as Selinski under-
stands it here, had much to do with the movement of individualistically
minded functionalists. Selinski does not make his demand based on soul
and expression (war has been declared on these factors in the new Russia;
see René Fülöp Miller: "Der kollektive Mensch," *Vossische Zeitung* 3, October
1923)—but for the sake of a setting for the new human collective. For this
reason we shall return to Selinski's essay later.

If for the functionalists the basis of every new building is forever new
and different, then it seems reasonable that in working they rely on eternal
nature. In fact their ideal is the total merger with nature: the building not
as a body foreign to nature but as its organic component.

Häring tries to design the rooms in his clubhouse in Rio de Janeiro in
such a way that they are not general, transposable, interchangeable spaces
but are fundamentally determined by their particular situation in nature.
The ocean bay, mountain structure, color of vegetation, coastline, qualities
of light, etc., should all play an active part in the quite particular, unique,
and nonrepeatable form of halls and rooms. Nature should be embraced

---

and ideologically embrace the entire content of the Revolution" (L. Trotsky, *Über
Lenin,* German edition [Berlin, 1924]).

within the building and likewise every room should be embraced in every other one—following the model of organic life. One is reminded of Chinese *fêng shui* and the interpretation that Ernst Boerschmann places on the concept.[69] The functionalist tends to depersonalize the building process. He is reluctant to adopt an imperatorial attitude toward the world. He integrates himself and his product. The person who builds is ultimately only the mediator. For him the perfect building would be one that grew out of the ground like an organic plant. (Finsterlin—an example is an issue on snail shells published by *Wendingen*.)

One could thus raise the objection here, contrary to what has been said above, that the functionalist is defined just by the idea of integration, by the negation of any form of individualism!

But no! For integration into nature means integration into endless ambiguity, that is to say, into everything and nothing; it does not contradict individualism, as the hermit demonstrates. Nature enthusiasts love solitude. Integration into nature is only a euphemism for individualism, for the rejection of society.

In the end experience shows that precisely in this functionalist attitude that wants to dehumanize architecture, anthropomorphism prevails—more so than in any other humanist approach. For it is always the human being that places one space next to another. And if he does not accept responsibility for this task because he finds it imperatorial and rejects it, but instead wants to let things evolve from the inner nature of the materials and the spaces, then (in order to be able to grasp it) he will always have to interpret this nature first, because this inner nature of spaces and materials will always remain foreign to him—and how else should he interpret it but according to his own human, indeed personal condition?!

In fact dehumanization is the very thing that leads to humanization, to anthropomorphism.

When steps collide with a wall and I prepare for the steps by means of contrasting stripes in the wall, I do not know whether the wall or the steps find this pleasing and whether I have done what is right for them: I am thus bringing precisely the subjectively human concepts that I wanted to avoid into the objective world.

Isolation, absolute individualism is the ultimate driving force behind consistent functionalism. Even its reference to the organic is not primary but simply the consequence of an individualistic attitude. Thus the deciding factor is the relationship with society!

Functionalist deliberations are correct so long as they concern a specific matter, and they go wrong as soon as things have to fit together. It is correct to say that a single rectangular room is uneconomical, that a curve is a better biological transcription of real usable space. But if it is a matter of arranging several rooms together, the result is different. If several oval, circular, or curved rooms are put together, far more space is lost than in a group of rectangular rooms that fit together much better. The honeycomb can be cited once more as an example from nature. In individual organisms the single organs are certainly curved, but they fit snugly together because they are made of flexible, pliable material.

Häring and Scharoun sometimes choose different widths for their corridors, allowing them, like living arteries, to narrow, to shrink, in places where there is less traffic. This is all right provided that traffic always follows this same path until the death of the building, that the same conditions prevail as on the first day, in the same way as is the case for blood corpuscles in an organism. But it is wrong, and the functional becomes antifunctional as soon as the traffic finds different conditions—such as through a change of owner or when purpose alters traffic requirements—whereby it could be heaviest in precisely those places where the plan requires it to be lightest.

Thus in view of the fact that an individual item, even if it functions excellently in and for itself, and even if it is competely adapted to an infinitely manifold nature, is not adequate for society's living requirements, it indeed closes itself to them because it is exaggerated for the sake of uniqueness in space, time, and personality and is not open to duration, change, and multiplicity. In such a case it is questionable whether the mechanical structures of rectangularity are not socially more correct in functional terms!

Once more then: the deciding factor is the attitude toward society.

The human being stands between nature and society. He opts for human community and thus places himself in a certain state of tension with nature. He opts for nature and is in a certain state of tension with society.

Expressed differently, the human being bases his actions and work either on the fact, the awareness of human community and his membership in it, or on a feeling of unity with nature. As a creator he works from the whole to the individual or from the individual to the whole!

According to this, two clear types can be distinguished: at their extremes are the rationalist and the romantic.

129

In the context of architecture we have identified the consistent function-alist as representing one of these types, the romantic.

His opposite is the consistent rationalist who has congealed into formalism.

When van de Velde referred to the machine, he saw it as the neat, concise, modern, and elegant form.

When the functionalist refers to the machine, he sees it as the moving tool, the perfect approximation to an organism.

When the utilitarian refers to the machine, he sees it as an economic principle of saving work, power, and time.

When the rationalist refers to the machine, he sees it as the representative and patron of standardization and typification.

Let us now turn to the clear-thinking representative of the Western view, the Swiss Charles-Edouard Jeanneret (b. 1887), who has already been quoted several times. He is known as a purist painter and publisher of *L'esprit nouveau* in Paris and is better known as an architect under the pseudonym Le Corbusier-Saugnier, who worked for Peter Behrens for a short time. Le Corbusier adopts a position of absolute *Sachlichkeit*. Naturally he rejects the facade: "Architecture has nothing to do with styles. Louis XIV, XV, XVI, or Gothic are to architecture as the feather on a woman's head—occasionally pretty but not always, and never more than that." He admires the work of modern engineers. "Without pursuing an architectural idea, guided only by the conditions of functional calculations derived from the laws that govern the universe, and by the concept of a living organism, modern engineers have taken the fundamental elements and by putting them together according to firm rules, they have come close to great works of art and allow the work of the human hand to resonate with the universal order."

In a series of essays in *L'esprit nouveau*, "Des yeux qui ne voient pas," Le Corbusier contrasted types of modern motorcars, airplanes, etc., with conventional contemporary architecture and came to this result: "If problems of the dwelling and its layout were studied like a chassis, we should very soon see our houses transformed and improved. If houses were produced industrially, serially like a chassis, we would see unexpected forms, but they would be healthy, defensible forms, and an aesthetic would be formulated with surprising precision."

A house: protection against heat, cold, rain, thieves, the curious—a receptacle for light and sun. A certain number of compartments for cooking, work, intimate life.

130

A room: a surface upon which one can move freely; a bed on which to stretch out; a chair for comfort and another for work; a table for work; drawers so that every object can quickly be put in its place. Number of rooms: one for cooking, one for eating, one for working, one for bathing, and one for sleeping. Such are the standards of a dwelling.

In order to arrive at a definition of a simple, clear, and defensible type for such "machines for living," Le Corbusier recommends the use of standards:

One has to set up a standard in order to face the problem of perfection. When a standard is established, competition immediately and violently comes into play. In order to win, one has to do things better than one's rival, in every part, in the line of the whole, and in every detail. That is what all parties are compelled to: progress! The standard is a necessity. The standard is based on sure foundations, not arbitrariness, but with the certainty of intention and with a logic controlled by experiment.... The establishment of a standard means exhausting all practical and reasonable possibilities, deriving a type that will be recognized as appropriate to the maximum performance of functions, using minimal means, as little hand assembly as possible, and a minimum of materials: words, sounds, colors, forms.

This emphasis on the type, on the universally valid, the need for a norm is what makes Le Corbusier fundamentally different from the functionalists. The basis of his work is the primary awareness of belonging to human society. To be sure, functionalists will agree with many, perhaps all, of Le Corbusier's pronouncements, but there then remains the distinction that what is heterogeneous for them is autogenous for Le Corbusier, to use Paul Tillich's terminology (*Das System der Wissenschaften nach Gegenständen und Methoden*).[70]

A recurring and vigorously emphasized aspect of Le Corbusier's approach is the importance of the floor plan, because it is the floor plan that primarily contains the social element of building.

"Mass and surface are determined by the plan. The plan is the generator. All the worse for those people with no imagination."

The whole structure rises on a foundation and develops according to a rule drawn on the ground in the floor plan. Good forms, variety of form, unity of a geometric nature, communication of harmonies — that is architecture. The plan is the basis.

131

Without a plan there can be no greatness of invention and of expression, no rhythm, no volume, no coherence. Without a plan we have only the sensation intolerable to man of formlessness, misery, disorder, and arbitrariness. The plan demands the most active invention. At the same time it demands the strictest discipline. The plan is the determining factor for the whole. It is the decisive moment. A plan is not a pretty thing to draw, like a Madonna's face. It is a severe abstraction, nothing but dry mathematics for the eye. But the work of the mathematician remains one of the highest activities of the human mind. The unity of the law is the law of the good floor plan—a simple, infinitely variable law.

What is already clear in these statements by Le Corbusier is his social view of architecture. His thinking moves from the whole to details, that is, for him the fundamental element is order, which is inseparable from any overview, whereas architecture can just as logically be directed toward expression, at the point where it creates and forms a single object, an individual body, something that exists for itself. Even an architect concerned with expression will, of course, draw plans and will not underestimate how very important they are, but it is right that we should hear a paean of praise to the plan from an architect who makes the totality his starting point. The plan is the element that fits the structure into the floor, the universal; it is the union of the enduring base with the earth common to all. But the elevation is the more individual element, the differentiating factor. A plan belongs to the world of the horizontal, an elevation to the world of the vertical.

The plan conveys, in the most compressed form possible, the order and overview of the building; the elevation conveys the construction. It is therefore not surprising that someone who lays such emphasis upon the plan should emphatically underline the element of order. "Architecture is art in the highest sense—mathematical order." "More and more, constructions and machines can be represented in proportions and in a play of volumes and materials; many of them are true works of art as they contain number—that is order."

Order—universal validity—rejection of all subjective elements in building, rejection of precisely that movement that van de Velde called "dramatic." "The cathedral is not a plastic work of art, it is a drama: a struggle against the law of gravity, concern with the sphere of emotions. For this reason we search in it for complementary values of a subjective nature beyond the plastic element." If order is to be visible in built space it needs elementary primary forms. For the architect concerned with expression, such demands do not exist: what is most irregular can at the same time be most expressive. Le Corbusier works with clear, recurring, unambiguously comprehensible masses: "Cube, cone, cylinder, sphere, and pyramid are the great primary forms that light reveals to advantage. They give us a clear and tangible image without ambiguity. For this reason these forms are beautiful forms, the most beautiful forms." "If the fundamentals of architecture are sphere, cone, and cylinder (one thinks of Cézanne's statement), as creators and emphasizers of form, they are purely geometrical by nature. But geometry frightens today's architect." The first European architect to recognize the positive role of geometry for architecture would seem to have been Berlage, who praised geometrical form as early as his Zurich lectures of 1907. It stands above the all too personal and often ugly character of the idiosyncratic because it is "not individual and essentially always beautiful in itself."

Something that is very important to our case now emerges, justifying and explaining the extent to which we have followed Le Corbusier's pronouncements: whereas an architect who is concerned with the individual work, and is therefore looking for expression, always places the demands of purpose clearly in the foreground and consequently stresses construction, the architect proceeding from the whole, and thus concerned with order, will stress an element that has no fundamental significance for functionalists — play! Functionalists want to make their buildings into tools, but rationalists (and this is surprising at first) are equally determined to see them as toys!

Expression isolates, is always serious by nature, and in attempting to overcome its seriousness does not transcend the half-measures of the grotesque.

The overview may well be able to be lighthearted. Play requires community, order, rules.

Le Corbusier does not expressly talk about these relationships, but the expression "play" repeatedly occurs in his writings — a concept that apparently seems to him to be the best analogy for his ideas. A sentence like this one: "Architecture is the masterly, correct, and magnificent play of masses brought together under light" recurs frequently in many variations,* and elsewhere Le Corbusier makes supplementary remarks on the subject of

---

* Emile Malespine writes similarly in *Manomètre*, Lyons, 1923, p. 50: "Health is line, surface, light, the great geometrical masses, which in their play give the impression of security, reason, and repose."

"purpose" and "construction" — not in Poelzig's romantically disapproving way but by integrating these important elements, which he continually stresses himself, into the whole and entirely rejecting their isolation and independence. (Isolation and independence of individual factors are potentially dangerous for German artists; for example the element of expression and mime is unquestionably part of dance, but it is a mistake to isolate this factor and make modern dance out of expressive mime.) Le Corbusier says:

> A commonplace for young architects states: one must express construction. And another: a thing is beautiful when it corresponds to its purpose. (Compare the much more correct version by Otto Wagner quoted above: "Something impractical can never be beautiful!") The good Lord may have emphasized joints and vertebrae, but there is still something else. Architecture has a different meaning and different tasks from showing constructions and fulfilling purposes. Purpose is here understood as a matter of pure utility, of comfort, and of practical elegance. Architecture is art in the highest sense, mathematical order, speculation, perfect harmony through the proportionality of all relationships: that is the "purpose" of architecture.

Therefore the conception of architecture as an art is the conscious representation of aesthetic demands, whereas functionalists and utilitarians will always tend to negate building as an art. Adolf Loos (b. 1870): "Only a very small part of architecture belongs to art: the gravestone and the monument. Everything else that serves a purpose must be eliminated from the ranks of art" (*Sturm,* 1911, p. 334).* [71]

Le Corbusier consciously starts with man. Human will is the decisive factor: "Brutal materiality can only accept the idea through the order that one imposes upon it." The aim of the human desire to build is standardization: "Every problem that will emerge tomorrow is a problem of synthesis; it requires a stricter standardization than any age has ever known."

Just as striving to dehumanize building, to eliminate the element of will, actually brings the functionalists to humanization, so the rationalists are led

---

* Other formulations by Adolf Loos, for example his reference to standardization, correspond very closely with those of Le Corbusier, who must have been stimulated by Loos in Vienna. Here are some pronouncements by Loos: "To change a form when no *sachlich* improvement is possible ... is the greatest absurdity. I can only invent something new when I have a new problem, in architecture, for example: a building for

by a conscious emphasis of human will to objectivity and *Sachlichkeit*. There is no doubt that someone whose starting point is the consciousness of human community is in a certain state of tension with nature. He is not inclined to make buildings harmonize with the existence of evolved organisms in a kind of mimicry, where the result can only be a hybrid, not an organism and not a building; he creates the embodiment of his human will. In opposing nature's rule, his house disputes nature's space and orders it according to human requirements: the house is in a state of tension with nature. The house has its own center and expresses its will almost aggressively (Mendelsohn: "Nature is organic development, the house individual will"). But far from standing brutal and alien in nature for this reason, it enters into closer unity with it as a result of tensions. The house is mathematics, and because it is mathematics—that is, law, order, purity, health, and logical consistency in its requirements and tendencies—it binds itself to the liveliness of nature, which is never possible through dissolution or relativization but always only through concentration and absolute architectural logic. "The more human creations move away from direct contact, the more strongly they incline to pure geometry. A violin or a car that touches our body has a low degree of geometrical rigor, but a city is pure geometry" (*L'esprit nouveau,* p. 18).

Here we must briefly mention the two French architects who taught Le Corbusier's generation (Mallet-Stevens, Guévrékian, Dufour, Lemaire, Jourdain, etc.): Auguste Perret of Paris, who works with his brother Gustave, and Tony Garnier of Lyons.[72] Perret was first and foremost a builder. The declaration that he wrote for the *Stavba* issue devoted to him (Prague, July 1923) is astonishingly reminiscent of Otto Wagner: "A living architecture is that which faithfully expresses its epoch. One looks for examples of it in every field of construction. One will choose works that are strictly subordinates to

---

turbines, hangars for airplanes. But a chair, table, wardrobe? I will never admit that we, for the sake of the imagination, should change forms tried and tested over centuries" ("Von der Sparsamkeit"). Loos's most important works are a theater project (1896); the Café Museum in Vienna (1898); the Steiner Villa in Hietzing (1898); the Goldmann and Salatsch Department Store in Vienna (1900); the American Bar in Vienna (1907); the design for the *Chicago Tribune* (1922); the Terrace Hotel project, "Babylon" (1923) (*L'architecture vivante*, Paris, 1923).

their use and are built with the judicious use of material, that achieve beauty by their design and harmonious proportions, and that are inspired by the necessary elements that compose them."[73]

Perret is from the same mold as Eiffel, whose spirit also recurs in the wonderful structure erected by Freyssinet in Orly for the great dirigible hangars.[74] Perret used ferroconcrete to create a skeleton into which walls are placed as light membranes. This technique is most consistently used in the church at Le Raincy. Perret's main works are the casino in Saint-Malo that has already been mentioned (1899/1900), an apartment house on the rue Franklin in Paris (1902/03), which was the decisive turning point in Perret's output, a garage on the rue du Ponthieu in Paris (1908/09), and the Théâtre des Champs Elysées in Paris (1911/12). The story of this build- ing has become a quarrel between Perret and van de Velde, in which not only German friends such as Karl Ernst Osthaus (who, however, does not do justice to Perret's achievement) took van de Velde's side but (among others) also Jacques Mesnil in an essay called "Henry van de Velde et le théâtre des Champs Elysées."[75] There can be no question but that the spatial design in the Théâtre des Champs Elysées was due to van de Velde. But the extent to which the forcing out of van de Velde was caused by personal intrigue on the part of the Perrets and how far (beyond the personalities) it represents a victory of modern construction over architecture can scarcely be decided from Mesnil's essay. More recent buildings by Perret are the docks in Casa- blanca (1916), the Esders Workshops (1919), a high-rise project (1922), the church at Le Raincy (1923), a bank for the Société Marseillaise de Crédit in Paris, and a decorator's studio also in Paris. All of these buildings show great imagination in their constructional design and at the same time offer bad taste in architectural form.

Garnier (b. 1869) is an architect through and through. In two large publi- cations he provides an insight into his work, which is admirable both for the grandeur of its concepts and for the most scrupulously detailed work in execution. The book *Les grands travaux de la ville de Lyon* contains buildings by Garnier that he erected or planned for that community when he was city architect: the Franco-American Sanatorium, the Grange-Blanche Hospital, the stadium, the art school, the slaughterhouses, the municipal residential buildings, the main post office, the telephone exchange, and the imposing Bourse du travail with its congress halls, libraries, museums, administration offices, etc.[76] Edouard Herriot, then mayor of Lyons, wrote a few introduc- tory sentences for the portfolio. Even more comprehensive and bold is the portfolio *Une cité industrielle, étude pour la construction des villes*, in which a modern industrial town with all its residential, traffic, hygiene, and educational problems is worked out in masterly and minute detail and with a wealth of valuable ideas.[77] This labor was completed in 1905. Whereas Herriot says in his foreword to the Lyons portfolio that "our French cities still lack all the institutions essential for their up-to-date functioning," one can praise the *Cité industrielle* for the fact that its creator, probably more than any other French architect, respected and liberated healthy function, as his plan for the sanatorium demonstrates in particular. On his relationship with German architecture Garnier says: "I have never had a chance to see the architectural designs that impressed me, but I noticed on the other hand the often great ingenuity in the technical installations that I have seen in Germany" (*Reisen in Deutschland,* 1907 and 1911).[78]

Nothing is more self-evident than that a rationalist should stress form. Form is nothing more than the consequence of establishing a relationship between human beings. For the isolated and unique figure in nature there is no problem of form. Individuals, even individuals in nature, are free. The problem of form arises when an overview is demanded. Form is the prerequisite under which an overview becomes possible. Form is an eminently social matter. Anyone who recognizes the right of society recognizes the right of form.

If humanity were just a sum of individuals, it would probably be possible to see the house as a pure tool, as purely functional. Anyone who sees a form in humanity, a pattern articulated in time and space, approaches the house with formal requirements, in which case "formal" is not to be confused with "decorative."

If every building is part of a built whole, then it recognizes from its aesthetic and formal requirements certain universally valid rules, rules that do not arise from its individual functional character [*Zweckcharakter*] but from the requirements of this whole. For here, in the social sphere after all, must lie the primeval elements of the aesthetic (Guyau: Art is tenderness).[79] A one-sided fulfillment of function [*Zweckerfüllung*] leads to anarchy. Where a building is perceived as part of a whole, the character of a toy is added to the character of a tool, the absolute to the relative element.

The concept of "form" does not deal with accessories, decoration, taste, or style (from Gothic to Biedermeier) but with the consequences arising from a building's ability to be an enduring structure. The functionalist prefers to exaggerate the purpose to the point of making it unique and

137

momentary (a house for each function!) but the rationalist takes the purpose broadly and generally as readiness for many cases, simply because
he gives thought to the enduring qualities of buildings, which perhaps see
many generations with changing requirements and therefore cannot live
without leeway. The rationalist is no more indifferent to purpose than the
functionalist. Although he does not have the perspective of the Baroque
genius opposing purpose, he avoids the tyrannical rule of purpose. As the
functionalist looks for the greatest possible adaptation to the most specialized purpose, so the rationalist looks for the most appropriate solution
for many cases. The former wants what is absolutely fitting and unique for
the particular case; the latter wants what is most fitting for general need,
the norm. The former is all for adaptation, relation, formlessness growing
from selflessness, and mimicry; the latter is also for personal will, self-
consideration, play, and form.

There is no doubt that the West leads in its determination to see architecture as a whole and from a social point of view. I quote from a program-
matic essay by Victor Bourgeois for the Brussels magazine *Sept arts:* "Since
the building is inseparable from its neighbor and since a street extends
into another street, all powerful architecture tends to style, that is to say,
a superior collective equilibrium."[80] The following passage explains how personal and psychological work comes to be rejected: "A modern architect
who is compelled to build today on any street in Brussels is almost insolent
with regard to his art if he realizes an interesting building—what progess is
this if this hostile architecture becomes an indifferent architecture."[81]

In Western Europe the feeling is not that an architect should work in a
special, original, and personal style (which he had best protect from imita-
tions by official patent). Here conspicuous work is considered bad eo ipso—
simply because it is conspicuous: "A home must be made a measure of
man" (Malespine) and "Originality is, moreover, a form of insubordination"
(Georges Linze).[82] From this point of view it is understandable when Roland
Holst emphatically points Dutch artists toward "the correction that the
romantic always and under all circumstances signifies" (*Architektura*,
February 1924).[83]

It is not surprising that Le Corbusier addresses the problems of the
modern metropolis, for these accord with the basic thrust of rationalism,
that is, working from an awareness of community, moving from the whole to
the individual. (It is precisely by this means that form emerges since form
is correspondence, and tact comes from *tangere* = to touch.) In his *Principes*

fondamentaux d'urbanisme moderne, Le Corbusier maintains the clarity of his rationalism throughout, but at the same time demonstrates that the consistent rationalist gets stuck in just the same cul-de-sac as the consistent functionalist.[84] Functionalism may court the danger of exaggerating to the point of becoming grotesque, but rationalism courts the danger of reducing everything to the schematic.

It is quite logical that the individual aiming at expression will arrive at moving curves with maximum fluidity, fulfilling every function, and will therefore see concrete as a plastic mass that can be modeled. Contrast this with R. van t'Hoff: "Only with ferroconcrete are the horizontal and vertical adaptations consistent" (*De Stijl* 2, no. 5).[85] The rationalist who is inclined toward an overview likewise emphasizes straight lines and right angles. "Why," asks Scharoun, "must everything be straight, when the straight line is produced only by the environment?" Le Corbusier might reply: "Precisely because nothing can remain isolated, because we all stand within an environment, everything must be straight and the curve is individualistic lack of discipline."

There is no question that only the straight line and right angle can be the basis of the modern creation, which seeks to eliminate arbitrariness and rejects all anthropomorphic curves—and yet it would be wrong to turn the straight line and right angle into a dogma or rigid principle. The modern metropolis sketched by Le Corbusier, which in fact hardly touches upon many problems, is certainly consistently straight-lined and right-angled down to the last detail, but it can be so only because and for as long as it remains on paper. Here Le Corbusier can certainly decree: "The curve—that's paralysis," but if he were to realize his plan and did not find a field as flat as a silver platter, he would be forced by every bend in a river or by every hill to depart from the rigid straight lines and strict right angles; otherwise one could say, "This straight line is senility," and thus the functionalist would be justified.

Le Corbusier's city plan shows fairly clearly the dangers of a consistent rationalism: form becomes an overbearing, life-constraining, stifling mask, and the result is no longer the integration into a living whole but an academic division that turns play into a show. And then it is time again to emphasize purpose and underline function to lead the way to recovery and reflection.

It seems to us that all building contains an element of compromise: between purpose and form, between individual and society, between economy and politics, between dynamics and statics, between forcefulness and uniformity, between mass and space—and that style in each case is nothing more than the particular version of this compromise. Kurt Schwitters's view (*Merz* 6) is similar in principle: "Style expresses the common will of many, ideally all, the democracy of the will to design. But since most people —even the occasional artist—are idiots by and large, and since idiots are usually most doggedly convinced about what they think, and as agreement by all can only take the middle road, so style is usually a compromise between art and non-art, between play and purpose."[86]

Today the East shows a passionate emphasis on the dynamic element. Such an emphasis is already hinted at in German functionalism. Just as the dynamic element here, in accordance with our entire constitution and past, is oriented individually, so we find in Russia that dynamism is collectively oriented, indeed dynamism seems to be virtually the means by which the life of collective human beings is expressed architecturally. Let us return to Selinski's essay "Baut Bewegung!" [Build movement!], from which I have already quoted.[87] It shows that this problem can be solved only with the aid of every possible technical and mechanical device, but it also lets us see that a strong emphasis on dynamism always tends toward the romantic-revolutionary. We share here the most important sections of Selinski's essay (*Neue Kultur-Korrespondenz* 1, nos. 4/5, Berlin 1923):

Stone is becoming extinct. Stone is becoming a retrograde element. It serves only to hinder the evolution of architecture and is thus becoming socially reactionary. Immobile, cramped, and crooked in its dynamic possibilities, stone cannot follow the rapid tempo of life. But life is becoming dynamic with enormous rapidity. Today people still move along city streets in carriages and traps. Tomorrow there will be moving sidewalks, just as advertisement boards, neon signs, pneumatic doors, etc., are already on the move. But a clay-footed colossus like the one proposed by architects (meaning the competition entries for the Palace of Labor in Moscow) will never contain within its gates the tens and hundreds of thousands of people who will surge to the Pantheon of the Revolution on November 7th. Its walls will stand too silent and immobile, its doors will be too narrow, its acoustics will be unsuited for the hundred thousand voices of the jubilant people.

Why not erect a gigantic building on an enormous, rotating steel foundation with removable glass and aluminium walls? Such a palace would be capable of guiding the masses of people from room to room, opening itself up to magnificent halls, bringing masses of listeners closer to speakers from its various platforms. Instead of elevators, continuously rotating spiral ladders will carry people up to the roof. Why should one not, for example, set up some rooms, classes, laboratories, and operation theaters that can in turn swing around to the south and the sun, and in the evening flood the street with light to be exploited for general artistic and educational purposes?

We must proceed to a new building material: steel, ferroconcrete, and especially Duralumin, glass, and asbestos. We now see a shift to these materials across the whole cultural front. It would be a disgrace to build a palace in the heart of Red Moscow, in the residence of the Federation of the Soviet Union, whose physiognomy is directed to the past when it should serve the revolutionary present.

Aside from dynamic building, a number of other constructional problems must be solved in the Palace of Labor. Acoustics in the large halls must be strengthened with an electric membrane. Walls must literally speak with the assistance of radio telephones. Walls, ceilings, and vestibule must become translucent when necessary. The radio must be exploited to full advantage. Radio waves must beam through glass corridors to activate electric motors driving ventilation and various other devices like cooking facilities, for example. The roof must be suitable for walking in the open air, cinema, lighting effects, sport, etc.[88]

(In discussing this, Akseiski said the following: "Things like this have not even been carried out in America. Without disputing the possibility in principle of such a building in the future, it must be said that it would be ridiculous to try to build it at the moment.") It is impossible to think of a sharper contrast with the Russian Selinski than the Frenchman Albert Gleizes, who in his *Vom Kubismus* writes in the chapter on "Dynamism": "A flower is immobile. It can be moved by outside forces—otherwise it remains static. A painting is a silent and immobile manifestation. To speak of dynamism when dealing with a painting is to give words a meaning that they do not have!" (p. 30).[89]

The element of movement is shared by German functionalism and Russian dynamism (biomechanics). (Italian Futurist architecture falls into the same category, although after the early death of Sant'Elia, killed in 1916, Virgilio Marchi is probably the only one who still represents it. Marchi emphasizes and underlines individualistic, dramatic, dynamic, and lyrical elements. "Every architect has his own rhythm and his own law that does not coincide with that of anyone else.")[90] In Germany one is dealing with movement as an expression of individual life, with a pseudo-organic, plastic movement working from within, whereas in Russia one is dealing with installation, montage, and constructing frameworks. Working from the outside like this, almost without a plan, produces ingenious constructivist works that ultimately remain always studio objects, as is seen, for instance in Ladovski's class at VKhUTEMAS Moscow.[91]

Plasticity and construction are both features of architecture, but they are not themselves architecture.

It is a feature common to the East and West that, in contrast to individualist Germany, they proceed from the collective. But the collective is fundamentally different here and there: France has a structurally articulated society; Russia is dominated by the masses. A by-product of this is that the plan is a major feature in the West but is addressed strikingly little in the East. There and in fascist Italy the plan is replaced by direct tension of masses.

The problem is to fuse the two tendencies, statics and dynamics. In an excellent essay "Der jung-europäische Staat" (*Vossische Zeitung*, 25 September 1923), Willy Hellpach recommended this task to Germany in terms of national law: "The remedy is not to compel emergent professional forces to submit to the imaginary authority of Platonic powers again—in history attempts of that kind always end with the complete ruin of the formal powers—but to create a new state with real authority by taking those forces that have emerged as a result of powerful spiritual processes of radical change in the nation and integrating them into the state as legal, synarchic forces, thus putting an end to their unlawful, anarchic effects."[92]

Heinrich Mann takes a similar line: "We are in the middle and it is our task to link East and West; one does not shut off nature. In the future we will be the republic in which representation of class and parliamentarianism are interlinked."[93]

The exclusive fulfillment of purpose, the one-sided focus on function makes the individual building dynamic and qualifies it. It becomes one "consequence" within a flow of biological dependencies, with a logical inclination to include the temporal factor. One-sided focus on form gives statics the rigidity of a general, abstract "law." Interpenetration of the two elements makes the building a living, concrete "form" [*Gestalt*].

"Consequence"—"law"—"form." This is the terminology of Paul Tillich's *Das System der Wissenschaften nach Gegenständen und Methoden*. The law: "The thinking person can look away from individual being to create some-

142

thing general, comprehensive" (physics). Consequence: "The individual becomes part of a (temporal) context" (history). Form: "The individual being becomes a general being. Form is actually the concrete, the real being" (technology) (Christian Herrmann in a critique of Tillich, *Sozialistische Monatshefte,* 1923, p. 569).*

Alfred Vierkandt in his *Dualismus im modernen Weltbild* [Dualism in the modern world image] seems close to such a view.[94] Christian Herrmann sums up his doctrine like this:

> In this sense every culture is by its very nature built upon a dualism of principles. For on the one hand culture represents the epitome of the meaning of life, derived from life, or aimed at its preservation and furtherance, in brief, things that exist from the point of view of utility; but on the other hand, such things have their own intrinsic value that opposes the content as that which formed it. Tension of this kind can be seen in all spheres of culture. This dysfunction between a utilitarian and a defined content and it's pure formation as form can be seen everywhere, in law, art, religion, economics, society, science, and technology. In the life of the soul we find the same dualistic confrontation, for on the one hand it is a process entirely determined by biology, on the other hand, however, it leads to patterns with their own meaning and value. Spiritual acts are causally determined by their antecedents, but they are also determined by the meaning that they serve. Thus human beings are closely attached to two worlds: the world of biological necessity, a dark natural bedrock full of hardships, and a spiritual world with specific content and substance. (*Sozialistische Monatshefte,* 1923, p. 287).** [95]

If we return to the building, we can say that its concrete form is a compromise between individual (function) and society (form). In its pure development this compromise is inhibited by "expression" and "soul." Its pure

---

* Similar trains of thought in Kurt Riezler, *Gestalt und Gesetz* (Munich, 1924), p. 171; Felix Weltsch, *Gnade und Freiheit* (Munich, 1920); Viktor Engelhardt, *Weltanschauung und Technik* (Leipzig, 1922–1923); S. Friedländer, *Schöpferische Indifferenz* (Munich, 1918); Albert Lewkowitz, "Simmels religiöses Denken," in *Religiöse Denker der Gegenwart* (Berlin, 1924); R. N. Coudenhove-Kalergi, *Apologie der Technik* (Leipzig, 1922).

** I add here a passage from Piet Mondrian's "Neue Gestaltung in der Musik und die futuristischen italienischen Bruitisten," German trans. Max Burchartz (*De Stijl* 6,

form is living equilibrium, realization of a behavior that plays to many sides, open and yet determined. We may join Theo van Doesburg in calling it "formless" provided that we do not confuse "formless" [*formlos*] with "shapeless" [*gestaltlos*].[96] Closed form in the sense of a "figure" is today no longer a satisfying element in art, either in architecture or in other fields. A drive toward the final fusion breaks the bounds of closed form (in painting this was done by Cubism) and tries to achieve pure relationships, spatial tensions that are never arbitrarily limited. "Art is equilibrium achieved by evaluation of all parts" (Schwitters). "Proportion" is the interpenetration of "function" and "form," that is, a plastics of proportion replaces a morphoplastics (Piet Mondrian). "As long as design uses any form, it is impossible to shape pure proportionalities. For this reason the new design has liberated itself from all creation of form" (Piet Mondrian).[97]

The younger generation of German architects insists on strict *Sachlichkeit.* Mies van der Rohe explains: "We reject all aesthetic speculation, all doctrine, and all formalism. Let form be shaped by the nature of the task, using the means of our time. That is our work." Otto Wagner had already insisted on the same thing in a very similar formulation.

The necessary and only sound approach is to reject aesthetic speculation, formalism, and doctrine, but it seems to us quite a frequent error to make this rejection from an anti-aesthetic point of view, even if we inveigh against the aestheticism of aesthetes one hundred times a day. Rejecting aesthetic demands (which is not the same as aesthetic speculation) would be to saw off the branch on which one sits. As long as individual objects are being dealt with, the fulfillment of purpose may suffice to create a healthy form. But if we accept the demands of a monumental architecture, that is, of an architectural whole, the bringing together of forms — even genuinely sound ones — does not suffice. The demand for unity is through and through an elementary aesthetic or artistic demand, and to assume that all strictly *sachlich* works "in themselves" would form a unity, even if they were developed in a vacuum, is to draw a false conclusion. The task is not merely an overview of new buildings but also an overview of their landscape or urban environment.

─────────

no. 1): "Pure expression of the new spirit always remains true to itself in life as in art. It is the exact and conscious protection of balance, accordingly the balance between the individual and the universal, between the natural and the spiritual."

House, human being, sun, and landscape form a complex of mutual relationships. Just as the individual form gets its face and body organically from these relationships, so, for the sake of the overall idea, must a housing complex, as an overall urban composition of a complicated organism, fulfill more and various environmental demands in order to absorb, integrate, and subordinate the personality of individual organisms converted to something impersonal. Only when they are all conjoined do the parts attain the validity and meaning each intends. The types that result from such architectural tasks are not a necessary evil of an anxious economy; they are a necessity of life in terms of what a housing complex demands and means and what the individual objects, considered within the same framework, must be, namely an organic unit (Richard Döcker, *Volkswohnung*, 10 July 1923).[98]

We should not abandon this demand because we are prejudiced — rightly! — against previous romantic methods of doing it justice. The demand itself remains as long as we do not abandon the full claim of design. A bridge over a river is not just a utilitarian problem but also a town planning problem, that is, the demand to insert its mass into the movement of the bank, into the rhythm of the streets and squares, by means other than formal nonsense and naturalistic mimicry is completely an artistic-aesthetic one. One can deny these demands only by including under the concept of utility the consideration of the optical and logical, of the perceptually correct. But then one has done nothing more than give aesthetic demands another name. In fact, according to utilitarian dogmatists, there is a double demand: the accord with *sachlich*-constructional demands and the accord with demands arising from the the nature of our organs of perception. And it is precisely these that we call aesthetic demands in the pure, original sense of the word (αἰσθάνομαι = I perceive). We do not doubt for a moment that these demands, just as much as *sachlich*-constructional ones, belong to the realm of human reason; these demands are not mystical and arbitrary nor are they in any way satisfied by that.

To care whether and if things relate to one another is under no circumstances a matter of utility. But if we abandon the demand for unity, we can no longer speak well of design. The problem is not solved by the fact that hitherto people have always tried to create unity in an emotional or romantic fashion, using only the values and realities of the landscape. We have to solve it on the basis of reason.

We find that German architecture is somewhat inclined to devote itself to an extreme that changes fairly frequently and then gives way to the opposite extreme—the consequence of inner uncertainty. It is all too rarely recognized that the aim should be to stabilize the strong dynamic tensions that living architecture must absorb in order not to become aesthetic, and this certainly includes tensions of extreme revolutionary power and force, the kind demanded by Selinski's essay.

It is erroneous to think that dynamism can only be expressed in the elevation, in the animated "form" [*Form*]; instead, it is to a great degree a matter of the floor plan. And it is just as erroneous to believe that structural requirements are assured by a quadrature of the plan, which often enough remains a drawing-board ornament. In contrast Mendelsohn says: "Architecture establishes the conditions of its animated masses from its own laws: the dynamic condition, movement of space (seen in outline as its linear element), the rhythmic condition, the relationship of masses (seen in elevation as its surface projection), and the structural condition or balance of movement (seen in plan and section as their structural elements)."

We find a clear and secure attitude in recent Dutch architecture as well as in recent Czech architecture, which is getting under way with surprising élan.

Theo van Doesberg, editor of *De Stijl*, stresses the double function of building: "Function from the perspective of practice; proportionality from the perspective of art." Function and play. "Intentional artistic design and utilitarian constructivism combine to produce complete equilibrium" (*De Stijl* 6, nos. 6–7).[99] Political realism and confidence of this kind spare Dutch architecture from swinging from extreme to extreme between opposing dogmas; it allows it the possibility of coping with all the dynamic tensions of our time openly and freely, without abandoning the demand for monumentality; it allows Dutch architecture the possibility of steady development.

Under the pressure of circumstances and through the expansion of aesthetic insight, it is only now that an architecture shaped by and through itself seems possible, an architecture in which the other arts will not be applied and thus subordinated but one that will work organically together with the other arts; it makes possible an architecture that from the beginning experiences beauty in its constructional functions, that is, an architecture that through the tension of its proportions raises the construction itself above its material necessity to aesthetic form (J. J. P. Oud).

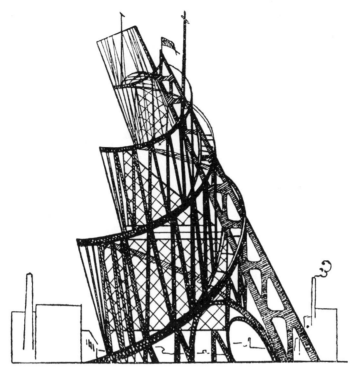

Tatlin: Model for the *Monument to the Third International*

Plates

The illustrations are arranged by country and within each country alphabetically by architects' names.

We should like to thank Messrs Theo van Doesburg (Paris), Karl Lönberg-Holm (Detroit), Professor Markalous (Brno), and Karl Teige (Prague), for kindly providing material; we should also like to thank the following publishers: Albert Levy, Paris (*L'architecte*); Ch. Massin, Paris (*Les grands travaux de la ville de Lyon*); Auguste Vincent, Paris (*Une cité industrielle*); Ernst Wasmuth, Berlin; Delphin, Munich; Photo-Libraire de France, Paris (Guévrékian and Mallet-Stevens); Franco Campitelli, Foligno (illustration in text p. 101); and Karl Peters, Magdeburg (*Frühlicht*, I. [J. J.] P. Oud factory, p. 37).

[In the interest of clarity, Behne's English captions have been minimally edited. His German and French captions remain essentially unchanged — ed.]

Frank Lloyd Wright

San Francisco, 1920
Design for a skyscraper
Projet pour une maison à forme de tour
Entwurf für ein Turmhaus

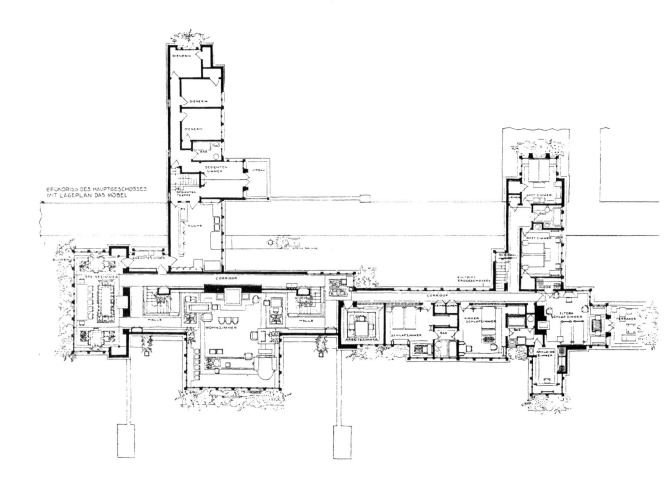

Frank Lloyd Wright

Avery Coonley [House], Riverside, Ill., 1908
Residence
Maison d'habitation
Wohnhaus

Albert Kahn

Seamless steel tubes, Detroit

Albert Kahn

Link Belt Co., Nicetown

Peter Behrens

Berlin, 1911/12
The AEG mounting hall (30 m wide)
Halle de montage de la AEG (30 m de largeur)
Montagehalle der AEG (Breite 30 m)

Peter Behrens

Berlin, 1910/11
Hallway of the small-motor factory of the AEG
Corridor de la fabrique de petits moteurs de la AEG
Flur der Kleinmotorenfabrik der AEG

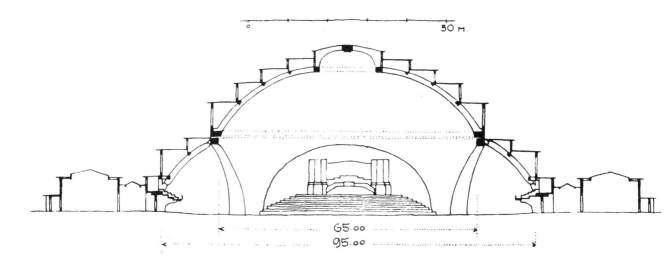

Max Berg

Breslau, 1913
Century Hall, sectional view and interior, height 40 m
Halle commémorative des fêtes du centenaire,
section et vue intérieure, hauteur 40 mètres
Jahrhunderthalle, Schnitt und Innenansicht, Höhe 40 Meter

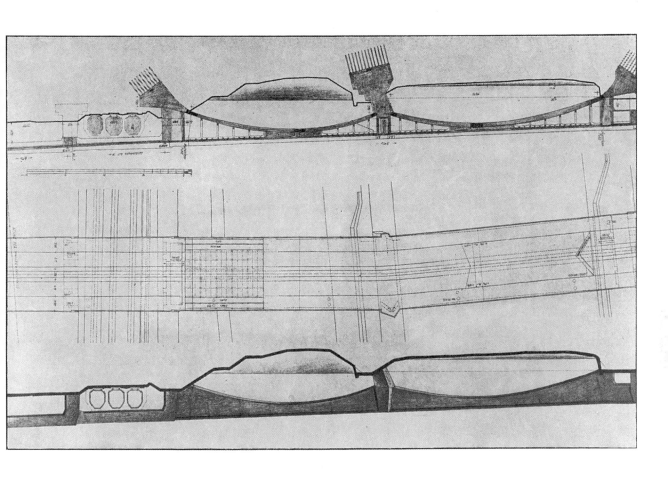

Richard Döcker

Zurich, 1924
Design for a bridge across the Limmat
Projet pour un pont sur La Limmat
Entwurf für eine Brücke über die Limmat

**Alfred Gellhorn, Martin Knauthe,
and Rudolf Belling**

Halle an der Saale, 1923
Gasoline tank
Réservoir à benzine
Benzintank

H[einrich] de Fries

Berlin, 1924
Competition design for the offices and businesses in the Prince Albrecht Gardens
Travaux de concours pour les constructions de bureaux et de magasins dans les jardins Prince-Albrecht
Wettbewerb für die Büro- und Geschäftsbauten in den Prinz-Albrecht-Gärten

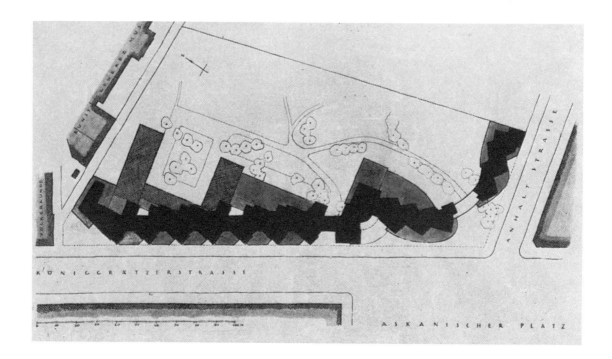

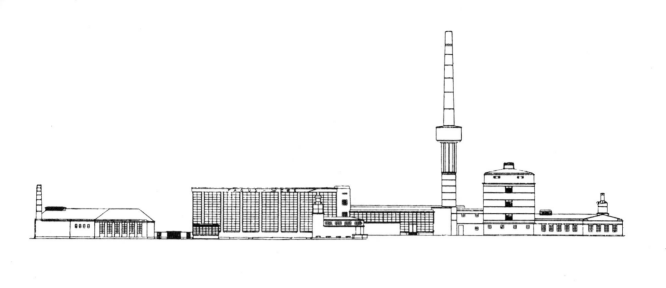

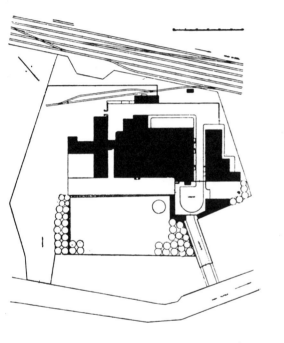

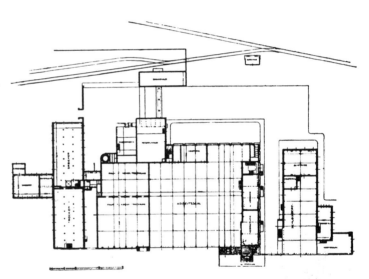

Walter Gropius and Adolf Meyer

Fagus Factory, Alfeld an der Leine, after 1913 [1911]
Factory producing shoe lasts and stamping molds, ground plan and elevation
Fabrique de formes pour chaussures et de couteaux d'estampe, plans et élévation
Schuhleisten-Fabrik und Stanzmesser-Fabrik, Grundriße und Aufriß

Walter Gropius and Adolf Meyer

Fagus Factory, Alfeld an der Leine, after 1913 [1911]
Staircase
Escalier
Treppenhaus

Walter Gropius and Adolf Meyer

Fagus Factory, Alfeld an der Leine, after 1913 [1911]
Machine hall
Halle des machines
Maschinenhaus

Walter Gropius and Adolf Meyer

Cologne, 1914
The exhibition buildings of the "German Werkbund," courtyard in front
of the engine hall and a view of the offices at the rear
Constructions pour l'exposition du "Deutscher Werkbund", cour devant
la halle des machines et face postérieure du bâtiment des bureaux
Bauten für die Ausstellung des "Deutschen Werkbundes", Hof vor der
Maschinenhalle und Rückseite des Bürogebäudes

Wilhelm Deffke

Bulgaria, 1922
Silo for Varna
Silo pour Varna
Silo für Varna

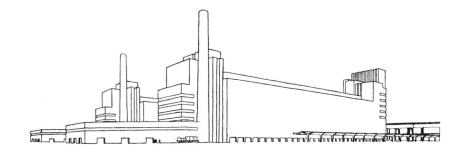

M. Luz

Königsberg, Prussia, 1922
Competition design for the stock exchange
Travail de concours pour le "Börsenhof"
Wettbewerbs-Arbeit für den "Börsenhof"

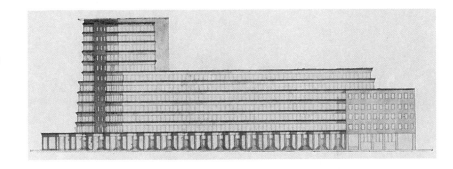

Hugo Häring

Berlin, 1922
Competition design for a business building
in the Tiergartenstraße
Travail de concours pour une maison
d'affaires dans la Tiergartenstraße
Wettbewerbs-Arbeit für ein Geschäftshaus
in der Tiergartenstraße

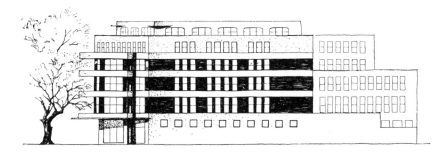

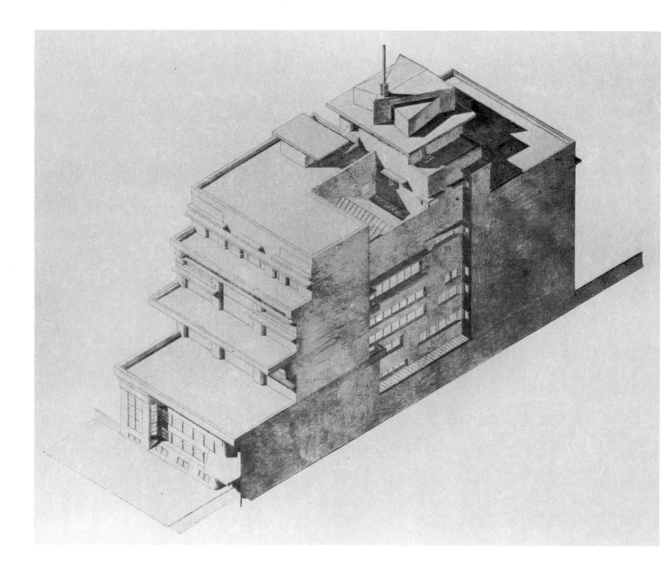

Hugo Häring

Rio de Janeiro, 1923
German Club Building
Maison pour le Club allemand
Haus für den Deutschen Club

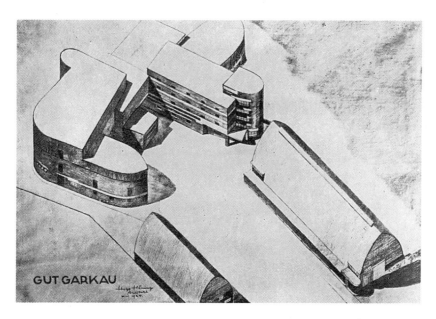

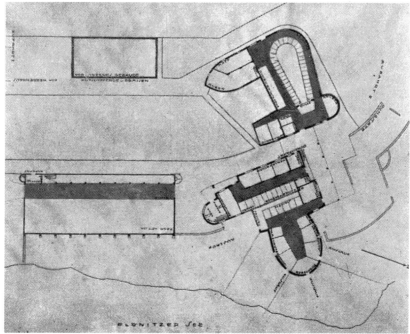

Hugo Häring

Garkau Property, Mecklenburg [Holstein], 1924
Farm buildings
Bâtiments pour l'exploitation rurale
Wirtschaftsbauten

UNTERGESCHOSS   HAUPTGESCHOSS   OBERGESCHOSS   BODENGESCHOSS.

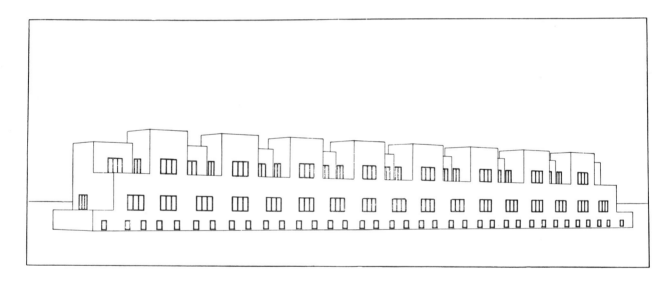

Ludwig Hilberseimer

Berlin, 1924
Row houses, plan and elevation
Maisons construites à l'alignement, plan et élévation
Reihenhäuser, Grundriß und Aufriß

Fritz [Friedrich] Kaldenbach with Breest & Co.

Dresden, 1918
Seck's [Sack's] millwright's workshop
Fabrique de moulins Seck
Mühlenfabrik Seck

Erich Mendelsohn

Luckenwalde near Berlin, 1921/23
Hat factory. View through the gatehouse to the dye works and factory halls
Fabrique de chapeaux. Vue de la porte de la conciergerie sur la teinturerie et les halles
Hutfabrik. Blick durch das Torhäuschen auf die Färberei und die Hallen

Erich Mendelsohn with Erich Laaser

Wüstegiersdorf, Silesia, 1922/23
Reconstruction of the textile works, part of building with tower
Reconstruction de la fabrique textile, corps de tour
Umbau der Textil-Werke, Turmtrakt

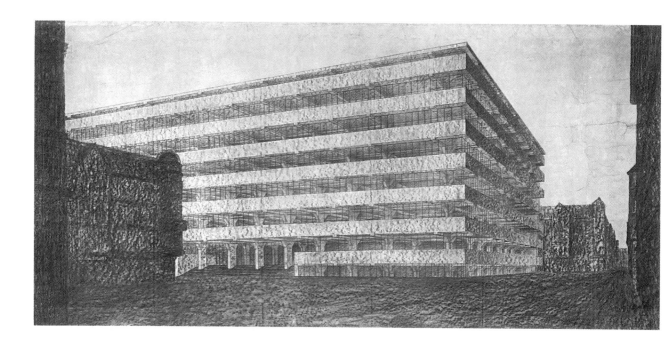

L. Mies van der Rohe

Berlin, 1923 [1922]
Business offices, concrete, iron, glass
Maison pour bureaux, béton, fer, verre
Bürohaus, Beton, Eisen, Glas

Note: The most functional layout of the working spaces
determined the depth of the room: 16 m. A two-way
frame with a span of 8 m and cantilever of 4 m, on all
sides, was found to be the most economical structural
principle. The trusses are 5 m apart. This system of
trusses carries the ceiling slab, which at the end of the
cantilevers turned upward to become the outer skin and
serves as the rear wall for the shelves, which were trans-
ferred from the interior to the outer walls to create an
open plan. Above the 2 m high shelves is a continuous
strip of ceiling-high windows.

Hans Poelzig

Lubań near Posen, 1911/12
Chemical works
Fabrique de produits chimiques
Chemische Fabrik

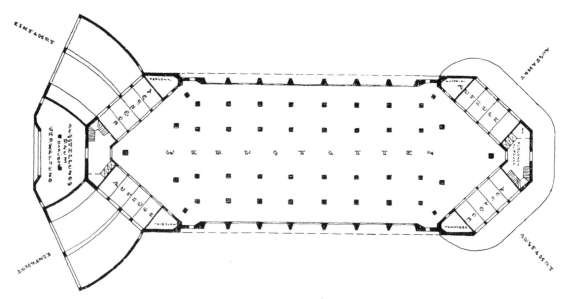

Adolf Rading

Breslau, 1922
Garage, model and plan of ground floor
Garage, modèle et plan du rez-de-chaussée
Garage, Modell und Erdgeschoß-Grundriß

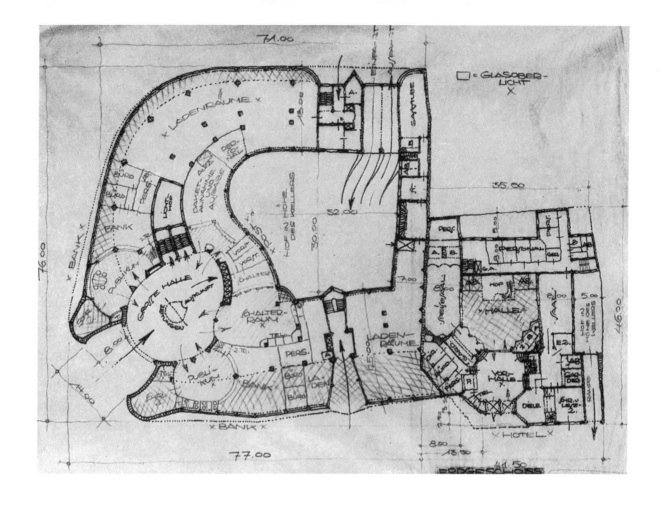

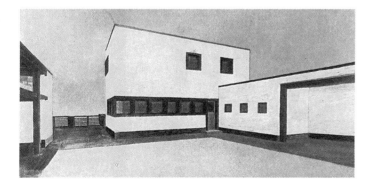

Hans Scharoun

Königsberg, Prussia, 1922
Competition design for the stock exchange (hotel, offices, post office, bank), plan of ground floor
Travail de concours pour le "Börsenhof" (hôtel, bureaux, poste, banque),plan du rez-de-chaussée
Wettbewerbs-Arbeit für den "Börsenhof" (Hotel, Büros, Post, Bank), Grundriß des Erdgeschosses

Karl Schneider

Hamburg, 1924
Joiner's workshop and residence
Atelier de menuiserie avec maison d'habitation
Tischlerwerkstätte mit Wohnhaus

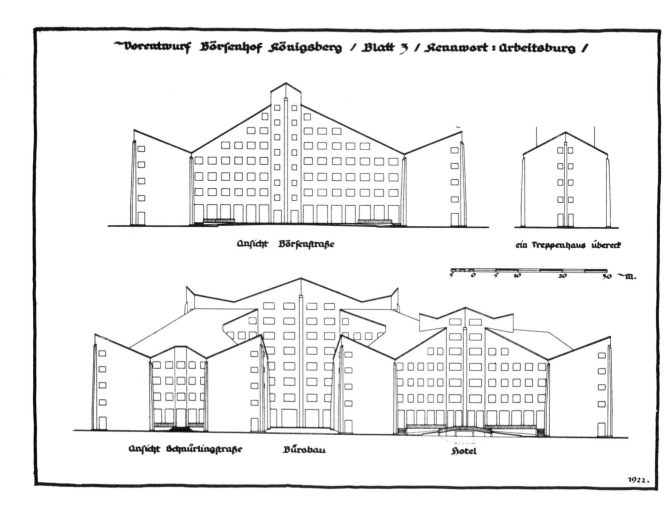

Hans Söder

Königsberg, Prussia, 1922
Competition design for the stock exchange
Projet de concours pour le "Börsenhof"
Wettbewerbs-Entwurf für den "Börsenhof"

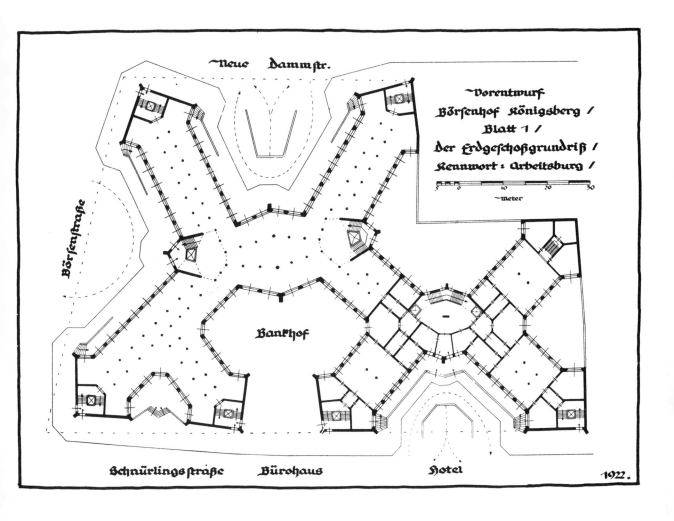

Neue Damm str.

Vorentwurf
Börsenhof Königsberg /
Blatt 1 /
der Erdgeschoßgrundriß /
Kennwort : Arbeitsburg /

5   0   10   20   30
~meter

Börsenstraße

Bankhof

Schnürlingstraße   Bürohaus   Hotel

1922.

179

Bruno Taut

Leipzig, 1913
Exhibition pavilion
Pavillon d'exposition
Ausstellungspavillon

J. D. Peters and K. Lönberg-Holm

Königsberg, Prussia, 1922
Model for the stock exchange, office, hotel, post office
Modèle pour le "Börsenhof", bureau, hôtel, poste
Modell zum "Börsenhof", Büro, Hotel, Post

Max Taut

Berlin, 1923/24
Offices of the "Allgemeiner Deutscher Gewerkschaftsbund," safe deposit vault
Bureaux du "Allgemeiner Deutscher Gewerkschaftsbund" trésor
Bürohaus des "Allegemeinen Deutschen Gewerkschaftsbundes" Tresor

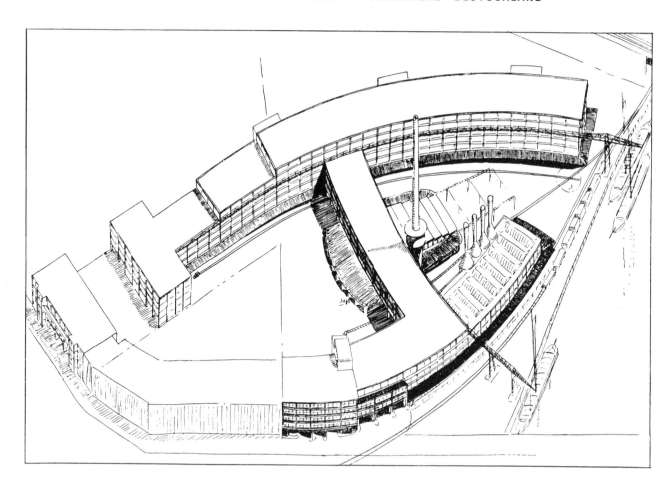

Max Taut

Berlin-Schöneberg, 1923
Competition design for the Norma Tool Factory
Plan de concours pour la fabrique d'outils "Norma"
Wettbewerbs-Entwurf für die Werkzeugfabrik "Norma"

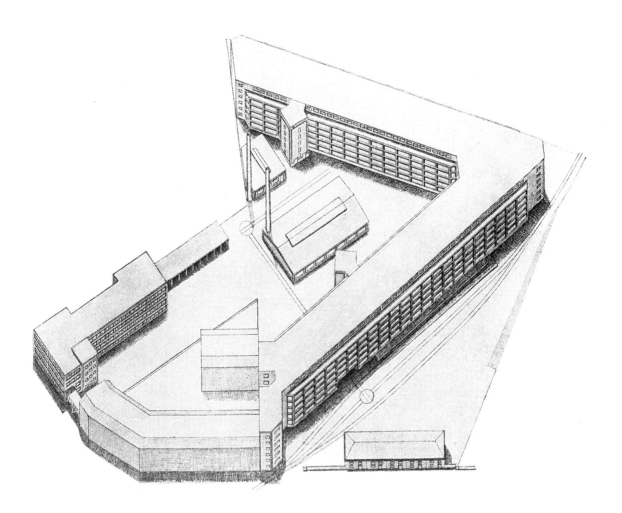

Hans and Wassili Luckhardt

Berlin-Schöneberg, 1923
Competition design for the Norma Tool Factory
Plan de concours pour la fabrique d'outils "Norma"
Wettbewerbs-Entwurf für die Werkzeugfabrik "Norma"

Karl Lönberg-Holm

Chicago-Tribune, 1923 [1922]
Competition design, side view, elevation,
and plan of ground floor
Projet de concours, façade latérale, façade
et plan du rez-de-chaussée
Wettbewerbs-Entwurf, Seitenansicht, Front
und Erdgeschoß-Grundriß

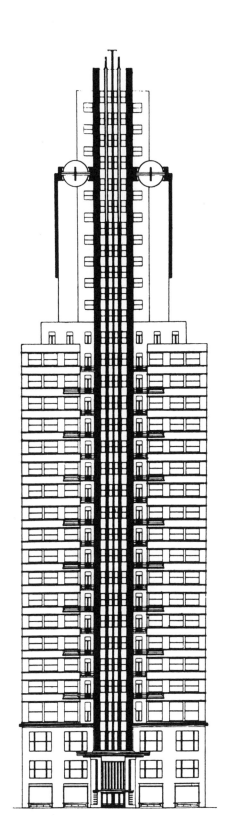

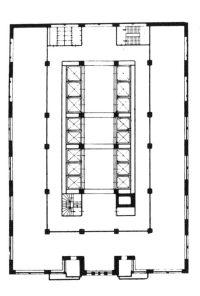

185

Robert Mallet-Stevens

Paris, 1924
Bookshop
Librairie
Buchladen

F. Le Coeur

Paris, 1923 [1911–1913]
Main telephone office
Administration centrale des téléphones [Central téléphonique "Bergère"]
Telephon-Hauptamt

Tony Garnier

Lyons, 1905 [25 May 1917]
Factories
Fabriques
Fabriken

Tony Garnier

Lyons, 1905 [3 July 1917]
Blast furnaces
Hauts-fourneaux
Hochöfen

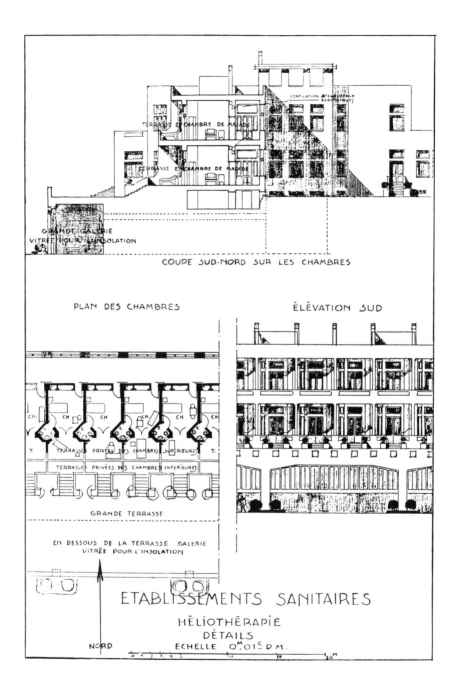

COUPE SUD-NORD SUR LES CHAMBRES

PLAN DES CHAMBRES

ÉLÉVATION SUD

GRANDE TERRASSE

EN DESSOUS DE LA TERRASSE GALERIE
VITRÉE POUR L'INSOLATION

NORD

ETABLISSEMENTS SANITAIRES

HÉLIOTHÉRAPIE
DÉTAILS
ECHELLE 0ᴹ,01ᴵᴰ D M.

Tony Garnier

Lyons, 1905
Pavilion for helio-therapeutics
Pavillon d'héliothérapie
Pavillon für Heliotherapie

Tony Garnier

Lyons, 1913
Slaughterhouse (80 m width, 210 m length)
Halle d'abbatoirs (80 m de largeur, 210 m de longueur)
Schlachthalle (80 m breit, 210 m lang)

Auguste and Gustave Perret

Paris, 1919
The Esders Workshops for ready-made clothing
Ateliers de confection Esders
Konfektions-Ateliers Esders

Auguste and Gustave Perret

Paris, 1919
Studio for decorative painting (51 m length, 12.85 m width)
Atelier de décoration (51 m de longueur, 12.85 m de largeur)
Dekorations-Atelier (Länge 51 m, Breite 12.85 m)

E[ugène] Freyssinet

Orly, 1924
Concrete and iron hall for dirigible airships (275 m length, 60 m height, 91 m width)
Halle de béton armé pour ballons dirigeables (275 m de longueur, 60 m de hauteur, 91 m de largeur)
Eisenbeton-Halle für Lenkluftschiffe (Länge 275 m, Höhe 60 m, Breite 91 m)

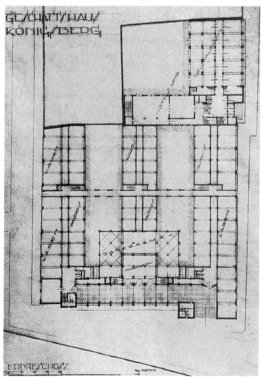

Mart Stam

Königsberg , Prussia, 1922
Competition design for the stock exchange, rendering and plan of the ground floor
Plan de concours pour le "Börsenhof", perspective et plan du rez-de-chaussée
Wettbewerbs-Entwurf für den "Börsenhof", Perspektive und Grundriß des Erdgeschosses

H. P. Berlage

Müller & Co., London, 1914
Office building
Maison pour bureaux
Bürohaus

G. W. van Heukelom

Utrecht, 1918/21
Head office of the Dutch Government Railways
Edifice de l'administration des Chemins de fer des Pays-Bas
Verwaltungsgebäude der Niederländischen Staatsbahnen

Karl [Cornelis] van Eesteren with Theo van Doesburg

1923
Design for a university hall, ceiling in colored glass (50 m width, 50 m length)
Plan pour la salle des fêtes dans une université, plafond en verre de couleurs (50 m de largeur, 50 m de longueur)
Entwurf für eine Universitäts-Aula, Decke in farbigem Glas (50 m breit und 50 m lang)

W. van Leusden

1923
Waiting hall for the electric tramway with kiosk
Salle d'attente des tramways avec kiosque
Wartehalle der Straßenbahn mit Kiosk

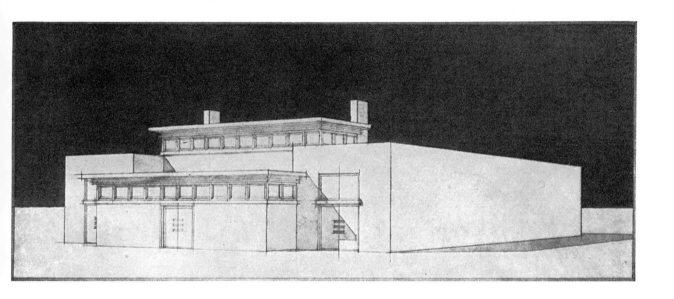

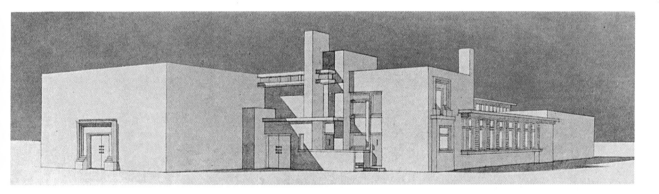

J. J. P. Oud

[Purmerend], 1919
Two factory designs: warehouse with distillery, factory with offices
Deux plans de fabrique: entrepôts avec distillerie, fabrique avec bureaux
Zwei Fabrik-Entwürfe: Lagerhaus mit eingebauter Brennerei, Fabrik mit eingebautem Kontor

R. D. Roosenburg

Eindhoven, 1923
Engineers' office at the Philips incandescent lamp factory
Bureau des ingénieurs de la fabrique d'ampoules électriques Philips
Ingenieur-Büro der Glühlampenfabrik Philips

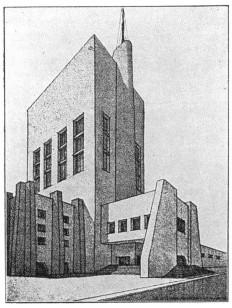

Antonio Sant'Elia

1914
Sketch for an office building
Plan d'une maison d'affaires
Geschäftshaus-Entwurf

Mario Chiattone

1919
Sketch of a factory
Plan de fabrique
Fabriks-Entwurf

Friedrich Kiesler

Vienna, 1924
System and construction of the *International Theater Exhibition*
Système et contruction de *L'exposition internationale du théâtre*
System und Aufbau der *Internationalen Theater-Ausstellung*

Adolf Loos

1923
Type of small house
Type de petite maison
Kleinhaus-Typ

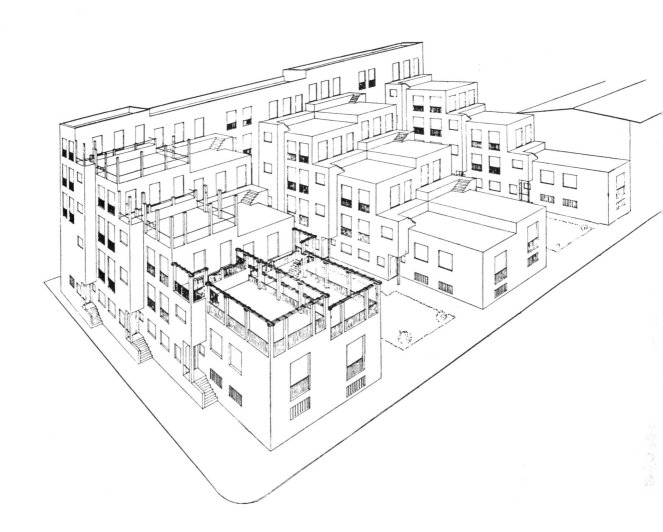

Adolf Loos

1924
Apartment block
Bloc de maison louée
Miethaus-Block

Otto Wagner

Vienna, 1905
Cashiers' windows of the Post Office Savings Bank
Salle des caisses de la "Caisse d'Epargne Postale"
Kassensaal der Postsparkasse

Gabriel Guévrékian

1924
Hotel with garages, model and plan of the lower and upper floors
Hôtel avec garages, modèle et plan du rez-de-chaussée et des étages supérieurs
Hotel mit Garagen, Modell und Grundriß des Erdgeschosses und der Obergeschosse

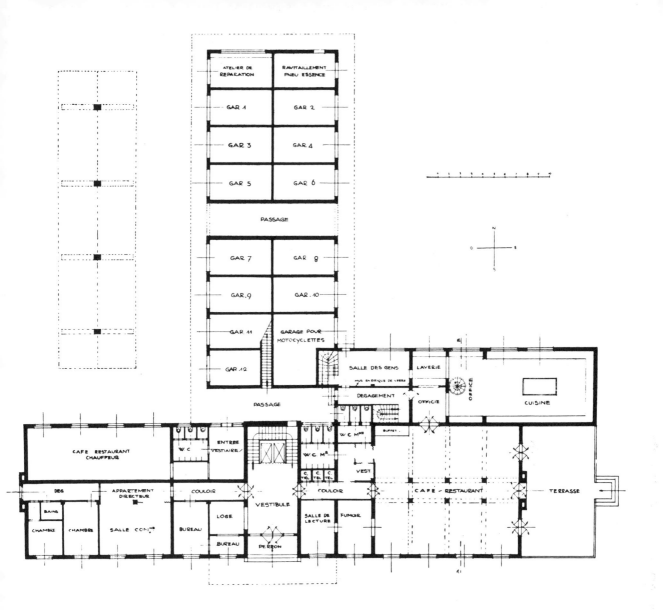
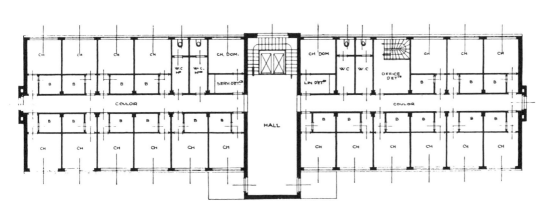

Ladovski

Architecture studio, VKhUTEMAS school of arts (former academy), Moscow, 1923
Tower for the chemical preparation of lyes
Tour pour emploi des lessives dans une fabrique chimique
Turm zur Verarbeitung von Laugen in einer chemischen Fabrik

Vesnin

1924
Competition design for the "Palace of Labor" in Moscow, third prize
Plan de concours pour le "Palais du Travail" à Moscou, IIIième prix
Wettbewerbs-Entwurf für das Palais der Arbeit" in Moskau, III Preis

Alexandra Exter

Moscow, 1923
"Isvestiia" pavilion at the *First Pan-Russian Exhibition*
Pavillon de la "Iswestija" dans la *Première exposition Pan-Russe*
Pavillon der "Iswestija" auf der *1. Allrussischen Ausstellung*

El Lissitzky Studio

"Unovis," 1920
Platform for public speakers
Tribune d'orateur
Rednertribüne

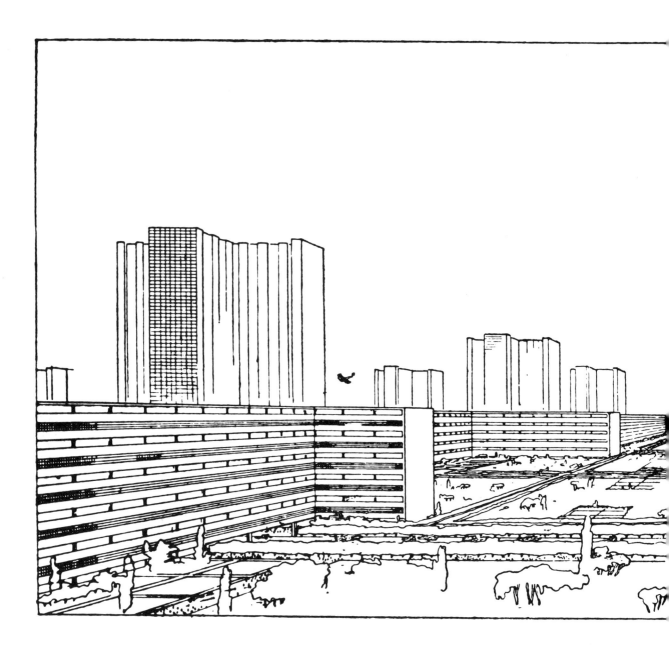

Le Corbusier-Saugnier [*sic*]

1912/1922
City skyscrapers and apartment blocks in a modern city
Maisons de ville avec nombreux étages et blocs de bâtiments d'une grande ville moderne
City-Hochhäuser und Wohnhausblöcke einer modernen Großstadt

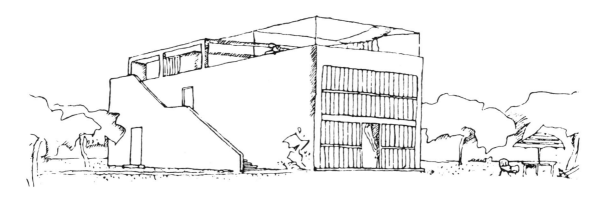

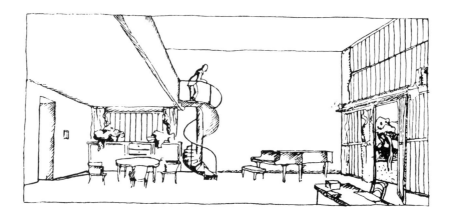

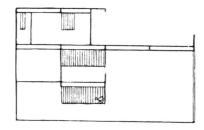

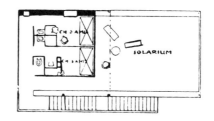

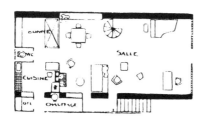

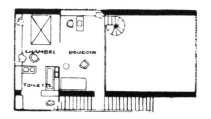

Le Corbusier-Saugnier [*sic*]

1922
Prototype for mass-produced housing
Projet de maison à bâtir par séries
Serienhaus-Entwurf

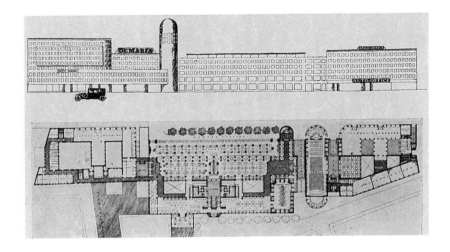

J. Krejcar

Prague, 1923
Design for a hotel on the Moldau, ground plan and elevation
Projet pour un hôtel au bord de la Moldau, plan et façade
Entwurf für ein Hotel an der Moldau, Grundriß und Aufriß

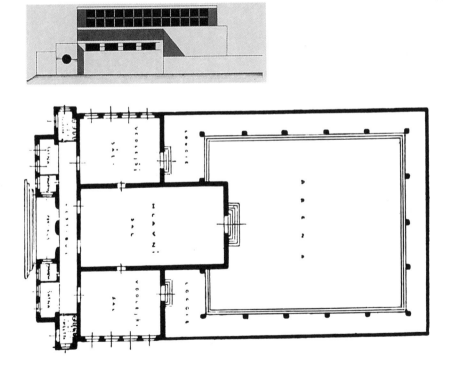

Vit Obrtel

Pavilion for art exhibitions, ground plan and elevation
Pavillon pour expositions artistiques, plan et élévation
Pavillon für Kunstausstellungen, Grundriß und Aufriß (Vordertrakt)

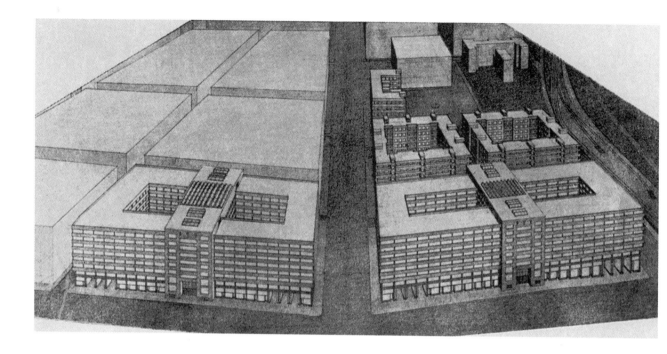

Oldrich Tyl

Prague, 1924
Competition design for the buildings of the Model Exhibition—first prize—bird's-eye view
Travail de concours pour les constructions de la foire d'échantillons—I^{ier} prix—Vue à vol d'oiseau
Wettbewerbs-Arbeit für die Bauten der Mustermesse—I. Preis—Vogelschau

Ladislaus Peri

Lenin Monument (mausoleum and museum), 1924
Concrete, red glass, black glass
Béton, verre rouge, verre noir
Beton, rotes Glas, schwarzes Glas

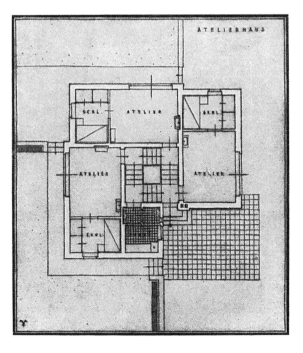

Fred Forbát

1923
Studio building, elevation and ground plan
Maison pour ateliers, élévation et plan
Atelierhaus, Aufriß und Grundriß

Fred Forbát

1923
Group of three studios
Groupe de trois maisons pour ateliers
Gruppe von drei Atelierhäusern

Bibliography

[Slight modifications have been made to Behne's bibliography in an attempt to render it more useful — ed.]

Ahlberg, Hakon. *Modern Swedish Architecture*. London: Ernest Benn Ltd., 1924.

Amsterdam, Publieke Werken. *Wendingen* 7 (1923).

Ashbee, C. R. *Frank Lloyd Wright*. Berlin: Ernst Wasmuth Verlag, 1911.

Behne, Adolf. *Holländische Baukunst in der Gegenwart*. Berlin: Ernst Wasmuth Verlag, 1922.

———— *Ruf zum Bauen*. Berlin: Ernst Wasmuth Verlag, 1920.

Behrendt, W. C. *Alfred Messel*. Berlin: Bruno Cassirer Verlag, 1913.

———— "Meyer Verwaltungsgebäude in Hannover-Vinnhorst." *Neubau* (10 January 1924).

Behrens, Peter. *Das Ethos und die Umlagerung der künstlerischen Probleme*. Darmstadt: 1920.

———— *Beziehungen der künstlerischen und technischen Probleme*. Berlin: 1917.

———— "Werbende künstlerische Werte im Fabrikbau." *Plakat* 11, no. 6 (June 1920): 269–73.

Berlage, H. P. *Grundlagen und Entwicklung der Architektur*. Berlin: Julius Bard Verlag, 1908.

———— "Frank Lloyd Wright." *Wendingen* (November 1921).

Blauw. "Finsterlin." *Wendingen* (1924).

Boerschmann, Ernst. *Baukunst und Landschaft in China*. Berlin: Ernst Wasmuth Verlag, 1923.

Bourgeois, Victor. "Architecture." *Sept arts* (Brussels), no. 1, (1922).

———— "L'urbanisme vivante." *Sept arts* (Brussels; December 1924).

Bouwkunde, Maandschrift der nieuwe ideen in de Architectuur. Antwerp.

La cité: Revue mensuelle Belge. "Urbanisme, Architecture, Art public" (Brussels, from 1920).

Cocteau, Jean. *Manomètre* (Lyons), no. 4 (1923).

Le Corbusier-Saugnier. "Des yeux qui ne voient pas." *L'esprit nouveau* (Paris, 1922).

Le Corbusier. *Vers une architecture*. Paris: G. Crès & Cie., 1924 [first published in 1923].

———— *Recherche des principes fondamentaux d'urbanisme moderne*. Paris: Ebendorf, 1923.

———— "Architektur-Wende." *Europa-Almanach*. Potsdam: Gustav Kiepenheuer Verlag, 1924.

Coudenhove-Kalergi. *Apologie der Technik*. Leipzig: Neuer Geist-Verlag.

Dietzel, Heinrich. *Technischer Fortschritt und Freiheit der Wirtschaft*. Bonn and Leipzig: Kurt Schröder Verlag, 1923.

Döcker, Richard. "Über Baukunst." *Die Volkswohnung* 5, no. 13.

———— *Kleinhaustypen-Pläne*. Stuttgart: Industrie-Verlag, 1922.

———— "Ein Beitrag zum städtebaulichen Weiterschaffen." *Der Städtebau*, nos. 3–4 (1921).

Doesburg, Theo van. "Tot een beeldende architectuur." *De Stijl*, nos. 6/7 (1924).

———— *Classique—Baroque—Moderne*. Paris: Leonce Rosenberg, 1921.

———— *Drie Voordrachten over de nieuwe beeldende Kunst*. Amsterdam: 1919.

Dormoy, Marie. "Auguste und Gustave Perret." *Kunstblatt* (October 1923).

Ehmig, Paul. *Das deutsche Haus*. Berlin: Ernst Wasmuth Verlag, 1914.

Ehrenburg, Elias. "Ein Entwurf Tatlins." *Frühlicht* (Magdeburg), no. 3 (1922).

Engelhardt, Viktor. *Weltanschauung und Technik*. Leipzig: Felix Meiner Verlag, 1922–1923.

Fierens-Gevaert. "L'architecture et l'art décoratif en Belgique." *La cité* (December 1923).

Finsterlin, Hermann. "Casa nova (Zukunfts-Architektur)." *Wendingen*, no. 3 (1924).

———— "Innen-Architektur." *Frühlicht*. Magdeburg: Karl Peters Verlag, 1921.

Ford, Henry. *Mein Leben und Werk*. Leipzig: Paul List Verlag, 1923.

Franz, W. "Industriebauten." *Städtebauliche Vorträge* (Berlin) 8, no. 5 (1919).

Frey, Dagobert. "Otto Wagner." *Österreichische Biographie*, 178 ff.

Friedländer, S. *Schöpferische Indifferenz*. Munich, 1918.

Fries, H. de. "Industrie-Baukunst." *Wasmuths Monatshefte*, 5, nos. 5–6.

Frobenius, Leo. *Das unbekannte Afrika*. Leipzig: 1923.

Garnier, Tony. *Une cité industrielle*. Paris: Vincent Press.

———— *Les grands travaux de la ville de Lyon*. Paris: Massin Press.

Gleizes, Albert. *Vom Kubismus*. Berlin: Verlag Der Sturm, 1921.

Gropius, Walter. "Die Entwicklung moderner Industriebaukunst." *Jahrbuch des Deutschen Werkbundes*, 1913.

Gropius, Walter, and Adolf Meyer. *Bauten*. Berlin: Ernst Wasmuth Verlag, 1924.

Hablik, Wenzel August. "Die Freitragende Kuppel." *Frühlicht* (Magdeburg), no. 3 (1922).

Hellpach, Willy. "Der jung-europäische Staat." *Vossische Zeitung* (25 September 1923).

Hellwag, Fritz. "Peter Behrens und die AEG." *Kunstgewerbe-Blatt* (Leipzig) 22, no. 8.

Herre, Richard. "Hochhäuser für Stuttgart." *Wasmuths Monatshefte* 7, nos. 11–12.

Herrmann, Christian. *Sozialistische Monatshefte* (1923): 382, 569.

Hilberseimer, Ludwig. "Großstadt-Architektur." *Der Sturm* 4 (1924).

Hoeber, Fritz. *Peter Behrens*. Munich: Georg Müller & Eugen Reutsch Verlag, 1913.

Van t'Hoff, Robert. "Architectuur." *De Stijl* 5, no. 12.

———. "Aanteekeningen (Antonio Sant'Elia, d. 1916)." *De Stijl* 10 (1919).

Jancu, Marcel. "Architectura noua." *Contimporanul* (Bucharest, February 1925).

———. "Une base à créer pour la nouvelle collaboration." *Architectura* (Amsterdam, 4 November 1925).

Kick, Paul, and Alphons Schneegans. "Geschäfts- und Kaufhäuser, Gebäude für Banken und andere Geldinstitute." *Handbuch des Architekten* (Leipzig, 1923).

Kiesler, Friedrich. Catalog, program, almanac. Internationale Ausstellung neuer Theatertechnik (Vienna, 1924).

De Klerk, M. "Uitgevoerde Bouwwerken." *Wendingen*, nos. 9–10 (1924).

Kubsch, Hugo. "Kunst und Technik." *Siemens' Wirtschaftlichen Mitteilungen*, no. 40.

Leurs, Stan. "De crisis in bouwkunst." Lecture at the Third Modern Art Congress (Bruges, 1822).

Lindner, Werner, and Georg Steinmetz. *Die Ingenieurbauten in ihrer guten Gestaltung*. Berlin: Ernst Wasmuth Verlag, 1923.

Lissitzky, El. "Architektur der S. S. S. R." *Kunstblatt* (Berlin, February 1925).

———. "Element und Erfindung." *A-B-C* (Zurich), no. 1 (1924).

Loos, Adolf. *Ins Leere gesprochen, 1897–1900*. Paris: Georges Crès & Cie., 1922.

———. "Ornament und Erziehung." *Wohnungskultur* (Brno) 1, nos. 6/8.

———. "Von der Sparsamkeit." *Wohnungskultur* (Brno, 1924): 17.

———. "Über Architektur." *Der Sturm* 1 (1911): 334.

——— *Richtlinien für ein Kunstamt.* Vienna: Verlag Richard Lanyi, 1919.

Lülwes, H. "Was muß beim Entwurf neuer Werke beachtet werden?" *Hawa-Nachrichten*, no. 1, in-house publication (Hannoverschen Waggonfabrik, January 1922).

Lux, Josef August. *Olbrich.* Berlin: Ernst Wasmuth Verlag, 1914.

——— *Otto Wagner.* Munich: Delphin-Verlag, 1914.

Märten, Lu. *Wesen und Veränderung der Formen (Künste).* Frankfurt am Main: Taifun-Verlag, 1924.

Mann, Heinrich. "Diktatur der Vernunft." *Vossische Zeitung* (Berlin, 11 October 1923).

Marchi, Virgilio. *Architettura Futurista.* Filigno: Franco Campitelli Editore, 1924.

Marilaun, Karl. *Adolf Loos.* Vienna: Wiener Literarische Anstalt, 1923.

Markalous, B. "Französische Künstler." *Wohnungskultur* (Brno, 1924).

——— "Adolf Loos." *Wohnungskultur* (Brno) 1, nos. 4–5.

Mendelsohn, Erich. "Die internationale Übereinstimmung des neuen Baugedankens oder Dynamik und Funktion." *Architectura* (Amsterdam, 2 and 9 February 1924).

——— "Bauten und Skizzen." *Wasmuths Monatshefte* 8, nos. 1–2.

——— "Gedanken zu der neuen Architektur." *De Nieuwe Kronick* (Amsterdam, 26 March 1921).

——— "Frank Lloyd Wright." *Architectura* (Amsterdam, 25 April 1925).

Mesnil, Jacques. *Henry van de Velde et le théâtre des Champs Elysées.* Brussels: G. van Oest, 1914.

Meyer. "Die Bedeutung der Mathematik in der Industrie." Paper read at the Verein zur Beförderung des Gewerbefleißes (Berlin, 9 November 1922).

Micic-Belgrad, Ljubomir. "Antisoziale Kunst muß vernichtet werden." *Wohnungskultur* (Brno) 1, nos. 6/8.

Mies van der Rohe, L. "Industrielles Bauen." *G. Zeitschrift für elementare Gestaltung* (Berlin), nos. 1–3 (1923/24).

Miller, René Fülöp. "Der kollektive Mensch." *Vossische Zeitung* (Berlin, 3 October 1923).

Mondrian, Piet. "Neue Gestaltung in der Musik." *De Stijl* 6, no. 1.

——— *Le neo-plasticisme.* Paris: Léonce Rosenberg, 1920.

Mumford, Lewis. "Imperialistische Architektur in Amerika." *Kunst und Künstler* (March 1925).

Muthesius, Hermann. *Die Werkbund-Arbeit der Zukunft.* Jena: Eugen Diederich, 1914.

Neutra, Richard. "Eine Bauweise in bewehrtem Beton an Neubauten von Frank Lloyd Wright." *Die Baugilde* (February 1925).

Osthaus, Ernst. *Henry van de Velde*. Hagen, Westphalia: Folkwang Verlag, 1920.

Oud, J. J. P. "Berlage und sein Werk." *Kunst und Kunsthandwerk* (Vienna), nos. 6/8 (1919).

———— "Over de toekomstige bouwkunst en hare architectonische mogelijkheden." *Bouwkundig Weekblad* (Amsterdam, February 1921; in French: *La cité* [Brussels, November 1923]).

———— "Ja und Nein, Bekenntnisse eines Architekten." *Europa-Almanach*. Potsdam: Gustav Kiepenheuer Verlag, 1924.

———— "Biographie." *Wohnungskultur* (Brno) 1, nos. 9/10.

Paulsen, Friedrich. "Briefe von einer Amerikareise." *Bauwelt* (Berlin, 1925).

Perret issue of *Stavba* (Prague), no. 7.

Pfleiderer, Wolfgang. *Die Form ohne Ornament. Werkbund-Ausstellung 1924.* Stuttgart: Deutsche Verlags-Anstalt, 1924.

Poelzig, Hans. Speech in Salzburg. *Kunstblatt* (Berlin), no. 3 (1921).

Redslob, Edwin. "Neue Industriebauten." *Neubau* (Berlin, 10 January 1921).

Riezler, Kurt. *Gestalt und Gesetz*. Munich: Musarion-Verlag, 1924.

Schliepmann, Hans. *Lichtspieltheater*. Berlin: Ernst Wasmuth Verlag, 1914.

Schlüter, Otto. "Staat, Wirtschaft, Volk, Religion in ihrem Verhältnis zur Erdoberfläche." *Zeitschrift für Geopolitik* (Halensee: Kurt Vowinkel Verlag), nos. 6/7 (1924).

Schneider. *Technik in der Kunst*. Stuttgart: Frankh's Technischer Verlag.

Schüler, Edmund. "Der Wolkenkratzer." *Kunst und Künstler* (March 1925).

Schwitters, Kurt. "Watch Your Step!" *Merz* (Hannover: Merz-Verlag), no. 6 (1923).

Selinski. "Stil und Stahl." *Neue Kultur-Korrespondenz* (Berlin) 1, nos. 4/5, (1923).

Staal, I. F., and Oskar Beyer. "Mendelsohn." *Wendingen* (Amsterdam, October 1920).

Stahl, Fritz. "Hans Poelzig." *Wasmuths Monatshefte* (Berlin, May 1919).

Stam, Mart. "Kollektive Gestaltung." *A-B-C* (Zurich), no. 1 (1924).

Stavba. Zeitschrift des Bundes Prager Architekten, ed. Karl Teige (Prague, from 1922)

Swaelman, van der. "Stedenbouw." *Het Overzicht* (Antwerp, September 1923).

Taut, Bruno and Fischmann. *Das Monument des Eisens*. Leipzig: Verlag des Stahlwerk-Verbandes und des Vereins Deutscher Brücken- und Eisenbau-Fabriken, 1913.

Tillich, Paul. *Das System der Wissenschaften nach Gegenständen und Methoden*. Göttingen: Verlag Vandenhock und Rupprecht.

Timmling, W. "Topik der Kunst." *Die Baulaterne* (Halle an der Saale, February 1925).

Velde, Henry van de. *Amo*. Leipzig: Insel-Verlag (Insel-Bücherei no. 3).

———— *Die drei Sünden wider die Schönheit*. Zurich: Verlag Max Rascher, 1918.

———— *Formules d'une esthétique moderne*. Brussels: L'Equerre Press, 1923.

———— "Das Folkwang-Museum." *Innen-Dekoration* (Darmstadt, 1902).

———— "L'orientation du goût en architecture." *Europe*. Paris: F. Rieder & Cie., 1923: 124.

———— "Devant l'architecture." *Europe*. Paris: F. Rieder & Cie., 15 July 1924.

———— "Vers une construction collektive!" Fifth manifesto of the De Stijl group (Paris, 1923).

Vierkandt, A. *Der Dualismus im modernen Weltbild*. Berlin: Pan-Verlag, 1923.

Wagner, Otto. *Die Baukunst unserer Zeit,* 4th ed. Vienna, 1914.

———— *Eine Studie über die Großstadt*. Vienna, 1912.

Weltsch. *Gnade und Freiheit*. Munich: Kurt Wolf Verlag, 1920.

Wright, Frank Lloyd. "Anmerkungen zu den Zement-Blockhäusern." *Baugilde* (Berlin), no. 4 (1925).

Wenzel August Hablik, Itzehoe: Exhibition building

Editor's Notes

In those instances where Behne does not provide full biographical or bibliographical data in his own bibliography, we have attempted to supply that information in these notes. In some cases this information is not available.

1. Elfriede Schneider.

2. Karl Friedrich Schinkel (1781–1841).

3. Henry van de Velde (1863–1957); August Endell (1871–1925); Joseph Maria Olbrich (1867–1908).

4. Otto Wagner (1841–1918): *Die Baukunst unserer Zeit*. Vienna: Anton Schroll, 1914), 44; translated in Otto Wagner, *Modern Architecture*, intro. and trans. Harry Francis Mallgrave (Santa Monica: The Getty Center for the History of Art and the Humanities, 1988), 82. This is the 4th ed. of Wagner's *Moderne Architektur*, which was first published in 1896.

5. Franz Heinrich Schwechten (1841–1924). The Anhalt Station (1877–1880) is by Schwechten, but the Stettin Station (1874–1876) is by Theodor Stein.

6. Ernst von Ihne (1848–1917).

7. Hendrik Petrus Berlage (1856–1934); Alfred Messel (1853–1909).

8. Perret brothers: Auguste (1874–1954) and Gustave (1876–1952).

9. The concepts embodied in the word *Sachlichkeit* and its adjectival form, *sachlich*, are central to Behne's argument in *Der moderne Zweckbau*. The Introduction attempts to present a nuanced view of the use of these terms in the early decades of the twentieth century. Please refer to pages 47–49 of the Introduction for more information regarding the changing meanings of these terms.

10. Petrus Josephus Hubertus Cuypers (1827–1921).

11. Hendrik Petrus Berlage, "The Foundations and Development of Architecture," in *Hendrik Petrus Berlage: Thoughts on Style, 1886–1909* (Santa Monica: The Getty Center for the History of Art and the Humanities, 1996). Original edition, *Grundlagen und Entwicklung der Architektur* (Berlin: Julius Bard, 1908).

12. Joseph Auguste E. Vaudremer (1829–1914): *L'architecte* (1924), 8: "*Mais Vaudremer n'eut pas la gloire d'engager définitivement les jeunes générations dans la voie d'une architecture française rationelle. Pour l'architecture hollandaise Berlage a cette gloire.*"

13. Dagobert Frey, "Otto Wagner," *Neue Österreichische Biographie, 1815–1918* (Vienna: Amalthea, 1923), 178ff.

14. Wagner 1914 (see note 4), 45; translated in Wagner 1988, 83–84.

15. Wagner 1914 (see note 4), 135–36 n. 155; this passage appears *only* in the 1914 edition of *Moderne Architektur*.

16. Bernhard Sehring (1855–1941).

17. Bruno Taut (1880–1938).

18. Charles Edouard Jeanneret, known as Le Corbusier (1887–1965).

19. Leo Frobenius (1873–1938): *Das unbekannte Afrika, Aufhellung der Schicksale eines Erdteils* (Munich: Beck, 1923).

20. Julius Raschdorff (1823–1914).

21. Frank Lloyd Wright (1867–1959); Louis Henry Sullivan (1856–1924).

22. Richard Herre.

23. Peter Behrens (1868–1940); Walter Gropius (1883–1969); Erich Mendelsohn (1887–1953); Ludwig Mies van der Rohe (1886–1969); J. J. P. Oud (1890–1963); Jan Wils (1891–1972); Robert van t'Hoff (1887–1979); W. Greve; Jaromír Krejcar; Oldrich Tyl; Jaroslav Fragner; Bedřich Feuerstein (1892–1936).

24. This is Behne's very loose translation of Wright's passage into German. Wright's actual words were as follows: "The machine is here to stay. It is the forerunner of the [real] democracy that is our dearest hope. There is no more important work before the architect now than to use this normal tool of civilization to the best advantage instead of prostituting it as he has hitherto done in reproducing with murderous ubiquity forms born of other times and other conditions and which it can only serve to destroy." See Frank Lloyd Wright, "In the Cause of Architecture," *Architectural Record* 23, no. 3 (March 1908): 163.

25. Wagner 1914 (see note 4), 47; translated in Wagner 1988, 86.

26. Karl Scheffler (1869–1951).

27. Walter Gropius, "Die Entwicklung moderner Industriebaukunst," in *Jahrbuch des Deutschen Werkbundes* (Jena: Eugen Diederichs, 1913), 17–22.

28. Gropius (see note 27), 21–22.

29. Henry Ford (1863–1947): *Mein Leben und Werk* (Leipzig: Paul List, 1923), 113 ff.

30. Ford (see note 29), 218.

31. Ford (see note 29), 104.

32. Ford (see note 29), 173.

33. Emil Rathenau (1838–1915).

34. Heinrich Zille (1858–1929).

35. Raphael (1483–1520); Hans Makart (1840–1884).

36. Peter Behrens, "Werbende künstlerische Werte im Fabrikbau," *Plakat* 11, no. 6 (June 1920): 269–73.

37. H. Lülwes: "Was muß beim Entwurf neuer Werke beachtet werden?" *Hawa-Nachrichten*, no. 1 (January 1922).

38. Heinz Stoffregen (1879–1929).

233

39. Hans Poelzig (1869–1936): "Rede in Salzburg," *Kunstblatt*, no. 3 (1921): 77 ff.

40. Gropius (see note 27), 20.

41. *Sept arts* (15 February 1923): "*Sans doute ne pourra-t-on jamais parvenir à quelque douce harmonie, mais il est nécessaire de tendre à une organisation rationelle de toute brutalité sonore.*"

42. Jean Cocteau (1889–1963): *Le coq et l'arlequin: Notes autour de la musique 1918* (Paris: Editions de la Sirène, 1918): "*Les machines et les bâtisses américaines ressemblent à l'art grec en ce sens, que l'utilité leur confère une sécheresse et une grandeur dépouillées du superflu. Mais ce n'est pas de l'art. Le rôle de l'art consiste à saisir le sens de l'époque et à puiser dans le spectacle de cette sécheresse pratique un antidote contre la beauté de l'inutile qui encourage le superflu.*"

43. Fritz [Friedrich] Kaldenbach (1887–1918).

44. Hermann Finsterlin (1887–1973): "Innen-Architektur," *Frühlicht*, no. 2 (winter 1921–1922): 36.

45. Henry van de Velde, *Die drei Sünden wider die Schönheit* (Zurich: Max Rascher, 1918), 41.

46. Henry van de Velde, "Das Folkwang-Museum in Hagen," *Innen-Dekoration* 13 (October–November 1902): 249–72 (October); 273–77 (November).

47. Van de Velde (see note 46), page reference unknown.

48. Van de Velde (see note 46), page reference unknown.

49. Samuel Bing (1836–1905); Edmond de Goncourt (1822–1896); Jules de Goncourt (1830–1870); Karl Ernst Osthaus (1874–1921): *Henry van de Velde* (Hagen, Westphalia: Folkwang, 1920).

50. Henry van de Velde, "Devant l'architecture," in *Europe* (Paris: F. Rieder & Cie., 1924).

51. Michel de Klerk (1884–1923); Johan Melchior van der Meij; Alexander Jacobus Kropholler (b. 1881); Hendrikus Theodorus Wijdeveld (b. 1885).

52. Richard Döcker (b. 1894); Luckhardt brothers: Hans (1890–1954) and Wassili (1889–1972).

53. Jan Frederik Staal (1879–1940): "Naar Aanleiding van Erich Mendelsohn's Ontwerpen," *Wendingen* (October 1920): 3: "*Het is het beste Duitsche, het behoort tot het beste persoonlijke werk, maar het is nog Duitsch en nog persoonlijk.*"

54. Erich Mendelsohn, "Problem einer neuen Baukunst," *Wasmuths Monatshefte* (1924): 3.

55. Richard Neutra (1892–1970).

56. Nikolai Fedorovich Lapshin.

57. Richard Döcker, "Über Baukunst," *Die Volkswohnung* 5, no. 13 (10 July 1923): 161–62.

58. Hugo Häring (1882–1958).

59. Johannes Ludovicus Matheus Lauweriks (1864–1932).

60. Hans Scharoun (1893–1972); Adolf Rading (1888–1957).

61. Michel Roux-Spitz.

62. Heinrich de Fries (1887–1938).

63. Lu Märten: *Resultate historisch-materialistischer Untersuchungen* (Frankfurt am Main: Taifun-Verlag, 1924).

64. Louis van der Swaelmen (d. 1929): "Stedenbouw," *Het Overzicht* (September 1923): *"Het gaat dus om functies en om organen"*; Georges-Eugène Haussmann (1809–1891).

65. Vladimir Evgrafovich Tatlin (1885–1953).

66. Elias Ehrenburg, "Ein Entwurf Tatlins," *Frühlicht*, no. 3 (spring 1922): 93.

67. Wenzel August Hablik (1881–1934).

68. K. Selinski: "Stil und Stahl," *Neue Kultur-Korrespondenz* 1, nos. 4–5 (1923).

69. Ernst Boerschmann (1873–1949). *Fêng shui* (literally, "wind-water") is the Chinese art of auspiciously siting buildings and placing elements within them according to natural forces.

70. Paul Tillich (1886–1965): *Das System der Wissenschaften nach Gegenständen und Methoden* (Göttingen: Vandenhoeck & Ruprecht, 1923).

71. Adolf Loos (1870–1933): "Über Architektur," *Der Sturm* 1 (1911): 334.

72. Robert Mallet-Stevens (1886–1945); Gabriel Guévrékian; Francis Jourdain (1876–1958); Tony Garnier (1869–1948).

73. *"L'architecture vivante est celle qui exprime fidèlement son époque. On en cherchera des exemples dans tous les domaines de la construction. On choisira les oeuvres qui strictement subordonnées à leur usage, réalisées par l'emploi judicieux de la matière, atteindront à la beauté par les dispositions, les proportions harmonieuses, inspirés des éléments nécessaires qui les composent."*

74. Gustave Eiffel (1832–1923); Eugène Freyssinet (1879–1962).

75. Jacques Mesnil: *Henry van de Velde et le théâtre des Champs Elysées* (Brussels: G. van Oest, 1914).

76. Tony Garnier, *Les grands travaux de la ville de Lyon* (Paris: Massin Press, 1919).

77. Tony Garnier, *Une cité industrielle: Etude pour la construction des villes* (Paris: C. Massin & Cie., 1939).

78. *"Je n'ai pas eu l'occasion de voir de grandes compositions architecturales qui m'aient impressioné, mais j'ai remarqué par contre très souvent beaucoup d'ingéniosité dans les installations techniques que j'ai vues en Allemagne."*

79. Guyau: *"L'art c'est de la tendresse."*

80. Victor Bourgeois (1897–1962): *Sept arts*: *"Puisque la maison est inséparable de sa voisine et qu'une rue prolonge une autre rue, toute architecture puissante tend au style, c'est à dire à un équilibre supérieur et collectif."*

81. Bourgeois (see note 80): *"Un architecte moderne obligé de construire actuellement dans une rue de Bruxelles commet presque une insolence à l'égard de son art, s'il réalise un édifice intéressant — quel progrès, si cette architecture hostile devenait une architecture indifférente."*

82. R. Malespine: "*Il nous faut des maisons à mesure d'homme*"; Georges Linze: "*L'originalité est du reste forme d'insubordination.*"

83. Richard Nicolaüs Roland Holst (1868–1939).

84. Le Corbusier, *Recherche des principes fondamentaux d'urbanisme moderne* (Paris: G. Crès & Cie., 1924).

85. Robert van t'Hoff, "Architektuur," *De Stijl* 2, no. 5: "*Bij gewapend beton zijn alleen de toepassingen in horizontale en verticale richtingen consequent.*"

86. Kurt Schwitters (1887–1948): "Watch Your Step!" *Merz,* no. 6 (1923).

87. Behne's reference to an earlier quotation from "Baut Bewegung!" is incorrect. No such passage from the Selinski essay appears in the preceding pages of the present volume.

88. K. Selinski, "Baut Bewegung!" *Neue Kultur-Korrespondenz* 1, nos. 4–5 (1923).

89. Albert Gleizes (1881–1953) and Jean Metzinger: *Du cubisme* (Paris: E. Figuière & Cie., 1912), 30.

90. Antonio Sant'Elia (1888–1916); Virgilio Marchi (1895–1960).

91. Nikolai Aleksandrovich Ladovski (1881–1941).

92. Willy Hellpach (1877–1955): "Der jung-europäische Staat," *Vossische Zeitung* (25 September 1923).

93. Heinrich Mann (1871–1950).

94. Alfred Vierkandt (1867–1953): *Der Dualismus im modernen Weltbild* (Berlin: Pan-Verlag, 1923).

95. Christian Herrmann (b. 1865): *Sozialistische Monatshefte* (1923): 287.

96. Theo van Doesburg (1883–1931).

97. Piet Mondrian (1872–1944).

98. Döcker (see note 57).

99. Theo van Doesburg, "Tot een beeldende architectuur," *De Stijl* 6, nos. 6–7: 78.

Illustration Credits

Every effort has been made to locate all copyright holders for the images reproduced in this book. The publishers invite any copyright holders they have not been able to reach to contact them so that full acknowledgment may be given in subsequent editions.

The following sources have granted permission to reproduce illustrations in this book (numbers refer to the pages where the illustrations appear; in the case where two or more images appear per page, letters are used to differentiate):

117   Stiftung Archiv der Akademie der Künste, Sammlung Baukunst, Berlin.

151, 152   The Frank Lloyd Wright Archives, Scottsdale, Arizona.

153, 154   Albert Kahn Associates, Inc., Detroit.

155a   Knud Lönberg-Holm Archive, New York.

155b   Chicago Architectural Photographing Company.

158, 159   AEG, Frankfurt.

162a   Elisabeth Weber-Belling, Munich.

165, 166a, b   Busch-Reisinger Museum (BR GA 3.4; BR GA 6.6; BR GA 6.3a), Harvard University Art Museums, Cambridge. Gift of Walter Gropius.

167a   Dr. T. Deffke, Germany, and B. Sülzen, Germany.

167c, 168, 169a, b   Stiftung Archiv der Akademie der Künste, Sammlung Baukunst, Berlin.

170a, b   The Art Institute of Chicago.

172, 173   Mrs. Esther Mendelsohn Joseph, San Francisco.

174   Ludwig Mies van der Rohe. Concrete Office Building, 1922. Perspective. Charcoal, crayon on tan paper, 54½ x 113¾". The Mies van der Rohe Archive. The Museum of Modern Art, New York. Gift of the architect. Photograph furnished by The Museum of Modern Art, New York.

175   Lichtbildverlag für Kunstgeschichte Dr. F. Stoedtner, Düsseldorf.

176a, b, 177a   Stiftung Archiv der Akademie der Künste, Sammlung Baukunst, Berlin.

177b   The Getty Research Institute for the History of Art and the Humanities, Santa Monica, Archive no. 850129, vol. B, no. 2.16. Photographer: Ernst Scheel, Hamburg. Courtesy The Getty Research Institute Resource Collections and Martha Scheel.

180   Prof. Dr. phil. habil. Heinrich Taut, Lehnitz.

181a Courtesy Architectural Drawing Collection, University Art Museum, University of California, Santa Barbara, and Knud Lönberg-Holm Archive, New York.

181b, 182, 183 Stiftung Archiv der Akademie der Künste, Sammlung Baukunst, Berlin.

184, 185a,b Knud Lönberg-Holm Archive, New York.

186 © 1994 Artists Rights Society (ARS), New York/SPADEM, Paris.

187 Marianne Le Coeur, Paris.

188–89 Musée des Beaux-Arts de Lyon, inv. no. 1952–38.

190–91 Musée des Beaux-Arts de Lyon, inv. no. 1952–39.

196, 197 © 1994 Artists Rights Society (ARS), New York/SPADEM, Paris.

202a Rotterdam, Nederlands Architectuurinstituut, Van Eesteren III.168. Wies van Moorsel, Amsterdam, and Nederlands Architectuurinstituut/ Collection Van Eesteren, Fluck en Van Lohuizenfoundation, The Hague.

202b Rijksdienst Beeldende Kunst, The Hague, inv. no. AB 9127. Courtesy Wies van Moorsel, Amsterdam.

203a,b Oud A2.23. © 1995 Estate of J. J. P. Oud/VAGA, New York.

205a Como, Museo Archeologico "P. Giovio," no. 295. Courtesy Museo Archeologico.

206, 207 Mrs. Lillian Kiesler, New York.

208a,b, 209 © 1994 Artists Rights Society (ARS), New York/VBK, Vienna.

210 Deutsche Fotothek, Sächsische Landesbibliothek, Dresden, no. 181 219.

217 © 1994 Artists Rights Society (ARS), New York/VG Bild-Kunst, Bonn.

218–19 *Cité contemporaine pour 3 millions d'habitants.* Fondation Le Corbusier, Paris, no. 30827. © 1994 Artists Rights Society (ARS), New York/SPADEM, Paris.

220a Maison Citrohan, 1922. Fondation Le Corbusier, Paris. © 1994 Artists Rights Society (ARS), New York/SPADEM, Paris.

220b © 1994 Artists Rights Society (ARS), New York/SPADEM, Paris.

220c Maison Citrohan, 1922. Fondation Le Corbusier, Paris, no. 20708. © 1994 Artists Rights Society (ARS), New York/SPADEM, Paris.

225 ArkitekturMuseet, Stockholm.

231 Wenzel-Hablik Stiftung, Itzehoe.

Bibliography of Works by Adolf Behne

With some corrections and additions, this bibliography is based on those provided by Janos Frecot in *Werkbundarchiv*, vol. 1, ed. Janos Frecot and Diethart Kerbs (Berlin: Werkbund-Archiv, 1972), 85–116, and by Haila Ochs in Adolf Behne, *Architekturkritik in der Zeit und über die Zeit hinaus: Texte, 1913–1946*, ed. Haila Ochs (Basel: Birkhäuser, 1994), 181–95. Behne's extremely broad interests and many publications in both the professional and popular press make the location of his complete oeuvre extremely difficult. In all probability, therefore, the following list remains incomplete.

Books and Contributions to Books

1912 *Der Inkrustationsstil in Toscana*. Berlin: Emil Ebering.

1914 *Die Kunst Asiens*. Berlin: Verlag des Zentralbildungsausschusses der Sozial-demokratischen Partei Deutschlands [three lectures].

1915 *Zur neuen Kunst*. Berlin: Verlag *Der Sturm* [a 2nd ed. was published in 1917].

1917 *Oranienburg: Ein Beispiel für Stadtbetrachtungen*. Flugschrift des Dürerbundes 171. Munich: Georg Callwey.

1919 "Alte und neue Plakate." In *Das politische Plakat*, 5–23. Berlin-Charlottenburg: Verlag Das Plakat.

Response to questionnaire. In *Ja! Stimmen des Arbeitsrates für Kunst in Berlin*, 14–16. Charlottenburg: Photographische Gesellschaft, 1919.

Volk, Kunst und Bildung: Eine Flugschrift. Berlin: "Der Arbeiterrat," ca. 1919.

"Die Wiedergeburt der Baukunst." In Bruno Taut, *Die Stadtkrone*, 115–31. Jena: Eugen Diederichs.

Die Wiederkehr der Kunst. Leipzig: Kurt Wolff.

1920 Introduction. In *Ruf zum Bauen: Zweite Buchpublikation des Arbeiterrats für Kunst*, 3–6. Berlin: Ernst Wasmuth.

Der Sieg der Farbe: Die entscheidende Zeit unserer Malerei in 40 farbigen Licht-drucken. Berlin: Photographische Gesellschaft [eight installments of five color plates each].

1921 "Das Freiheitsbild in der Kunst und seine Vorgeschichte." In *Die Befreiung der Menschheit: Freiheitsideen in Vergangenheit und Gegenwart*, 1–44. Leipzig.

1922 *Holländische Baukunst in der Gegenwart.* Berlin: Ernst Wasmuth [a 2nd ed. was published in 1929].

1923 *Die Sammlung Gabrielson.* Göteborg.

1924 *Ausstellung J. Ryback: Berlin, 1923–1924.* Berlin: Lutze & Vogt.

1925 *Blick über die Grenze: Baukunst des Auslandes.* Bausteine 2–3. Berlin: Otto Stollberg.

    Heinrich Zille. Graphiker der Gegenwart 12. Berlin: Willy Weise.

    Die Überfahrt am Schreckenstein: Eine Einführung in die Kunst. Berlin: Arbeiter-Jugend Verlag.

    "Vom neuen Bauen." In *Flemmings Knabenbuch.* Vol. 6. Berlin.

    Von Kunst zur Gestaltung: Eine Einführung in die Kunst. Berlin: Arbeiter-Jugend Verlag.

1926 *Der moderne Zweckbau.* Berlin: Drei Masken-Verlag.

1927 *Max Taut: Bauten und Pläne.* Berlin: F. E. Hübsch.

    Neues Wohnen — Neues Bauen. Prometheus-Bücher. Leipzig: Hesse & Becker [a 2nd ed. was published in 1930].

1928 *Die frühen Meister: Eine Einführung in die Schönheiten alter Bilder.* Berlin: Deutsche Buch-Gemeinschaft.

    Eine Stunde Architektur. Stuttgart: Akademischer Verlag Fritz Wedekind.

1929 *Berlin in Bildern.* Edited by Adolf Behne. Vienna: Hans Epstein [photographs by Sasha Stone].

    Das neue Berlin: Monatshefte für Probleme der Großstadt. Edited by Adolf Behne and Martin Wagner. 12 vols. Berlin: Deutsche Bauzeitung [also appeared as *Das neue Berlin: Großstadtprobleme.* Berlin: Deutsche Bauzeitung, 1929].

1930 "Kind und lebendige Gegenwart." In *Museum und Schule,* 44ff. Berlin.

1931 *Wochenende und was man dazu braucht.* Schaubücher 26. Zurich: Orell Füssli.

1935 Introduction and selection and explanation of illustrations. In Dimitij Sergeevic Mereschkowskij, *Leonardo da Vinci: Historischer Roman.* Liebhaberdrucke der Deutschen Buch-Gemeinschaft 3. Berlin: Deutsche Buch-Gemeinschaft.

1936 Postscript and selection of illustrations. In Johann Wolfgang von Goethe, *Briefe an Frau von Stein, nebst den Tagebüchern aus Italien und Briefe von Frau von Stein.* 2 vols. Berlin: Deutsche Buch-Gemeinschaft.

1938 *Die Stile Europas: Von den Griechen bis zum Ausgang des Barocks.* Berlin: Deutsche Buch-Gemeinschaft.

1940 *In Stein und Erz: Meisterwerke deutscher Plastik von Theoderich bis Maximilian.* Edited by Adolf Behne. Berlin: Deutsche Buch-Gemeinschaft.

1943 *Alte deutsche Zeichner: Meisterwerke deutscher Graphik von den Karolingern bis zum Barock.* Berlin: Deutsche Buch-Gemeinschaft.

1945 "Entartete Kunst — eine Hitler-Lüge." Lecture at opening ceremony, Volkhochschule Wilmersdorf, Berlin, 30 June [reprinted in *Entartete Kunst.* Berlin: Carl Habel Verlagsbuchhandlung, 1947].

Introduction. In *Gemälde, Plastik, Graphik.* Exh. cat. Vol. 1.

1946 "Die Freiheit der Kunst." In Rathaus Berlin-Weißensee, *Kunstchau, Malerei, Graphik, Plastik,* 7–10. Exh. cat.

Heinrich Ehmsen. Edited by Adolf Behne. Kunst der Gegenwart 2. Potsdam: Eduard Stichnote.

Introduction. In *Ausstellung Berliner Künstler in Potsdam,* 3–4. Exh. cat.

1947 *Entartete Kunst.* Berlin: Carl Habel Verlagsbuchhandlung.

Heinrich Zille. Edited by Adolf Behne. Hefte der Kunst 1. Halle: E. Morgner.

Introduction. "150 Jahre soziale Strömungen in der bildenden Kunst." In *Kunstausstellung, Kulturwoche des FBGB,* 5–10. Berlin.

Introduction. In *Ludwig Waldschmidt.* Exh. cat. Berlin.

Karl Hofer. Künstler unserer Zeit. Berlin: Deutscher Kunstverlag.

Max Dungert zum Gedächtnis. Exh. cat. Berlin.

1948 "Heinrich Zille." In *Berliner Almanach,* 37–43. Berlin.

Introduction. "Karikaturen, Plakate, Portraits 1848." In *Ausstellung des Kulturbundes zur demokratischen Erneuerung Deutschlands.*

Josef Hegebarth, Graphik und Temperabilder. Exh. cat. Berlin.

Werner Scholz, Gemälde und Pastelle. Exh. cat. Berlin.

Werner Scholz. Kunst der Gegenwart. Potsdam: Eduard Stichnote.

1949 *Festgabe an Carl Hofer zum siebzigsten Geburtstag 11. X. 1948.* Edited by Adolf Behne and Gerhart Strauss. Potsdam: Eduard Stichnote. [Behne began the editing, which was completed after his death by Strauss.]

Heinrich-Zille-Studien. Edited by Adolf Behne. Berlin: Das neue Berlin.

1963 "Architekten." In *Bruno Taut: Frühlicht: Eine Folge für Verwirklichung des neuen Baugedankens, 1920–1922,* edited Ulrich Conrads, 126–35. Ullstein Bauwelt Fundamente 8. Berlin: Ullstein [this essay originally appeared in *Frühlicht* 2 (winter 1921–1922): 55–58].

1964 *Der moderne Zweckbau.* Edited by Felix Schwarz and Frank Gloor. Ullstein Bauwelt Fundamente 10. Berlin: Ullstein [reprint of edition of 1926 with a few less illustrations and an introduction by Ulrich Conrads].

1969 "Dammerstock." In *"Die Form": Stimme des Deutschen Werkbundes, 1925–1934,* edited by Felix Schwarz and Frank Gloor, 168–74. Ullstein Bauwelt Fundamente 24. Gütersloh: Bertelsmann Fachverlag Reinhard

Mohn [this essay originally appeared in *Die Form* 5, no. 6 (1930): 163–66].

1972 "Bibliographische Berichte: Adolf Behne." In *Werkbundarchiv*, vol. 1, edited by Janos Frecot and Diethart Kerbs, 81–128. Berlin: Werkbund-Archiv. [In addition to being a first basic Behne bibliography, this publication contains reprints of several published and unpublished essays, as well as letters written to Behne.]

1984 *Eine Stunde Architektur*. Architextbook 5. Berlin: Archibook-Verlag [contains reprints of *Eine Stunde Architektur*. Stuttgart: Heinrich Fink, 1928 (abridged); "Von der Sachlichkeit," introduction to *Max Taut: Bauten und Pläne*. Berlin: F. E. Hübsch, 1927; and "Dammerstock," *Die Form* 5, no. 6, 1930: 163–66].

1988 *Das neue Berlin: Großstadtprobleme*. Edited by Adolf Behne and Martin Wagner. Introduction by Julius Posener. Basel: Birkhäuser [reprint of *Das neue Berlin: Großstadtprobleme*. Berlin: Deutsche Bauzeitung, 1929].

1990 "Art, Craft, Technology." Translated by Christiane Crasemann Collins, in Francesco Dal Co, *Figures of Architecture and Thought: German Architecture Culture, 1880–1920*, 324–28. New York: Rizzoli [originally published as "Kunst, Handwerk, Technik," *Die Neue Rundschau* 33, no. 2 (1922): 1021–37].

1994 *Architekturkritik in der Zeit und über die Zeit hinaus: Texte, 1913–1946*. Edited by Haila Ochs. Basel: Birkhäuser.

Periodicals

1910 "Ein erzieherisches Museum." *Die Hilfe* 16: 835–36.

"Landschaften von Otto Reiniger." *Die Hilfe* 16: 244.

"Der Museumskatalog: Prinzipien einer populären Abfassung." *Die Hilfe* 16: 272–74.

1911 "Häusliche Kunstsammlungen." *Wissenschaftliche Rundschau* 2 (1911–1912): 229–32.

"Im Kampfe um die Kunst." *Wissenschaftliche Rundschau* 2 (1911–1912): 77–81.

"Lovis Corinths Golgatha-Bild." *Die Hilfe* 17: 30–31.

"Max Klingers neue Blätter 'Vom Tode.'" *Die Hilfe* 17: 255.

"Max Liebermann." *Wissenschaftliche Rundschau* 2 (1911–1912): 372–74.

"Max Slevogt." *Die Hilfe* 17: 461.

"Peter Behrens und die toskanische Architektur des 12. Jahrhunderts." *Kunstgewerbeblatt*, n.s., 23 (1911–1912): 45–50.

1912   "Bruno Taut." *Pan* 3, no. 23 (1912–1913): 538–40.

"El Greco." *Die Hilfe* 18: 286–87.

"Kunstliteratur." *Die Hilfe* 18: 477–78.

"Kunst und Gesetzmäßigkeit." *Wissenschaftliche Rundschau* 3 (1912–1913): 49–52.

"Die neue Sezession." *Die Hilfe* 18: 207.

Review of *Architektur und Kunstgewerbe in Alt-Holland*, by A. Jolles. *Kunstgewerbeblatt*, n.s., 24 (1912–1913): 220.

"Sammelreferat kunstwissenschaftliche Neuerscheinungen." *Wissenschaftliche Rundschau* 3 (1912–1913): 1–2 [supplement].

1913   "Die aesthetischen Theorien der modernen Baukunst." *Preussische Jahrbücher* 154 (October): 274–83.

"Die Bedeutung der Farbe in Falkenberg." *Gartenstadt* 7, no. 12: 249.

"Die Berliner Herbstausstellung." *Die Gegenwart* 84: 778–80 n.

"Der Berliner Herbstsalon." *Die neue Kunst* 1 (1913–1914): 223–25.

"Die Berliner Sezession." *Die Gegenwart* 83, no. 42: 343–45.

"Die Botschaft in Washington." [Unknown periodical] 7, no. 3: 429–31.

"Der erste deutsche Herbstsalon." *Die Tat* 5 (1913–1914): 841–43.

"Fortschritte in der Kunstkritik." *Kunstgewerbeblatt*, n.s., 24: 46–50.

"Die grosse Berliner Kunstausstellung." *Die Gegenwart* 84: 435ff. and 454ff.

"Der Herbstsalon." *Die Gegenwart* 84: 668–69.

"Heutige Industriebauten." *Velhagen und Klasings Monatshefte* 28, no. 2 (1913–1914): 53–64.

"Die Juryfreie." *Die Gegenwart* 84: 587–89.

"Der Kaiser und die Kunst." *Die Tat* 5 (1913–1914): 576–87.

"Kunst und Milieu." *Die Gegenwart* 84: 599–619.

"Die Leipziger Baufach-Ausstellung." *Die Tat* 5 (1913–1914): 504–7.

"Der Maler Franz Marc." *Pan* 3, no. 26: 616–18.

"Der Märchenbrunnen." *Die Hilfe* 19: 586.

"Max Pechstein." *Die Hilfe* 19: 139.

"Max Pechstein." *Die neue Kunst* 1 (1913–1914): 221–23.

"Moderne Kunstbücher." *Die Tat* 5 (1913–1914): 936–42.

"Das Monument des Eisens auf der Leipziger Baufachausstellung." *Die Um–schau* 17: 619–21.

"Populäre Kunstwerke." *Sozialistische Monatshefte* 19, no. 1: 423–25.

"Romantiker, Pathetiker und Logiker im modernen Industriebau." *Preussische Jahrbücher* 154 (October): 171–74.

"Vom Kunstschriftsteller." *Kunstgewerbeblatt*, n.s., 24: 154–55.

1914 "Arbeitsdarstellungen in der Kunst." *Die neue Zeit* 31: 129–33.

"Biologie und Kubismus." *Der Sturm* 5, nos. 11–12 (1914–1915): 68–71.

"Bruno Taut." *Der Sturm* 4, nos. 198–99: 182–83 [reprinted in *Die Berliner Moderne, 1885–1914*, edited by J. Schutte, 592–96. Stuttgart: Sprengel, 1987].

"Deutsche Expressionisten." *Der Sturm* 5, nos. 17–18 (1914–1915): 114–15.

"Deutsche Werkbund-Ausstellung in Köln." *Allgemeiner Beobachter* 4, no. 7: 90–93.

"Dürfen wir uns noch mit Kunst beschäftigen?" *Sozialistische Monatshefte* 20, no. 2: 1181–84.

"Das Ende der Berliner National-Galerie." *Die Gegenwart* 85: 201–3 n.

"Die erste Ausstellung der freien Sezession." *Die Gegenwart* 85: 261–64.

"Expressionismus." *Allgemeiner Beobachter* 3: 273–74.

"Geh. Baurat Otto Wagner — Wien." *Deutsche Kunst und Dekoration* 35 (1914–1915): 382–84, 390.

"Das Glashaus." *Die Umschau* 18: 712–16.

"Die grosse Berliner Kunstausstellung." *Die Gegenwart* 86: 423–25.

"Heutige Industriebauten." *Die Welt des Kaufmanns* 10: 215–19.

"Der Inkrustationsstil zu Lucca." *Zeitschrift für Geschichte der Architektur* 7 (1914–1919): 14–26.

"Inkrustation und Mosaik." *Monatshefte für Kunstwissenschaft* 7: 55–60.

"Kinoarchitekturen." *Bild und Film* 4, nos. 7–8 (1914–1915): 133–39.

"Die Kölner Werkbundausstellung." *Die Gegenwart* 86: 501–6.

"Kunst, Geschmack und Nachahmung." *Kunstgewerbeblatt*, n.s., 26 (1914–1915): 142–44.

"Los von Paris." Ein Beitrag zur deutschen Mode." *Die Gegenwart* 86: 665–67.

"Die Maler Munch." *Die Gegenwart* 85: 127–28.

"Das Monument des Eisens von Taut und Hoffmann auf der Internationalen Baufachausstellung in Leipzig." *Kunstgewerbeblatt*, n.s., 25: 86–88.

"Museen als Volksbildungsstätten." *Die Tat* 6 (1914–1915): 63–71.

"Die neue Nationalgalerie." *Die Tat* 6 (1914–1915): 442–45.

"Die neue Sezession." *Die Gegenwart* 85: 390–92.

"Ein neues Hausl." [Unknown periodical] 1 (March): 32–33 [reprinted under the title "Bruno Taut," in *Die Berliner Moderne, 1885–1914*, edited by J. Schutte, 592–96. Stuttgart: Sprengel, 1987].

"Die Säule." *Kunstgewerbeblatt*, n.s., 25: 144–46.

"Ungerechte Selbstvorwürfe." *Deutsche Kunst und Dekoration* 35 (1914–1915): 54ff., 65, 68.

"Volkstümliche Kunst." *Allgemeiner Beobachter* 4, no. 2: 18–19.

"Zur neuen Kunst." *Der Sturm* 5, no. 1 (1914–1915): 2–3 [advance section from *Zur neuen Kunst,* Sturm-Buch 7, 1915].

1915 "Expressionistische Architektur." *Der Sturm* 5, nos. 19–20 (January): 175.

"Die Fabrik." *Illustriertes Jahrbuch* (Berlin): 863–66.

"Gartenstadt-Architekturen." *Illustriertes Jahrbuch* (Berlin): 196–209.

"Gedanken über kunst und Zweck, dem Glashause gewidmet." *Kunstgewer-beblatt,* n.s., 27 (1915–1916): 1–4.

"Der Hass der Neutralen." *Die Tat* 7: 340–41.

"Das Können in der primitiven Kunst." *Kunstgewerbeblatt,* n.s., 27 (1915–1916): 44–46.

"Der Krieg in der bildenden Kunst." *Illustriertes Jahrbuch* (Berlin): 788–92, 828–33.

"Der Krieg und die künstlerische Produktion." *Die Umschau* 19: 268–73.

"Kunst und Biographie." *Deutsche Kunst und Dekoration* 36: 360–66.

"Majorität und Qualität." *Kunstgewerbeblatt,* n.s., 27 (1915–1916): 190–96.

"Ostpreussische Architekten in Berlin: Max Taut." Newspaper report [reprinted in *Max Taut, 1884–1967: Zeichnungen, Bauten,* 54ff. Berlin: 1984].

"Paul Scheerbart." *Zeit-Echo* 5 (1915–1916): 77.

1916 "Emmichs Grab." *Die Tat* 8 (1916–1917): 1032–33.

"Franz Marc zum Gedächtnis." *Die Tat* 8 (1916–1917): 1028–29.

"Museen als Volksbildungsstätten." *Der Kunsthandel* 8: 264–66.

"Stilbemerkungen zur modernen Kunst." *Die neue Rundschau* 27, no. 1: 553–60.

"Stil und Naturalismus." *Die Werkstatt der Kunst* 16: 131–33.

"Über Kunstkritik." *Sozialistische Monatshefte* 22, no. 3: 1305–8.

"Unsere Baukunst und das Morgenland." *Sozialistische Monatshefte* 22, no. 1: 155–57.

"Zu den Soldatenfriedhöfen Leberecht Migges in Brüssel-Evere und Wilhelmshaven." *Bau-Rundschau:* 193–205.

1917 "Biologie und Kubismus (Über Jakob von Uexküll: Bausteine zu einer biologischen Weltanschauung)." *Die Tat* 9 (1917–1918): 694–705.

"Einleitung zu einer Betrachtung des Morgenlandes." *Sozialistische Monatshefte* 23, no. 2: 588–90.

"Ist das Schwäche? (Über die russische Revolution)." *Sozialistische Monatshefte* 23, no. 2: 1285–88.

"Kritik des Werkbundes." *Die Tat* 9: 430–38 [reprinted in *Werkbund Archiv* 1, edited by Janos Frecot und Diethart Kerbs, 118–28. Berlin: Werkbund-Archiv, 1972].

"Paul Klee." *Die weissen Blätter* 4: 167–69.

"Das reproduktive Zeitalter." *Marsyas* 3 (November–December): 219–26.

"Rom als Vorbild?" *Sozialistische Monatshefte* 23, no. 1: 588–90.

"Vom einheitlichen Ziel der Kunst." *Deutsche Kunst und Dekoration* 41 (1917–1918): 18–29.

"Wem gehört die Gotik?" *Sozialistische Monatshefte* 23, no. 2: 1126–29.

1918   "Arnold Topp." *Neue Blätter für Kunst und Dichtung* 10, no. 2 (1918–1919): 625–27.

"Die Einheit der russischen Kunst." *Sozialistische Monatshefte* 24, no. 2: 745–48.

"Heinrich Zille." *Sozialistische Monatshefte* 24, no. 2: 1072–77.

"Hermann Essig." *Die Tat* 10, no. 1 (1918–1919): 341–49.

"Die Kathedrale von Reims." *Sozialistische Monatshefte* 24, no. 1: 346–51.

"Kunst oder Sentimentalität?" *Neue Blätter für Kunst und Dichtung* 1 (1918–1919): 3–7.

"Kunstwende?" *Sozialistische Monatshefte* 24, no. 2: 946–52.

"Die russische Aesthetik." *Sozialistische Monatshefte* 24, no. 2: 894–96.

"Die russische Kirche." *Sozialistische Monatshefte* 24, no. 2: 790–94.

"Die russische Kunst und die europäische Kunstgeschichte." *Sozialistische Monatshefte* 24, no. 2: 691–94.

"Über den Dichter Hermann Essig." *Sozialistische Monatshefte* 24, no. 1: 34–37.

"Die Überwindung des Tektonischen in der russischen Baukunst." *Sozialistische Monatshefte* 24, no. 2: 833–37.

"Zum Thema Kunst und Kultur des Altertums." *Der Kunstfreund* 6, nos. 1–3 (1918–1919): 12–18.

1919   "Aufruf." *Cicerone* 11: 264 [reprinted in *Arbeitsrat für Kunst, 1918–1921*, 103. Berlin: Akademie der Künste, 1980].

"Ausschreibewesen." *Sozialistische Monatshefte* 25, no. 1: 683ff.

"Ausstellung von Mosaiken." *Cicerone* 11: 141–42.

"Baukultur." *Sozialistische Monatshefte* 25, no. 1: 423ff.

"Die Berliner Sezession." *Die neue Rundschau* 30: 880–84.

"Bruno Taut." *Neue Blätter für Kunst und Dichtung* 2 (1919–1920): 13–15.

"Das degenerierte Frankreich und das junge Deutschland." *Sozialistische Monatshefte* 25, no. 2: 1220–22.

"Denkmalschutz." *Sozialistische Monatshefte* 25, no. 1: 851.

"Einfacher Hausrat." *Freiheit* 189: 2.

"Expressionismus für Arbeiter." *Freiheit* 378: 2.

"Farbfreudigkeit." *Sozialistische Monatshefte* 25, no. 1: 684.

"Farbiges Bauen." *Sozialistische Monatshefte* 25, no. 1: 1119.

"Frankreichs Wiederaufbau." *Sozialistische Monatshefte* 25, no. 1: 849–51.

"Der Gang der deutschen Malkunst seit Dürer." *Sozialistische Monatshefte* 25, no. 1: 262–65.

"Geschmack und Kunst." *Sozialistische Monatshefte* 25, no. 1: 1120ff.

"Graphik und Plastik von Mitgliedern der Novembergruppe." *Menschen* 2 (December).

"Hermann Essig." *Feuer* 1, no. 2 (1919–1920): 665–74.

"Historische, aesthetische und kristische Kunstbetrachtung." *Das hohe Ufer* 1, no. 1 (January): 134–36.

"Der Isenheimer Altar von M. Grünewald." *Die freie Welt* 32: 4ff., 8.

"Kunstausstellung Berlin 1919." *Freiheit* 352: 2.

"Lyrische oder architektonische Buehne?" *Die neue Schaubühne* 1: 77–80.

"Die Pflicht zur Wahrhaftigkeit." *Sozialistische Monatshefte* 25, no. 2: 720–24.

"Poelzig." *Sozialistische Monatshefte* 25, no. 1: 131–34.

"Siedelungsbau." *Sozialistische Monatshefte* 25, no. 1: 1120.

"Die Überwindung der Kunst-Akademie." *Freiheit* 198: 3.

"Unbekannte Architekten." *Sozialistische Monatshefte* 25, no. 1: 422–223.

"Unsere moralische Krisis." *Sozialistische Monatshefte* 25, no. 1: 34–38.

"Vorschlag einer brüderlichen Zusammenkunft der Künstler aller Länder." *Sozialistische Monatshefte* 25, no. 1: 155–57.

"Die Waffen nieder!" *Süddeutsche Freiheit, München* 1, nos. 15–16 (March).

"Was wird aus den Musen?" *Freiheit* 151: 2–3.

"Werkstattbesuche: Fritz Stuckenberg." *Cicerone* 11: 281–86.

"Werkstattbesuche: Jefim Golyscheff." *Cicerone* 11: 722–26.

"Zeitdokumente." *Sozialistische Monatshefte* 25, no. 1: 682ff.

"Zirkus." *Freiheit* 210: 2–3.

"Zum Tode Wilhelm Lehmbrucks." *Freiheit* 156: 2.

"Zu Rembrandts 250. Geburtstag." *Die freie Welt* 20 (October): 4–5.

"Zu Rembrandts 250. Todestag." *Die Gewerkschaft* 23: 827–29.

"Zur neuen Kunst." *Freiheit* 539: 2–3.

1920   "Baukultur." *Sozialistische Monatshefte* 26: 70ff.

"Dada." *Freiheit*, no. 269: 3.

"Emil Nolde." *Freiheit*, no. 123: 2.

"Expressionistenschau in Scheveningen und Arnhem." *Cicerone* 12: 726–27.

"Fabrikbau als Reklame." *Das Plakat* 11, no. 6: 274–76.

"Heinrich Zille." *Jahrbuch der jungen Kunst*: 110–16.

"Kunstausstellung für Arbeiter." *Freiheit* (January) [reprinted in Akademie der Künste, *Arbeitsrat für Kunst, 1918–1921*, 111. Exh. cat. Berlin: Akademie der Künste, 1980].

"Kunstbericht." *Freiheit*, no. 521: 2.

"Kunstpflege." *Sozialistische Monatshefte* 26: 991ff.

"Kunstunterricht." *Sozialistische Monatshefte* 26: 1041ff.

"Kurt Schwitters." *Freiheit*, no. 140: 2.

"Laubenkolonien." *Sozialistische Monatshefte* 26, no. 1: 439–40.

"Nein Kokoschka!" *Freiheit*, no. 123: 2.

"Neues Bauen." *Illustrierte Zeitung* (Leipzig) 154, no. 4000: 13.

"Neues Bauen." *Sozialistische Monatshefte* 26, no. 1: 629–30.

"Olbrich." *Sozialistische Monatshefte* 26: 310ff.

"Oud: Over de toekomstige bouwkunst en haar architectonische mogelijkheden." *Opbouw* (February).

"Paul Gösch." *Cicerone* 12: 150–54.

"Paul Gösch." *Jahrbuch der jungen Kunst*: 68–72.

"Reichskunstwart." *Sozialistische Monatshefte* 26: 990ff.

"Siedlungswesen." *Sozialistische Monatshefte* 26, no. 1: 70.

"Sozialisierung von Kunst und Wissenschaft." *Sozialistische Monatshefte* 26, no. 1: 191–94.

"Stadtschönheit (Dresden)." *Sozialistische Monatshefte* 26, no. 1: 438–39.

"Von holländischer Baukunst." *Feuer* 2 (1920–1921): 279–92.

"Ein Vorschlag (Über die politische Verantwortung der Presse)." *Sozialistische Monatshefte* 26: 260–63.

"Weimar (Bauhaus)." *Sozialistische Monatshefte* 26, no. 1: 69.

"Werkbund." *Sozialistische Monatshefte* 26, no. 1 (January): 68–69 [reprinted in *Werkbund Archiv* 1, edited by Janos Frecot und Diethart Kerbs, 138–40. Berlin: Werkbund-Archiv, 1972].

"Werkstattbesuche: Heinrich Zille." *Cicerone* 12: 271–77.

"Wolkenkratzer." *Sozialistische Monatshefte* 26: 1040ff.

1921 "Architekten." *Frühlicht* 2 (winter 1921–1922): 55–58 [reprinted in *Bruno Taut: Frühlicht: Eine Folge für die Verwirklichung des neuen Baugedankens, 1920–1922*, edited by Ulrich Conrads, 126–35. Ullstein Bauwelt Fundamente 8. Berlin: Ullstein, 1963].

"August Macke." *Freiheit* 116: 2–3.

"Bauwesen." *Sozialistische Monatshefte* 27: 783.

"Berlin-Bauten." *Sozialistische Monatshefte* 27, no. 1: 165–66.

"Berlin: Friedrichstadt." *Sozialistische Monatshefte* 27: 1079.

"Bild und Buchstabe." *Das Plakat* 12: 338–44.

"Buchkultur." *Sozialistische Monatshefte* 27, no. 2: 780–83.

"Cuypers †." *Sozialistische Monatshefte* 27: 372f.

"Danzig: Wolkenkratzer." *Sozialistische Monatshefte* 27: 862ff.

"Deutschland und die europäische Kunstbewegung." *Sozialistische Monatshefte* 27, no. 1: 297–301.

"Dresden: Hygienemuseum." *Sozialistische Monatshefte* 27: 166ff.

"Europa und die Architektur." *Sozialistische Monatshefte* 27, no. 1: 28–33.

"Fassaden-Erneuerung." *Sozialistische Monatshefte* 27, no. 2: 1077–78.

"Der Film als Kunstwerk." *Sozialistische Monatshefte* 27, no. 2: 1116–18.

"Der Film am Dienstag." *Freiheit* 452: 2.

"Holländische Baukunst der Gegenwart." *Wasmuths Monatshefte für Baukunst* 6 (1921–1922): 1–38.

"Industriebaukunst." *Sozialistische Monatshefte* 27, no. 1: 167–68.

"Kaldenbach." *Sozialistische Monatshefte* 27: 519.

"Kleinmietshaus." *Sozialistische Monatshefte* 27: 518ff.

"Kunst der Strasse." *Die freie Welt* 39: 307–9.

"Kunst und Naturanschauung." *Feuer* 3 (1921–1922): 145–50.

"Kunst und Schule." *Sozialistische Monatshefte* 27, no. 2: 607–11.

"Mittelalterliches und modernes Bauen." *Soziale Bauwirtschaft* (15 July).

"Mode." *Sozialistische Monatshefte* 27, no. 1: 373–74.

"Die neue Aufgabe der Kunst." *Die freie Welt* 51: 406f.

"Die neue Aufgabe der Kunst." *Sozialistische Monatshefte* 27, no. 2: 813–15.

"Neue Kräfte in der Architektur." *Feuer* 3 (1921–1922): 269–76.

"Ornament." *Sozialistische Monatshefte* 27: 783.

"Oskar Fischer." *Jahrbuch der jungen Kunst*: 149–52.

"Osthaus †." *Sozialistische Monatshefte* 27: 372.

"Poelzig: Großes Schauspielhaus." *Sozialistische Monatshefte* 27, no. 1: 164–65.

"Qualität und Luxus." *Sozialistische Monatshefte* 27: 374.

"Sozialismus und Expressionismus." *Die freie Welt* 23: 179f.

"Städtebau." *Sozialistische Monatshefte* 27: 518.

"Städtebau." *Sozialistische Monatshefte* 27: 1079.

"Städteverunstaltung." *Sozialistische Monatshefte* 27, no. 2: 1078–79.

"Walter Kampmann." *Das Plakat* 12: 319–34.

"Werkstattbesuche: Oskar Fischer." *Cicerone* 13: 210–14.

"Zeitgemäße oder unzeitgemäße Erziehung?" *Sozialistische Monatshefte* 27, no. 2: 890–93.

"Die Zukunft unserer Architektur." *Sozialistische Monatshefte* 27, no. 1: 90–94.

"Zum Fall Picasso." *Die neue Rundschau* 32, no. 2: 783–84.

1922 "Ackerscholle wider Futurismus." *Seidels Reklame* (September): 181ff.

"Ausstellungen." *Sozialistische Monatshefte* 28: 901f.

"Baukultur." *Sozialistische Monatshefte* 28: 327f.

"Baukultur." *Sozialistische Monatshefte* 28: 431f.

"Baukultur." *Sozialistische Monatshefte* 28: 902f.

"Breslau: Bebauungsplan." *Sozialistische Monatshefte* 28: 757f.

"Buchkultur." *Sozialistische Monatshefte* 28, no. 1: 145–46.

"Buchkultur." *Sozialistische Monatshefte* 28: 903f.

"Das bunte Magdeburg und die 'Miama.'" *Seidels Reklame* (October): 201–6.

"Die Deutsche Baukunst seit 1850." *Soziale Bauwirtschaft:* 146–49, 173–74, 186–87, 203–6, 229–31 [reprinted in abridged form as "'Vom Anhalter Bahnhof bis zum Bauhaus' 1922." *Bauwelt* 41–42 (1961): 1160ff].

"Entwürfe und Bauten von Walter Gropius." *Zentralblatt der Bauverwaltung* (December): 637–40.

"Expressionismus als Selbstzweck." *Sozialistische Monatshefte* 28, no. 1: 578–82.

"Farbige Fassaden." *Sozialistische Monatshefte* 28, no. 1: 430–31.

"Feininger und Corinth." *Freiheit* 46: 2–3.

"Der Grundriss." *Freiheit* 92: 2–3.

"Heinrich Zille als Plakatmaler." *Seidels Reklame* (December): 261–65.

"Hochhauspläne." *Sozialistische Monatshefte* 28: 759.

"Hochhausprobleme." *Sozialistische Monatshefte* 28: 326f.

"Holland." *Sozialistische Monatshefte* 28: 148.

"Ingenieurbauten." *Sozialistische Monatshefte* 28: 149.

"Junge französische Architektur." *Sozialistische Monatshefte* 28, no. 1: 512–19.

"Kritisches Programm." *Die Weltbühne* 18, no. 2: 6–7.

"Kunst, Handwerk, Technik." *Die neue Rundschau* 33, no. 2: 1021–37 [translated by Christiane Crasemann Collins as "Art, Craft, Technology," in Francesco Dal Co, *Figures of Architecture and Thought: German Architecture Culture, 1880–1920,* 324–38. New York: Rizzoli, 1990].

"Mode." *Sozialistische Monatshefte* 28: 149.

"Die neue Form der Eisenbahnreklame." *Die Eisenbahnreklame:* 30.

"Ein neuer Naturalismus? Eine Umfrage des Kunstblattes." *Das Kunstblatt* 6: 383–84.

"Neues vom Plakat." *Seidels Reklame* (July): 111–15.

"Das Plakat des Monats I." *Seidels Reklame* (November): 235.

"Das Plakat des Monats II." *Seidels Reklame* (December): 259.

"Plakate." *Sozialistische Monatshefte* 28: 150.

"Reklame." *Sozialistische Monatshefte* 28: 150f.

"Siedelungswesen." *Sozialistische Monatshefte* 28: 148.

"Der singende Fisch." *Freiheit* 4: 2.

"Der Staatsanwalt schützt das Bild." *Die Weltbühne* 18, no. 2: 545–48.

"Städtebau." *Sozialistische Monatshefte* 28: 758.

"Tagungen." *Sozialistische Monatshefte* 28: 432.

"Der Wettbewerb der Turmbau-Gesellschaft." *Wasmuths Monatshefte für Baukunst* 7 (1922–1923): 58–67.

"Wolkenkratzer." *Sozialistische Monatshefte* 28, no. 1: 147–48.

1923   "Allgemeines Niveau." *Sozialistische Monatshefte* 29: 453.

"Amerikanische Architektur." *Sozialistische Monatshefte* 29: 198–200.

"Amerikanische Architektur." *Vossische Zeitung* (April).

"Architektur." *MA* 8, Deutsches Sonderheft, nos. 5–6: 7.

"Ausstellung des Volkskommissariats für Kunst und Wissenschaft in Moskau." *Architectura*: 23f.

"Bauhausresumée." *Sozialistische Monatshefte* 29: 542–45.

"Das Bauhaus Weimar." *Die Weltbühne* 19, no. 2: 289–92.

"Baukultur." *Sozialistische Monatshefte* 29: 645.

"Die Bedeutung Cézannes." *Sozialistische Monatshefte* 29: 166–71.

"De Duitsche Tarenhis Bouw." *Wendingen* 5, no. 3: 15–17.

"Erfinder und Ölgötzen." *Die Weltbühne* 19, no. 1: 212–14.

"Farbe und Architektonik." *Sozialistische Monatshefte* 29: 69.

"Frankreich." *Sozialistische Monatshefte* 29: 646.

"Holland." *Sozialistische Monatshefte* 29: 453f.

"Die internationale Architektur-Ausstellung im Bauhaus zu Weimar." *Die Bauwelt*, no. 37: 533.

"Justi und die Modernen." *Die Weltbühne* 19, no. 1: 746–48.

"Kollegen — Kameraden." *Die Weltbühne* 19, no. 1: 133–35.

"Kriegserinnerungsmale." *Sozialistische Monatshefte* 29: 70f.

"Kroniek van de Duitsche Bouwkunst sedert het Einde van de Oorlog I, Chronik der Deutschen Baukunst seit Kriegsende II." *Bouwkundig Weekblad*: 29–34, 193–96, 211–12.

"Kronika nemeckého Stavebního umení po valcé." *Stavba*: 97–100.

"Das Kronprinzenpalais." *Die Weltbühne* 19, no. 1: 721–23.

"Kunst in Jena." *Vossische Zeitung* (August).

"Max Krause." *Architectura:* 144–46.

"Das moderne deutsche Plakat." *Deutscher Buch- und Steindrucker* 30 (1923–1924): 397–400.

"Das Musterwohnhaus der Bauhaus-Ausstellung." *Die Bauwelt,* no. 41: 591–92.

"Nemecky dopis." *Stavba:* 47–49.

"Neubauaufgaben." *Sozialistische Monatshefte* 29: 643–45.

"Die neue Nationalgalerie." *Die Weltbühne* 19, no. 1: 685–88.

"O Stavbe mest." *Stavba:* 145.

"Paula Modersohn und der Übergang zur Bildkonstruktion." *Sozialistische Monatshefte* 29: 294–99.

"Raffke baut." *Das Tagebuch* 4: 594–97.

"Siedelungswesen." *Sozialistische Monatshefte* 29: 645f.

"Städtebau." *Sozialistische Monatshefte* 29: 69f.

"De Tentoonstelling van 'Das Bauhaus' te Weimar." *Architectura:* 194ff.

"Tschechien." *Sozialistische Monatshefte* 29: 454.

"Über Städtebau." *G: Material zur elementaren Gestaltung* 2 (September): 2.

"Umenír Rusku." *Stavba:* 172–74.

"Verzamelaars en Musea." *Architectura:* 51f.

"Wohnkultur." *Sozialistische Monatshefte* 29: 70.

"Ein Wolkenkratzer-Wettbewerb." *Illustrierte Zeitung* (April).

"W.U.R." *Architectura:* 144.

1924 "Architektura." *Stavba* (1924–1925): 58f [Czech translation of "Architektur." *MA* 8, Deutsches Sonderheft, nos. 5–6 (1923): 7].

"Arthur Segal." *Die Weltbühne* 20, no. 2: 520–21.

"Baukultur." *Sozialistische Monatshefte* 30: 408f.

"Belgische Modernisten." *Die Bauwelt* 47: 1174–76.

"Deutsche Kunst in Moskau." *Die Weltbühne* 20, no. 2: 481–82.

"Deutschland boykottiert Paris." *Die Weltbühne* 20, no. 2: 961–62.

"Erarbeitete — oder gekaufte Schönheit?" *Almanach:* 41–49.

"Funktion und Form." *Sozialistische Monatshefte* 30: 767–68.

"Der gekränkte Kunstkenner." *Die Weltbühne* 20, no. 2: 639–40.

"Große Berliner Kunstausstellung." *Die Weltbühne* 20, no. 2: 66–68.

"Heinrich Zille." *Die Weltbühne* 20, no. 2: 560–61.

"Hoffmann, Taut, Gropius, Merz." *Die Weltbühne* 20, no. 1: 471–73.

"Karl Scheffler." *Die Weltbühne* 20, no. 2: 781–82.

"Kultur, Kunst und Reklame." *Der Pelikan* 19: 3–6.

"Die Kunst unter dem Strich." *Das Tagebuch* 5: 1601–2.

"Die moderne Fabrik." *Illustrierte Zeitung* (February).

"Moskauer Ausstellungsbauten 1923." *Die Bauwelt* 5: 65–66.

"Neubauten und Antiquitäten. Das Mosse-Haus. Das neue Gewerkschafts-haus. Die Sammlung neuer Kunst in Weimar. Berliner Sezession." *Die Weltbühne* 20, no. 1: 625–27.

"Die neue Tanzlegende." *Die Weltbühne* 20, no. 1: 307–8.

"Preußische Kunstverwaltung." *Die Weltbühne* 20, no. 2: 333–34.

"Provinz Berlin: Stadtbaurat Methusalem" [reprinted in *Bauwelt* 33 (1977): 1089].

"Publikum in Rußland." *Das neue Rußland* 1–2: 26–27.

"Reichskunstwart." *Das Tagebuch* 5: 212–13.

"Reklame." *Sozialistische Monatshefte* 30: 409f.

"Reklame als Bilder-Rätsel." *Das Tagebuch* 5: 844–48.

"Rußische Kunstberichte." *Die Weltbühne* 20, no. 1: 813–15, 852–53, 897–98.

"Rußlands Kunst von heute." *Die Bauwelt* 7: 99–100.

"Seddin." *Die Weltbühne* 20, no. 2: 747–49.

"Separatismus im Kronprinzenpalais." *Das Tagebuch* 5: 193–94.

"Snob und Antisnob. George Grosz, Franz Marc, Oskar Schlemmer, Moholy-Nagy." *Die Weltbühne* 20, no. 1: 34–37.

"Städtebau." *Sozialistische Monatshefte* 30: 406f.

"Die Strömungen in der gegenwärtigen deutschen Kunst." *Internationale Arbeiterhilfe*: 11–17 [in Russian].

"Über die moderne Baukunst Frankreichs." *Sozialistische Monatshefte* 30: 374–79.

"Der Unsinn der Kunst-Kommissionen." *Das Tagebuch* 5: 1006–7.

"Wettbewerb." *Sozialistische Monatshefte* 30: 806.

"'Wucht!' (Über Kriegerdenkmäler)." *Das Tagebuch* 5: 1156–57.

1925   "Abbau der Kunst." *Die Weltbühne* 21, no. 1: 57–59.

"Abschied vom Bauhaus von Weimar." *Die neue Erziehung* 7: 139f.

"Bilanz der Ausstellungen. (Juryfreie Ausstellung, Novembergruppe.)" *Die Weltbühne* 21, no. 2: 60–62.

"Das Bild als kategorischer Imperativ." *Sozialistische Monatshefte* 31: 627–31.

"Braucht Berlin eine Städtische Galerie?" *Die Weltbühne* 21, no. 2: 994–96.

"Das denkende Bild." *Die Weltbühne* 21, no. 1: 816–18.

"Der Film und die Bildkunst." *Der Kunstwanderer* 7: 377–79.

"Die Hauptstadt der Republik." *Sozialistische Monatshefte* 31: 410–13.

"Künstlerische Aktivität." *Sozialistische Monatshefte* 31: 26–29.

"Kunst und Klasse." *Kulturwille* 2: 154–55.

"Kunst, Wissenschaft, und Europa." *Sozialistische Monatshefte* 31: 223–25.

"Die Kunst zwischen Tod und Leben." *Das Schiff* 10 (October): 76.

"Ludwig Hoffmann; oder, Zum Thema Architektur-Kritik." *Wasmuths Monatshefte für Baukunst* 9: 352–54.

"Meyerhold." *Die Weltbühne* 21, no. 2: 727–28.

"Das moderne Buch und seine Montage." *Typographische Jahrbücher* 46: 368–71.

"Neues Bauen." *Das Schiff* 10 (October): 73–75.

"Der neue Stadtbaurat." *Das Tagebuch* 6: 277–78.

"Paul Scheerbart. Zur zehnten Wiederkehr seines Todestages." *Ostdeutsche Monatshefte* 6, no. 2 (1925–1926): 735–37.

"Preislisten." *Das Tagebuch* 6: 844–45.

"Schlachtfeld und Museumsinsel." *Die Weltbühne* 21, no. 2: 180–82.

"Schreibmaschine, Frans Hals, Lillian Gish, und Anderes." *Die Weltbühne* 21, no. 2: 456–58.

"Der Sieg der Farbe." *Die Form* 1, no. 2: 31–32.

"Der Stadtbaurat." *Die Weltbühne* 21, no. 2: 529–51.

"Die Stadt Berlin kauft Bilder." *Die Weltbühne* 21, no. 1: 32–33.

"Stagniert die Kunst?" *Sozialistische Monatshefte* 31: 758–61.

"Vernunft oder Repräsentation im Städtebau?" *Sozialistische Monatshefte* 31: 352–54.

"Vorsicht! Frisch gestrichen!" *Die Weltbühne* 21, no. 1: 596–97.

1926 "150 Sturm-Ausstellung." *Die Weltbühne* (February): 36.

"Der Abbau der Mietskaserne." *Das Tagebuch* 7, no. 2: 1613–14.

"An den Verein kommunistischer Kunstmaler." *Die Weltbühne* 22, no. 2: 460–61.

"Architekt und Mieter." *Sozialistische Monatshefte* 32: 767–68.

"Architekturpremiere." *Die Weltbühne* (January): 194–95.

"Ballhornbaut." *Die Weltbühne* (February): 831–32.

"Das Bauhaus in Dessau." *Reclams Universum* 43 (1926–1927): 318–19.

"Die Flagge." *Die Weltbühne* 22, no. 1: 944.

"Für Deutschland bearbeitet." *Die Weltbühne* (January): 635.

"Gehört die Zukunft der angewandten Kunst, dem Handwerk oder der Maschine?" *Farbe und Form* 11, nos. 6–7: 74.

"Das Haus." *Der Aufbau* 1: 101–2.

"Die Illustrierten: Bilderzeitungen oder Magazine?" *Die Weltbühne* 22, no. 2: 187–89.

"Ist der Stadtbaurat Frontoffizier?" *Die Weltbühne* (January): 77–78.

"Kriegsopfer und Verschönerungsverein." *Das Tagebuch* 7, no. 2: 1074–76.

"Kultur, Kunst und Reklame." *Das neue Frankfurt* 1 (1926–1927): 57–60.

"Kunst in der Gemeinschaft." *Die Tat* 18 (1926–1927): 685–93.

"Die Kunst muß die Gewalt beseitigen." *Der Zwiebelfisch* 19: 169–73.

"Muß ein Museum eine Tür haben?" *Das Tagebuch* 7, no. 1: 644–46.

"Neue Baukunst." *Ostdeutsche Monatshefte* 7 (1926–1927): 1004–10.

"Oberbürgermeister-Kunst." *Das Tagebuch* 7, no. 2: 1333–34.

"Die Stellung des Publikums zur modernen deutschen Literatur." *Die Weltbühne* 22, no. 1: 774–77.

"Tempelhofer Feld und Wedding (Kunstausstellung Wedding)." *Die Weltbühne* 22, no. 2: 346–48.

"Von Bode." *Die Weltbühne* (January): 116–17.

"Warten und Haine." *Die Weltbühne* (February): 475.

"Worin besteht die Not der Künstler?" *Sozialistische Monatshefte* 32: 36–38.

"Das Zimmer ohne Sorgen: Wie unsere Kinder wohnen werden." *Ubu* 3: 22–35.

"Zum Umbau des Berliner Opernhauses." *Sozialistische Monatshefte* 32: 387–90.

"Zur Äesthetik des flachen Daches" (Sonderheft "Das flache Dach"). *Das neue Frankfurt* 1 (1926–1927): 163.

"Zur Berufung ausländischer Architekten nach Rußland." *Die Bauwelt* 16: 374–75.

"Zwei holländische Arbeiten auf der Großen Berliner Kunstausstellung." *Die Bauwelt* 20, Sonderteil: Die Baukunst der Berliner Kunstausstellung: 13–16 [essay by Behne listed without his name].

"Zwei Sportplätze." *Das Tagebuch* 7, no. 1: 840–41.

1927 "Akademischer Frühling." *Die Weltbühne* 23, no. 1: 791–92.

"Ist die neue Bauart unbehaglich?" *Berliner Illustrierte Zeitung* (March): 515–16.

"Die moderne Fabrik." *Der Schünemann-Monat* 2: 160–67.

"Neue Landhausbauten." *Das ideale Heim*: 327–32.

"Otto Nagel." *Die Weltbühne* 23, no. 1: 77–78.

"Schlote zwischen Burgen — Gedanken zum Thema: Industriebauten am Rhein." *Rheinische Heimatblätter* 4, no. 8: 320–31.

"Türme." *Reclams Universum* 44 (1927–1928): 385–88.

"Wege zu einer besseren Wohnkultur." *Sozialistische Monatshefte* 33, no. 1: 121–23.

"Die Wohnung als Instrument." *Reclams Universum* 44 (1927–1928): 189.

1928 "Acht Architekten suchen einen Stil." *Das Tagebuch* 9, no. 1: 34–35.

"Berlin. Bericht über neue Graphik." *Das neue Frankfurt* 2, no. 10: 185f.

"Berlin-Bilderbericht von Adolf Behne." *Das neue Frankfurt* 2, no. 2: 37f; no. 6 (1928): 110 [reprinted in *Neues Bauen, Neues Gestalten*, 233f. Berlin (West): Elefanten Press, 1984].

"Berlin: Der Film als Wohltäter." *Das neue Frankfurt* 2, no. 4: 72.

"Berliner Öl-Kapitalismus." *Das Tagebuch* 9, no. 1: 415–17.

"Bilanz der Ausstellungen." *Humboldt-Blätter* 10: 186–87.

"Bildende Kunst in Deutschland, 1918–1928." *Die literarische Welt* 4, no. 45: 349f.

"Die Bundesschule des ADGB in Bernau bei Berlin." *Bauhaus* 2–3: 12.

"Die Bundesschule des Allgemeinen Deutschen Gewerkschaftsbundes in Berlin-Bernau." *Das neue Frankfurt* 2: 112–13.

"Die Bundesschule des Allgemeinen Deutschen Gewerkschaftsbundes in Bernau." *Zeitschrift für Gewerkschaftspolitik und Wirtschaftskunde* 5: 378f.

"Denkmal Ehrensache." *Das Tagebuch* 9, no. 2: 2000–1.

"Denkmals-Krise." *Humboldt-Blätter* 1: 20–22.

"Dürer und Grünewald." *Das Tagebuch* 9, no. 1: 500–2.

"Der Film als Pädagoge." *Das neue Frankfurt* 2: 203–5.

"Die Gewerkschaftsschule in Bernau bei Berlin." *Zentralblatt der Bauverwaltung* 48: 397–402.

"Kunst als Waffe." *Kunst der Zeit* 5–6 (1928–1929): 117.

"Die Kunstgeschichte am Ende und am Anfang." *Sozialistische Monatshefte* 34, no. 2: 980–83.

"Luxus oder Komfort?" *Das neue Frankfurt* 2: 6–7.

"Das moderne Museum." *Sozialistische Monatshefte* 34, no. 1: 42–45.

"Politik lobenswert ... Ästhetik mangelhaft." *Das neue Frankfurt* 2, no. 4: 73.

"Salon Justi." *Das Tagebuch* 9, no. 2: 1533–36.

"Die versteckten Watteaus." *Das Tagebuch* 9, no. 2: 1144–45.

"Vom Bauhaus in Dessau." *Humboldt-Blätter* 4 (January): 57–59.

"Vom Wesen des Stiles." *Der Kreis um das Kind* 3: 35–40.

"Zweck contra Nimbus." *Zentralblatt der Bauverwaltung* 48: 173–76.

1929 "50 Jahre 'Verein Berliner Kaufleute und Industrieller' 1879–1929." *Das neue Berlin* 11: 233.

"Adolf Meyer gestorben." *Welt am Abend* (August).

"Alexander Calder (USA)." *Das neue Frankfurt* 6 [reprinted in *Neues Bauen, Neues Gestalten*, 308. Berlin (West): Elefanten Press, 1984].

"An das 'Neue Frankfurt.'" *Das neue Berlin* 4: 86.

"Ausstellung der AHAG am Fischtalgrund." *Das neue Berlin* 1: 20.

"Das Berliner Wohnungsproblem. Ein Interview des Schriftleiters (A. Behne) mit Stadtbaurat Martin Wagner." *Das neue Berlin* 3: 50–57.

"China." *Die neue Rundschau* 40, no. 1: 430–31.

"Gibt es einen Weg aus der Wirrnis 'Deutscher' Kunstanschauungen? Eine Entgegnung (Zu Hans Rosenthal: Gibt es einen Weg aus der Wirrnis unserer deutschen Kunstanschauungen? Eine Besprechung des Buches *Kunst und Rasse* von Prof. Schultze-Naumburg)." *Deutsche Bauzeitung* 63, no. 1: 750–51.

"Heinrich Zille." *Das neue Berlin* 1: 189–92.

"In welcher Ebene ist Kunst politisch?" *Sozialistische Monatshefte* 35: 225–26.

"Karl Scheffler und das Kronprinzenpalais." *Die Weltbühne* 26, no. 1 (1929–1930): 882–83.

"Kunstausstellung Berlin." *Das neue Berlin* 1: 150–52.

"Kurt Kroner." *Das neue Berlin* 7: 147.

"Moderner Städtebau." *Das neue Berlin* 4: 86.

"Moderner Zweckbau." *Obelisk-Almanach*: 4–8 [supplement].

"Neu-Inszenierungen von Hoffmanns Erzählungen in der Kroll-Oper. (Bühnenbilder von Moholy-Nagy)." *Das neue Berlin* 1: 44–45.

Review of *Berliner Architektur der Nachkriegszeit,* by Elisabeth Maria Hajos and Leopold Zahn. *Das neue Berlin* 4: 87.

Review of *Das Gesamtschaffen des Architekten,* by Erich Mendelsohn. *Das neue Berlin* 12: 245.

"Die Städtische Kunst-Deputation kauft." *Das neue Berlin* 3: 62.

"Und was wird aus dem Reichstag und aus dem Platz der Deutschen Republik?" *Das neue Berlin* 3: 65.

"Wilhelm Leibl." *Sozialistische Monatshefte* 35: 411–14.

"Die Zehlendorfer Siedlung der Gehag." *Die Form* 4, no. 1: 4–8.

1930 "Adolf Loos." *Die Weltbühne* 26, no. 2: 960.

"Akademiepräsident Liebermann." *Die Weltbühne* 26, no. 2: 58.

"Architektur-Diskussion in Sowjetrußland." *Das neue Rußland* 7, nos. 5–6: 50–51.

"Das auf dem Pergamonaltar geopferte Deutsche Museum." *Die Weltbühne* 26, no. 2: 583–85.

"Aus der Rangliste der Kunst." *Die Weltbühne* 26, no. 2: 488–89.

"Berliner Berichte: Das Kronprinzenpalais." *Das neue Frankfurt* 4–5 [reprinted in *Neues Bauen, Neues Gestalten,* 306ff. Dresden: 1984].

"The Bernau Schule. The German Federated Trades Unions Build Their First Ideal College. An Example of Current German Architectural Design." *The Studio* 100, no. 451 (October): 302–6.

"Die Bremen." *Die Form* 5, no. 4: 108–9.

"Dammerstock." *Die Form* 5, no. 6: 163–66 [reprinted in *"Die Form": Stimme des Deutschen Werkbundes, 1925–1934*, edited by Felix Schwarz and Frank Gloor, 168–74. Ullstein Bauwelt Fundamente 24. Gütersloh: Bertelsmann Fachverlag Reinhard Mohn, 1969; and in *Eine Stunde Architektur*, 163–66. Architextbook 5. Berlin: Archibook-Verlag, 1984].

"Dammerstock-Schlusswort." *Die Form* 5, no. 18: 494.

"Das gerahmte Bild im Museum." *Das Tagebuch* 11: 1438–39.

"Ist Grünewald noch modern?" *Sozialistische Monatshefte* 36: 570–73.

"'Kollektiv' — und 'en gros': Zu einem neuen Wohnblock von P. R. Henning in Berlin." *Wohnungswirtschaft* 7: 406–8.

"Kronprinzenpalais." *Das Tagebuch* 11: 1395–96.

"Künstler des Proletariats (8): Wilhelm Morgner." *Eulenspiegel* 3, no. 10 (October): 135.

"Künstler des Proletariats (10): Jean Francois Millet." *Eulenspiegel* 3, no. 12 (October): 167.

"Kunstpolitik." *Sozialistische Monatshefte* 36: 679–80.

"Der Kunstsalon." *Die Weltbühne* 26, no. 2: 694.

"Die Museumsinsel." *Das Tagebuch* 11: 509–10.

"Die Museumsinsel: Eine Tragödie des Berliner Städtebaues." *Das neue Frankfurt* 4: 211–13.

"Neues Bauen in Rußland." *Das neue Rußland* 7, nos. 3–4: 71–72.

"Neues Wohnen — Neues Bauen." *Wohnungswirtschaft* 7: 69–100.

"Das preußische Kriegermal." *Sozialistische Monatshefte* 36: 891–93.

"Saison." *Sozialistische Monatshefte* 36: 995–96.

"Sportanlagen des SCC in Eichkamp. Dipl. Ing. Fred Forbát, Architekt BDA, Berlin." *Die Baugilde* 12: 2228–33.

"Synopsis der Kunst-Ausstellungen." *Das Kunstblatt* 14: 286–88.

"Über Kunstkritik." *Sozialistische Monatshefte* 36: 148–54.

"Verkehr und Tradition." *Sozialistische Monatshefte* 36: 256–58.

"Werner Scholz." *Die Weltbühne* 26, no. 2: 840–41.

"Zehn Jahre Bauhaus." *Wohnungswirtschaft* 7: 254–56.

"Zeitlupe. Was ist nationalsozialistische Kunst?" *Das Kunstblatt*: 154.

"Zu dem Block Baumschulenweg von Architekt BDA Henning." *Die Baugilde* 12: 2129–33.

1931 "Die Akademie am Scheideweg." *Die Weltbühne* 27, no. 2: 344–45.

"Albert Sigrist." Review of *Das Buch vom Bauen,* by Alexander Schwab. *Die Form* 6, no. 4: 160.

"Arbeiten von S. van Ravenstejn — Utrecht." *Die Form* 6, no. 5: 187–92.

"Bundesschule in Bernau bei Berlin." *Zentralblatt der Bauverwaltung* 51: 213–22.

"(Deutsche Bauausstellung Berlin 1931) Abteilung 'Die Wohnung unserer Zeit.'" *Zentralblatt der Bauverwaltung* 51: 733–35.

"Für und gegen Schinkel." *Die Weltbühne* 27, no. 1: 435–37.

"Karl Friedrich Schinkel (1781–1841)." *Die Sendung* 8: 153–55.

"Die Kunst als Waffe." *Die Weltbühne* 27, no. 2: 301–4.

"Die Kunst im Trommelfeuer der politischen Parteien." *Sozialistische Monatshefte* 37: 779–82.

"Künstler des Proletariats (14): C. Meunier." *Eulenspiegel* (April): 63.

"Künstler des Proletariats (15): Kurt Weinhold." *Eulenspiegel* (May): 79.

"Künstler des Proletariats (16): John Heartfield." *Eulenspiegel* (June): 95.

"Max Taut's Gewerkschaftshaus in Frankfurt am Main." *Wasmuths Monatshefte für Baukunst* 15: 481–84.

"Nationales und Internationales im neuen Bauen." *Moderne Bauformen* 30: 209–12.

"Nationales und Internationales im neuen Bauen." *Sozialistische Monatshefte* 37: 32–37.

"Otto Müller." *Die Weltbühne* 27, no. 1: 885–86.

"Über Käthe Kollwitz." *Sozialistische Monatshefte* 37: 904–7.

"Die Welt von unten oder Zweierlei Öl." *Die Weltbühne* 27, no. 2: 754–55.

1932 "15 Jahre Sowjetkunst." *Das neue Rußland* 9, nos. 7–8: 72–74.

"Die Auferstehung in der bildenden Kunst." *Die Sendung* 9, no. 3: 276.

"Edouard Manet." *Die Sendung* 9, no. 3: 49–50.

"Edouard Manet, 1832–1932." *Sozialistische Monatshefte* 38, no. 1: 58–61.

"Europäische Hauptstädte: Berlin." *Die neue Stadt* 3.

"Formel — Form — Gestalt." *Zentralblatt der Bauverwaltung* 52: 61.

"Ein Gegenstand und vier Ecken." *Sozialistische Monatshefte* 38, no. 2: 1023–26.

"Ist der Impressionismus undeutsch?" *Sozialistische Monatshefte* 38, no. 1: 522.

"Kann die Kunst im Leben aufgehen?" *Sozialistische Monatshefte* 38, no. 1: 138–43.

"Das Kronprinzenpalais in Oslo." *Die Weltbühne* 28, no. 1: 22–24.

"Künstler und Gesellschaft." *Sozialistische Monatshefte* 38, no. 1: 332–34.

"Ludwig Hoffmann gestorben." *Die Weltbühne* 28, no. 1: 779–80.

"Noch einmal Oslo." *Die Weltbühne* 28, no. 1: 365–69.

"Nur eine Reproduktion. (Matthias Grünewald)." *Sozialistische Monatshefte* 38, no. 2: 689–91.

"Vortrag auf der Protestveranstaltung 'Kunsterziehung in Not' des Reichsbundes deutscher Kunsterzieher am 30 Nov. 1931." *Kunst und Jugend* 1: 12.

"Das wachsende Haus." *Die Umschau* 36: 490–94.

"Zweierlei Anschauung." *Sozialistische Monatshefte* 38, no. 2: 840–42.

1933 "Architekten-Bücher (Über Le Corbusier, Mendelsohn, Bruno Taut)." *Die neue Rundschau* 44, no. 1: 287–88.

"Ist eine Soziologie der Kunst möglich?" *Die Form* 8, no. 1: 2–7.

"Künstler und Auftraggeber." *Sozialistische Monatshefte* 39: 120–25.

"Kunst nach Breitengraden." *Die Weltbühne* 29, no. 1: 288–90.

"Sankt Georg zu Limburg an der Lahn." *Atlantis* 5: 653–56.

"Wie werde ich lebendig und deutsch?" *Die Weltbühne* 29, no. 1: 104–6.

1934 "Haus Schminke in Löbau (Architekt Hans Scharoun)." *Innendekoration* 45: 84–89.

"H. P. Berlage, 1856–1934." *Deutsche Bauzeitung* 68, no. 2: 656.

"Eine Villa in Süddeutschland (Architekt F. A. Breuhaus)." *Innendekoration* 45: 111–12.

1935 "Caspar David Friedrich: Der Maler deutscher Landschaft." *Bibliothek der Unterhaltung and des Wissens* 59, no. 11: 144–70.

"Haus Matern in Bornim bei Potsdam. (Architekt Hans Scharoun)." *Deutsche Bauzeitung* 69, no. 1: 53–58.

"Paul Scheerbart gestorben am 15.10.1915." *Deutsche Zukunft* (October): 20.

"Phillip Otto Runge: Der Maler der Romantik." *Bibliothek der Unterhaltung and des Wissens* 59, no. 7: 155–82.

"Wie ein deutscher Meister entdeckt wurde: 100 Jahre Hausbuchmeister-Forschung." *Atlantis* 7: 50–54.

1936 "Der Bamberger Altar von Veit Stoß." *Lesestunde* 13 (December).

"Stilkunde V: Die Gotik." *Lesestunde* 13 (December).

1937 "Genie ohne Grenzen." *Lesestunde* 14 (December).

"Karl Blechen: Tarantella." *Lesestunde* 14 (April).

"Rubens: Die Söhne des Künstlers." *Lesestunde* 14 (December).

"Stilkunde VI: Die Bauten der Araber in Spanien." *Lesestunde* 14 (January).

"Stilkunde VIII: Der Barockstil." *Lesestunde* 14 (March).

"Stilkunde IX: Das Rokoko." *Lesestunde* 14 (April).

"Stilkunde X: Klassizismus." *Lesestunde* 14 (May).

1938 "Albrecht Dürer als Meister des Holzschnittes." *Lesestunde* 15 (March).

"Dürers Holzschnitt des Ritters Georg." *Lesestunde* 15 (March).

1942 "Das Problem der Sichtbarkeit." *Das Werk* (Zurich) 29: 145–48.

1947 "Christian Rohlfs." *Sonntag* 2, no. 41.

"Edvard Munch." *Sonntag* 2, no. 21.

"Ernst Ludwig Kirchner." *Sonntag* 2, no. 9.

"In Memoriam Max Dungert." *Sonntag* 2, no. 21.

"Joh. Wüsten †." *Sonntag* 2, no. 50.

"Schmitt-Rottluff." *Sonntag* 2, no. 24.

"Soziale Kunst." *Sonntag* 2, no. 45.

"Ungelöste Probleme der Kunstgeschichte." *Bildende Kunst* 1: 20–21.

"Von Hatschepsut bis Heckel: Wiedersehen mit Museumsgut." *Sonntag* 2, no. 4.

1948 "Haus Baluschek zum Gedächtnis." *Sonntag* 3, no. 14.

"Max Dungert." *Bildende Kunst* 2, no. 3: 27.

"Mensch und Kreatur (Zu Renée Sintenis' 60. Geburtstag)." *Aufbau* 4: 247–48.

"'Rinnsteinkunst' (Über den Simplicissimus)." *Aufbau* 4: 402–7.

"Vincent van Gogh und seine Mission." *Bildende Kunst* 2, no. 4: 3–7.

"Was will die moderne Kunst?" *Bildende Kunst* 2, no. 1: 3–5.

"Wunder der menschlichen Gestalt: Zu Georg Kolbes Tod." *Aufbau* 4: 60–61.

"Zeitstil oder neue Freiheit?" *Sonntag* 3, no. 8.

Index

The Modern Functional Building
Introduction by Rosemarie Haag Bletter
Translation by Michael Robinson

Rosemarie Haag Bletter received her doctorate from Columbia University with a dissertation on Bruno Taut's architecture and his relationship with the Expressionist writer Paul Scheerbart. She has taught at Columbia University and the Institute of Fine Arts at New York University. Presently, she is a professor in the departments of Art History and Modern German Studies at the City University of New York Graduate Center. Her publications include *Skyscraper Style* (with Cervin Robinson, 1975) and *El Arquitecto Josep Vilaseca* (1977). She has also published essays on Paul Scheerbart, Frank Gehry, Robert Venturi, American car culture, and Expressionist architecture. Professor Bletter was a guest curator for the Whitney Museum of American Art's *High Styles* exhibition in 1985 and has collaborated on three documentary films about contemporary architecture: *Beyond Utopia* (1983), *The Architecture of Arata Isozaki* (1985), and *James Stirling* (1987).

Michael Robinson graduated with a degree in German from Durham in 1964 and pursued a teaching career until 1984. At that time he left to work as a freelance translator and theater director. He directed his own translation of Arthur Schnitzler's *Anatol* at the Gate Theatre in 1987. Subsequently this performance was broadcast on BBC Radio and published by the Absolute Press. It was followed by other works for the stage and numerous translations of books on art, design, and architecture. Robinson's version of the Brecht/Weill musical *Happy End* has been approved for performance and publication by the Brecht and Weill Foundations. His translation of Gottfried Semper's *Der Stil in den technischen und tektonischen Künsten* will be published by the Getty Research Institute as part of its TEXTS & DOCUMENTS series.

Designed by Bruce Mau with Chris Rowat.
Coordinated by Suzanne Watson Petralli.
Type composed by Archetype in Scala, News Gothic, and Grotesque.
Printed and bound by Thomson-Shore, Inc., on Cougar Opaque.

TEXTS & DOCUMENTS
Series designed by Laurie Haycock Makela and Lorraine Wild.

TEXTS & DOCUMENTS

A series of the Getty Research Institute Publication Programs
Julia Bloomfield, Thomas F. Reese, Salvatore Settis, *Editors*
Kurt W. Forster, *Consultative Editor*

Few individuals better chart the path of European Modernism in the first decades of this century than Adolf Behne (1885–1948). Before World War I, Behne was active in the German Werkbund. As a critic, he explored differences in high, commerical, and popular culture, publishing frequently in periodicals such as *Der Sturm* and *Sozialistische Monatshefte*. In the 1920s Behne went on to become one of the most incisive and eloquent theorists of Modernism and, together with Bruno Taut and Walter Gropius, organized the Arbeitsrat für Kunst (Work council on the arts). Behne would also become an early critic of both the Werkbund and the Bauhaus.

Written in 1923, Behne's *Modern Functional Building* clarifies the concepts of German Modernism at their very inception, especially the crucial distinctions between functionalism, rationalism, and utilitarianism. In this text, Behne advocates a functionalism that is not technocentric but is comparable to the social ideas espoused by Max Weber and Georg Simmel. This broad concern with functionalism signifies a shift from older aristocratic value systems to the everyday and common experience as paradigmatic.

Introduced by Rosemarie Haag Bletter, this seminal text conveys the grit and complexity of early modernist aspirations — qualities for the most part filtered out in subsequent historical interpretations. It is essential reading for anyone interested in this phase of the modern discourse.

Otto Wagner, *Modern Architecture* (1902)
Introduction by Harry Francis Mallgrave
(Hardback, ISBN 0-226-86938-5. Paperback, ISBN 0-226-86939-3)

Heinrich Hübsch, Rudolf Wiegmann, Carl Albert Rosenthal, Johann Heinrich Wolff, and Carl Gottlieb Wilhelm Bötticher, *In What Style Should We Build? The German Debate on Architectural Style* (1828–1847)
Introduction by Wolfgang Herrmann
(Hardback, ISBN 0-89236-199-9. Paperback, ISBN 0-89236-198-0)

Nicolas Le Camus de Mézières, *The Genius of Architecture; or, The Analogy of That Art with Our Sensations* (1780)
Introduction by Robin Middleton
(Hardback, ISBN 0-89236-234-0. Paperback, ISBN 0-89236-235-9)

Claude Perrault, *Ordonnance for the Five Kinds of Columns after the Method of the Ancients* (1683)
Introduction by Alberto Pérez-Gómez
(Hardback, ISBN 0-89236-232-4. Paperback, ISBN 0-89236-233-2)

Robert Vischer, Conrad Fiedler, Heinrich Wölfflin, Adolf Göller, Adolf Hildebrand, and August Schmarsow, *Empathy, Form, and Space: Problems in German Aesthetics, 1873–1893*
Introduction by Harry Francis Mallgrave and Eleftherios Ikonomou
(Hardback, ISBN 0-89236-260-x. Paperback, ISBN 0-89236-259-6)

Friedrich Gilly: Essays on Architecture, 1796–1799
Introduction by Fritz Neumeyer
(Hardback, ISBN 0-89236-280-4. Paperback, ISBN 0-89236-281-2)

Hermann Muthesius, *Style-Architecture and Building-Art: Transformations of Architecture in the Nineteenth Century and Its Present Condition* (1902)
Introduction by Stanford Anderson
(Hardback, ISBN 0-89236-282-0. Paperback, ISBN 0-89236-283-9)

Sigfried Giedion, *Building in France, Building in Iron, Building in Ferroconcrete* (1928)
Introduction by Sokratis Georgiadis
(Hardback, ISBN 0-89236-319-3. Paperback, ISBN 0-89236-320-7)

Hendrik Petrus Berlage: Thoughts on Style, 1886–1909
Introduction by Iain Boyd Whyte
(Hardback, ISBN 0-89236-333-9. Paperback, ISBN 0-89236-334-7)

In Preparation
Walter Curt Behrendt, *The Victory of the New Style of Architecture* (1927)

Jacob Burckhardt, *Italian Renaissance Painting According to Genres*

LIBRARY OF CONGRESS CATALOGING-IN-PUBLICATION DATA

Behne, Adolf, 1885–1948.
[Der moderne Zweckbau. English]
The modern functional building / Adolf Behne; introduction by
Rosemarie Haag Bletter; translation by Michael Robinson.
p. cm. — (Texts & documents)
ISBN 0-89236-363-0 (cloth). — ISBN 0-89236-364-9 (paper)
1. Functionalism (Architecture) 2. Architecture, Modern— 20th Century.
I. Title. II. Series
NA682.F8B4513 1996
724'.6–dc20   96-1970
                                                               CIP